RISK MANAGEMENT

An Accountability Guide for University and College Boards

Second Edition

Janice M. Abraham

with Sarah Braughler, Liza Kabanova, and Justin Kollinger

AGB   The Association of Governing Boards of Universities and Colleges (AGB) is the premier membership organization that strengthens higher education governing boards and the strategic roles they serve within their organizations. Through our vast library of resources, educational events, and consulting services, and with nearly 100 years of experience, we empower 40,000 AGB members from more than 2,000 institutions and foundations to navigate complex issues, implement leading practices, streamline operations, and govern with confidence. AGB is the trusted resource for board members, chief executives, and key administrators on higher education governance and leadership. For more information, visit www.AGB.org.

 United Educators (UE), a reciprocal risk retention group, is a licensed insurance company owned and governed by more than 1,600 member schools, colleges, and universities throughout the United States. Members range from small independent schools to multicampus public universities. UE partners with its members to reduce risk through education-specific insurance coverage and risk management programs. UE's comprehensive suite of resources are designed to engage the entire campus community—faculty, staff, and students—in managing risk. For more information, visit www.ue.org.

This publication is designed to provide accurate and authoritative information with regard to enterprise risk management for higher education. It is sold with the understanding that the publisher is not engaged in rendering legal services. If legal advice or other expert assistance is required, the services of a competent professional person should be sought.

©2020 by Association of Governing Boards of Universities and Colleges, and United Educators Insurance, a Reciprocal Risk Group

AGB | 1133 20th Street, N.W., Suite 300 | Washington, DC 20036 | 202.296.8400 | www.AGB.org
UE | 7700 Wisconsin Avenue, Suite 500 | Bethesda, MD 20814 | 800.346.7877 | www.ue.org

All rights reserved. No part of this publication maybe reproduced or transmitted in any form or by any means, electronic or mechanical, including photocopying, recording, or using any information storage and retrieval system, without permission in writing from AGB and United Educators.
Printed in the United States of America
ISBN 978-1-7336368-3-4

Contents

Preface—First Edition v
Preface—Second Edition ix

Part I Fundamentals of Risk Management — 1

Chapter 1 Good Risk Management is Good Governance — 3
Chapter 2 Enterprise Risk Management: A Guide for Administrators — 9
Chapter 3 External and Internal Stakeholders in Risk Management — 29
Chapter 4 Enterprise Risk Management Maturity — 45

Part II Risk from the Board's Perspective — 57

Chapter 5 Risks to Effective Governance — 59
Chapter 6 Risks to Strategic Direction (and Shared Risks) — 73
Chapter 7 Risks to Institutional Resources — 91
Chapter 8 Risks to the Student Experience — 135
Chapter 9 Advancing Reputation — 175

Conclusion Lessons for Boards — 187

Chapter 10 A Call to Action — 189

Appendices

Appendix A AGB/UE Enterprise Risk Management Risk Registers — 191
Appendix B Sample Universitywide Risk Management Committee Charter — 199
Appendix C Sample List of Insurance Policies for Colleges and Universities — 203
Appendix D Models for Managing Compliance — 207

Resources — 213
Notes — 223
About the Author — 235
About the Contributors — 237
Author Acknowledgments — 239

Preface—First Edition
(April 2013)

Just when I think I have seen it all, something happens that surprises me.

Over my more than 30-year career serving education, I have become well aware of the bad things that can happen at a college or university. Incidents related to alcohol, hazing, and athletic scandals, while thankfully not common, also are not so obscure as to be outside of the realm of possibility.

But when a tenure denial leads to an incident of workplace violence, or sexual allegations are made, or a shooting incident occurs on campus, I'm disheartened. Equally alarming is a culture that exists on too many campuses that protects individuals and traditions, ignores ethics and values, and leaves the most vulnerable people at great risk of harm. Trustees, administrators, faculty, staff, students, and alumni all have roles to play in questioning even iconic programs, people, and traditions. No individual or tradition should be exempt from precautionary policies—not athletic stars, future (or current) Nobel laureates, a beloved Mr. Chips, tailgating, or initiation rites.

Left unheeded, societal trends of shifting demographics, declining state support, and competition from new education providers are also emerging risks for colleges and universities. Some trends are not necessarily risks or crises, until they are. Advising higher education administrators and board members on how to best prevent bad things from happening consumes much of my time and is the purpose of this book.

Preface—First Edition

In my career and volunteer work, I move between the two distinct worlds of running a business that serves higher education and serving as a college trustee. As a former administrator at a large research university and a liberal arts college, I try to be deliberate and intentional in remembering which hat I am wearing in these different roles. Transitioning between the two worlds of business and volunteer service can be difficult for any board member; the labyrinth-like decision-making process at colleges and universities can be challenging and sometimes frustrating. "High velocity" is not a term frequently ascribed to higher education administration or governance, but it seems more relevant today than at any other time in my long service to education. Balancing mission and change is the challenge for all who serve in education. The core values of higher education—the focus on mission, long-term horizon, and shared decision-making—serve institutions well. Retaining those values, while being more intentional and focused on risks and change, is our challenge.

As a trustee, I, like many of you, prefer to focus energy on the upside of risk. Guiding the college or university in taking strategic risks is a large part of the board's role. Adding new programs, building new facilities, or rebranding the institution can help ensure appropriate long-term enrollment levels, endowment funding, and community support. I encourage you to continue your oversight of strategic risk-taking, inspiring administrators to think broadly as they shape the future of their institutions.

I also encourage you to pay greater attention to other risks on campus—the risk of bad things happening—that can tarnish the institution's reputation and negatively impact the ability to achieve its mission. Too often, board members are unaware of the risks inherent in higher education. This is not due to an intentional lack of interest or attention to important risks, but rather to a lack of understanding. For too many colleges and universities, risks are unappreciated, cross-functional risks have no clear oversight responsibility, and mitigation plans are either not put into practice or are ineffective.

This book lays out principles and a process for the board to support a culture within the institution that embraces and prepares for risk. It is also designed to help senior administrators develop and support the board in providing appropriate board oversight and responses related to a myriad of risks. After reading this book, board members should be able to:

1. Support college and university administrators in implementing a streamlined process to identify, assess, manage, and report risks.

Part I introduces the importance of institutional risk management, an Enterprise Risk Management (ERM) process model that administrators can use to assess and manage institution-wide risks and the external and internal forces that shape the risk environment for higher education. A good ERM program executed by senior administration should result in reports addressed at the board level on the most critical risks to achieving an institution's strategic plan and/or mission.

2. Understand the complexity and breadth of risks that colleges and universities face and engage in meaningful discussions with campus leaders—asking the difficult questions that will help the administration better manage risks.

Part II introduces specific risks that are likely to appear on most "risk registers" used by college and university administrators to identify, assess, and plan for risks during an ERM process. The background information and questions provided equip trustees with both context and the right questions to ask to help ensure that administrators are closing gaps and focusing on the right issues.

One additional comment on vocabulary: I am well aware of the different preferences within higher education, but for the sake of simplicity, I have used the following titles and designations throughout this book:

- *Institution* refers to a college, university, system, or institutionally related foundation. (Because foundations do not have direct responsibility for academics, certain sections of this book may not be relevant for their boards and administrative teams.)
- *Board member* refers to the individuals who serve on the board. In practice, they may be called trustees, regents, governors, or directors.
- *President* refers to the chief executive at the helm of the institution. This person may be the president of an independent institution, chancellor of a public institution or system, or executive director of a foundation.

Not every risk discussed here will be relevant to every college, university, system, or foundation, and your institution's leadership

Preface—First Edition

may identify additional risks not discussed here. But if this book serves as an introduction to the world of higher education risks, fosters an appreciation for the tough jobs higher education administrators face, and challenges boards to take risk management seriously, I will have accomplished what I set out to do.

Preface—Second Edition
(March 2020)

Is there a need for a second edition of *Risk Management: An Accountability Guide for University and College Boards*? Have higher education and the world in general changed enough to merit a fresh look at the role governing boards and senior leadership should play in risk management?

A view of the landscape since 2013 yields an emphatic Yes. The economic, social, and political landscape has shifted dramatically in the intervening years, adding increased volatility, greater media and public scrutiny, and Generation Alpha getting ready to arrive at our campuses. "Is the business model of higher education sustainable?" is the most frequent question governing board members ask as we travel throughout the country. The answer, we believe, is no—not in its current structure. No, because the math doesn't work, there won't be enough high school graduates to spread around the country to fill the seats vacated by Millennials, and the public (families and legislators) isn't willing to pay the money required to support the traditional higher education experience (four or five years of college after high school and perhaps followed by a graduate degree).

What changed? COVID-19 pandemic, demographic change, technology finally offering quality learning opportunities, scandals that knocked colleges from the pedestal, an ever-expanding social economic divide, shifting needs of employers, global competition, and higher education's reluctance to take these external risks and opportunities seriously and adapt when it still had the luxury of time.

Preface—Second Edition

Is this an existential threat for all of higher education? Another emphatic no. But the reality is stark, and higher education must adapt to survive. We believe that boards and campus leaders that take the principles of risk management seriously have a better chance of thriving in this tumultuous environment. While research on the return on investing in enterprise risk management (ERM) for higher education has not been completed, more research is quantifying returns in the corporate sector.

> "The results suggest that an ERM framework and an ERM implementation can help companies improve performance by enabling executives to manage the company better. From a practical standpoint, companies ask how ERM adds value. Our results show that value comes from implementing the process, which then enables the company to make better decisions."
>
> —Paul L. Walker, James J. Schiro / Zurich Chair in Enterprise Risk Management Executive Director, Center for Excellence in ERM, St. John's University Tobin College of Business

As more higher education institutions embrace (or consider embracing) ERM, I am pleased that this second edition of the *Accountability Guide* continues to evolve in order to remain relevant and useful to governing boards. Part I of the guide now has a chapter on ERM program maturity, and Part II includes new discussions on compliance and reputational risk—areas where boards are increasingly shifting their focus. In addition, the risks discussed in Part II are reorganized to reflect a growing practice to establish board committees focused on the broad goals of the board rather than the functional areas of the institution. While we maintain our commitment to a "noses in and fingers out" approach to board governance, the increasingly precarious environment for colleges and universities create a call for boards to encourage and engage in a robust and comprehensive ERM program at the institutions they serve.

Janice M. Abraham

PART I | Fundamentals of Risk Management

"The word 'risk' derives from the early Italian *risicare* which means 'to dare.' In this sense, risk is a choice rather than a fate!"
—Peter L. Bernstein, author of *Against the Gods: The Remarkable Story of Risk*

Chapter 1
Good Risk Management is Good Governance

> "In the future, we will look at risks affecting the whole of an organization and its place in the community. We will address both upside and downside consequences, and our view will be enterprisewide, integrated and holistic. The result will be a more intelligent balance between potential benefits and harms. We will increase the confidence of stakeholders in our organizations and make them more resilient in a day and age of increased uncertainty. This is the real goal of risk management."
> —H. Felix Kloman, editor and publisher, *Risk Management Reports*

The Future Is Here

AT ITS CORE, RISK MANAGEMENT IS A governance and management discipline—not an end but a means to the end, the end being the accomplishment of the institution's mission. What is risk management from the board's perspective? Just as good financial management is more than a clean audit opinion, good risk management is more than not getting sued and having adequate insurance policies in place. Effective risk management prepares an institution to weather literal and figurative storms and sets the course for accomplishing the institution's strategic plan.

Whether you have just been appointed to a board position or have long served as a board member for a college or university, you no doubt recognize the increasing responsibilities being placed on boards for better institutional oversight.

When things go wrong, the board should have known that all was not well. Even if the wrongdoing falls beyond the scope of traditional board responsibility, finger-pointing by the media, alumni, parents, students, and others now means that every board must have a thorough understanding of the risks at its institution and up-to-date knowledge of how well the administration is working to mitigate those risks.

Historically, colleges and universities have had a strong track record of successfully weathering catastrophic events, which speaks to their resilience and historic place in society. But while the past decade has been difficult for many institutions, today's environment is different. Public perception of higher education, once universally seen as a public good, has declined as tuition and student debt have grown, each new scandal or controversy inflicting further harm. The rapid pace of change and innovation, the 24/7 news cycle and insatiable appetite for information, the litigation climate, and increasing scrutiny by politicians and regulators all place more pressure on boards to get it right.

In this climate, boards must set the tone for the importance of risk management. Once it seemed unlikely that a single long-term trend or catastrophic event could close an institution, but as increasing numbers of colleges run out of resources and face closure, unmanaged risk is now an existential threat to many. The margin of error is significantly narrower as weak finances and increased competition for a shrinking pool of students become more common.

Benign neglect or poor preparation for major risks can weaken and undermine an institution, leaving it with a diminished reputation, an inability to respond, and plans once embraced by the community unfulfilled. Boards are most effective if they operate with a clear set of priorities and concentrate on strategic oversight. Risk management should be on every board's to-do list for oversight.

The Role of Risk Management

With myriad demands resting on the shoulders of boards and senior administrators, it is reasonable to ask: Why invoke risk management as yet another process in a process-laden structure? Will it really make a difference in how the institution plans or functions?

While no one can effectively calculate the total cost of risk, consider these costs of failing to prepare for events that history proves are inevitable:

- *What were the opportunity costs* as the board and senior leadership huddled in meetings to chart a recovery after a significant risk was realized?

- *How much money was spent*, excluding insurance or outside sources, to try to speed the recovery?
- *What was the loss of promising faculty* who decided to accept competing offers?
- *How many people made decisions to enroll elsewhere* who might have become future alumni?
- *Which donors held back on major gifts* until the institution could sort things out—or didn't give at all?
- *How did rating agencies respond?* Was a bond rating lowered, or not raised, in turn raising questions about the financial strength of the institution?
- *How much additional effort must now be expended to instill future confidence* in the institution?[1]

An effective institutional or enterprise risk management (ERM) program, which has the full support and engagement of the governing board, will increase the likelihood that a college, university, or system will achieve its plans, increase transparency, and enable better allocation of scarce resources. Good risk management is good governance.

Evolution of Risk Management

The field of risk management is evolving. The transformation began in the late 20th century, when the focus was risk transfer and loss control, and an institution's exposure to losses drove the thinking about risk management. Where could the institution suffer a loss, usually defined by a lawsuit, fire, flood, or accident? How could the institution reduce its exposure? Addressing these questions meant buying insurance and signing contracts with service providers to transfer risks. Campus loss control focused on safety, physical injury from slips and falls, and property damage from natural disasters.

ERM in Higher Education

Enterprise Risk Management took hold in the corporate world in the early years of the 21st century. Models developed by the Committee of Sponsoring Organizations (COSO) of the Treadway Commission and the International Standards Organization (ISO) established the framework that is the foundation of most ERM practices today. The goal of ERM was, and is, to move away from viewing risk in silos and instead look across the enterprise for risks, paying particular attention to risks that occur in the gaps between the silos.

ERM advanced to colleges and universities as governing board members brought their business experiences to higher education boardrooms. As they worked with ERM in their companies and on corporate boards, they began to recognize the applicability and relevance of using a holistic approach to risk management in academic institutions.[2] The original COSO framework assigns risks to one of four categories: strategic, operations, reporting, or compliance. Many in higher education modified these categories to strategic, operations, finance, and compliance. If any of these risks occur on a major scale, reputational harm is sure to follow.

In today's environment ERM is a combination of strategic planning, traditional risk management, and internal controls. A consensus definition, and one used for this book, is the following:

> **Enterprise Risk Management (ERM)** is a business process, led by senior leadership, that extends the concepts of risk management and includes:
> - Identifying risks across the entire enterprise;
> - Assessing the impact of risks to the operations and mission;
> - Developing and practicing response or mitigation plans; and
> - Monitoring the identified risks, holding the risk owner accountable, and consistently scanning for emerging risks.

Over the past decade ERM has impacted higher education, helping institutions:

- Ensure every major risk has an owner and an action plan;
- Address obscure risks without obvious owners and the potential to derail strategic plans;
- Address critical but intractable risks that have remained untouched for years;
- Direct resources to mundane but potentially devastating natural disasters rather than the headline-making risks of the day;
- Use expertise and staff already available to enact meaningful risk mitigation;
- Identify and adopt best practices from their peers; and
- Know when to say "yes" or "no" to innovative ideas.

Insight: You Don't Have to Call It ERM

Because of its corporate origins, ERM can be a hard sell in academia. If the phrase "enterprise risk management" feels too corporate, institutions can brand it as something more appropriate to their culture. We've seen institutions name their programs "institutional risk management," "holistic risk management," "community of practice," "strategic risk management," and others. One institution pairs risk management with institutional effectiveness. The important thing is that faculty and staff respond favorably to the program, whatever you call it.

This book will help institutions without ERM experience these benefits, and it will show institutions that have ERM in place how to get more out of existing programs.

Moving Forward

The evolution of risk management continues today as both a grassroots and grasstops initiative. Best practice now is to have broad-based ownership of risk management from top to bottom and throughout the institution. The board and president jointly articulate a commitment to risk management, and the senior administration implements an enterprisewide process of identifying and analyzing risks and communicating and increasing awareness about risks across the institution's operation. The focus now is on establishing roles and responsibilities so that everyone on campus considers risk in their day-to-day activities.

The board has a role in this evolving risk management model: to engage senior leadership and integrate risk management into the work of board committees and full board deliberations, and to require risk management discussion as part of major program and project reviews and strategic planning. Board discussions need to consider both the upside of risk (opportunities to enhance the institution's mission and operations) and the downside of risk (circumstances that prevent the institution from accomplishing its plans and achieving its mission). How intentionally a board and administration think about risk, and how well they respond when the unexpected occurs, is the ultimate test of a sound risk management program.

Insight: All Risk is Not Local

How has risk management evolved on campuses?

"Over recent decades risk management has moved beyond the campus to the larger community of Ithaca, then over state borders to where it is now, encompassing global programs run by Cornell—all with regular oversight by the board."

—Former director of risk management at a private research university

Chapter 2
Enterprise Risk Management: A Guide for Administrators

INSTITUTIONWIDE ENTERPRISE RISK MANAGEMENT (ERM) SHOULD be part of every college or university's operations and planning[1] An institution that has not established an ERM discipline and structure is an institution without a plan. Without the discipline of identifying risks, assigning ownership, consulting with subject-matter experts, and monitoring progress to reduce risks, institutions will falter when the inevitable crisis occurs. ERM also supports an institution taking on new programs and initiatives with the confidence that risks have been vetted and communicated. ERM is a discipline for campus administrators, led by the president, for risk identification, assessment, mitigation, and reporting responsibilities and, ultimately, for informing board members of the most significant institutional risks. (See Exhibit 1.)

Step 1: Risk Identification—Compiling a Risk Register

Risks can be identified in many ways, but starting from a blank slate is the least efficient. After two decades of ERM programs on campuses, many comprehensive lists exist that can be used as a starting point. Institutions often spend too much time and energy involving large numbers of faculty and staff in identifying a long list of 100 to 200 (or more) risks but spend too little of it on the real work of thoughtfully assessing those risks and then developing treatment or mitigation plans.

Exhibit 1: Key Steps in Enterprise Risk Management (ERM)

The risk identification process led by senior administrators should identify no more than 20 key risks across the institution. Of the top 20 risks the senior administration identifies, approximately 10 should be reported to the board and its committees. Experience shows that focus is diluted and follow-through is weak if an institution's risk register is larger than that. (See Exhibit 2 and Appendix A.)

When identifying risks, it is also important to focus on uncertainties that can impact your institution's objectives. Many institutions new to ERM end up capturing a list of problems that require straightforward fixes, such as faulty refrigeration for medications or deteriorating sidewalks. Such problems are not risks, and while they require attention, they do not impact the institution's ability to achieve its mission. ERM should focus on preparing the institution for coming challenges through cross-departmental collaboration, not creating accountability for fixing known problems the institution simply needs to address.

Colleges and universities with the greatest success in incorporating risk management into ongoing operations and involving the board at the appropriate point report that they start small. They begin with a group of knowledgeable individuals at a senior level within the administration—a senior risk management committee—and use existing lists of risks to identify, assess, mitigate, and

---

Insight: Invert the 80/20 Rule

Institutions tend to spend 80 percent of their risk management time identifying risks and 20 percent doing something about those risks, such as assessing the impact of risks, assigning owners to the risks, developing plans to reduce risk, and tracking risk. But best practice calls for reversing the 80-20 allocation of effort. Using the lists in this book and information gleaned from other institutions, institutions can jump-start the risk identification process and limit it to 20 percent of the effort. Spending the remaining 80 percent on assessing the likelihood, impact, and risk mitigation strategies (rather than reinventing the work done by others) is a far more efficient use of everyone's time.

monitor their own top risks. (See Exhibit 2 and Appendix B.)

A senior risk committee, working across the campus at a senior level, is an essential starting point for effective ERM. (See Appendix B for a sample committee charter.) While the process of risk identification can be repeated and extended to the broader community in future years, the board should gain comfort that the biggest risks—the risks with the greatest likelihood of severely impacting the mission and ongoing operations of the institution—are addressed first and brought forward for the board's review.

Risk identification is not a "one and done" exercise but rather a process that should be incorporated into the ongoing governance and management of an institution. Administrators should also use the ERM process to evaluate launch plans for new programs and initiatives—identifying, assessing, and mitigating risks to academic programs, capital campaigns, or joint ventures.

Ideally, the risk identification process is repeated or reviewed every few years or as events dictate. In subsequent years, after the top risks are identified and the board and senior administration gain confidence in the process, going deeper into the institution to identify additional risks is recommended. Members of the campus risk committee can conduct focus groups and individual interviews with managers and faculty leaders. Asking "What keeps you up at night?" and similar questions can be a revealing process for grassroots risk identification. This approach offers the opportunity to uncover potential risks that the central administration may not have recognized as significant.

If a broader net of grassroots risk identification process is initiated, the campus must be prepared to embark on the next steps of assessing the risks and developing risk-mitigation plans for each risk identified.

Insight: You Don't Have to Have a Committee

Not all institutions opt for a committee approach. Rather than form a committee to identify new or emerging risks, the risk officer at a private liberal arts college meets individually with the institution's top 30 leaders every 12 to 16 months. Using a qualitative interview process, the risk officer calibrates the likelihood and impact of every risk they share with him. Leadership then uses his results as a key input when it comes time to set their top mitigation priorities each year.

Insight: News You Can Use

To identify emerging risks, a university system campus focuses on headline news. For any major news event involving risk, from the Flint water crisis to measles outbreaks in areas with antivaccine families, the institution's risk intelligence committee identifies top headline risks. Then they ask how those risks would potentially impact their institution, highlighting risks that the institution is not mitigating. Repeating this exercise annually enables them to keep their risk register up to date and to get ahead of emerging risks.

Who Serves on the Senior Risk Management Committee?

A senior group of administrators, with experience and accountability across the functions of the institution, is best positioned to serve as a risk management team and risk owners.

Senior risk management committees often consist of the chief academic officer, general counsel, and officers from such areas as student affairs, technology, development, athletics, finance, and administration. Adding a campus risk manager, internal auditor, and compliance officer to this group of senior administrators can augment its expertise. (For additional resources from AGB, see "Five Unsung Campus Heroes Every Trustee Should Know or Know About" by Lawrence White in the May/June 2012 issue of *Trusteeship*.) Some campuses also include vice presidents of facilities, research, campus police, investments, and/or the medical director as part of the senior risk management committee. As social media and technology propel risk events into the news cycle more quickly than ever before, communications leaders play an important role on the committee, assisting it in identifying institutional risks and in updating the institution's crisis response planning.

This team will provide the breadth and depth needed to identify, assess, and assign ownership of the top risks facing the institution. Ownership by a senior administrator of each risk is important as it creates accountability and responsibility for developing mitigation plans, testing those plans, and monitoring adherence to them.

Identifying risks without the appropriate follow-through could create potential liability exposure and a credibility gap in the community.

Step 2: Risk Assessment—Scoring the Risks

After identifying the risks, the next step for senior administrators is to assess: 1) the likelihood that the risk or event will occur and 2) the impact it could have on the institution's ongoing operation. This sorting and classification process creates a roadmap to help administrators identify the strategic risks that should be shared with the board to ensure appropriate oversight.

Risk assessment can be simple or complex, depending on the risks involved, as well as available resources and culture of the institution. It is not an exact science, but rather a process to develop priorities for the institution. The goal is to arrive at a shared understanding of each risk's impact and likelihood relative to other important risks. This

Exhibit 2: Sample Risk Registers

To start the process of risk identification, use the risk registers currently in use by other institutions to build your own.

Public University

1. Tuition dependent business model
2. Deferred maintenance
3. Cybersecurity
4. Talent recruitment and retention
5. Student enrollment
6. Campus climate
7. IT infrastructure

Independent Technical University Risk Register

1. Student well-being
2. Recruitment and retention of human capital
3. Data and cybersecurity
4. Public safety (students, staff, visitors)
5. Noncompliance (domestic, international, NCAA)
6. Tuition dependency
7. Crisis management
8. Student attainment and experience

Independent Research University Risk Register

1. Data protection
2. Graduate program enrollment
3. Research funding
4. Regulatory compliance
5. Financial stability & cost management
6. Undergraduate enrollment management
7. Legacy practices
8. Alumni & core constituent relations
9. Capital plan & facilities maintenance
10. IT infrastructure
11. Emergency preparedness
12. Student experience
13. Talent attraction and retention

Community College

1. Financial risk: Enrollment and demographic decline
2. Reputational risk: Inconsistent messaging and application of procedures
3. Strategic risk: Aging workforce, lack of succession planning, large number of looming retirements
4. Financial risk: Current funding and capital needs
5. Operational risk: Lack of disaster preparedness and business continuity plans
6. Operational risk: minors on campus
7. Strategic risk: Misalignment between operations and strategic plans
8. Operational risk: Lack of data governance

Exhibit 2: Sample Risk Registers *(continued)*

9. Operational risk: Outside violence coming onto campus
10. Financial risk: Further state and local budget cuts
11. Operational risk: Wasteful and duplicative budget cuts

Independent Liberal Arts College Risk Register (*Example 1*)

1. Student demand for programs in academic portfolio
2. Faculty governance
3. Strategic budgeting
4. Fraternity and sorority life
5. Employee development
6. Adequate academic space & deferred maintenance
7. Perception of College's response to sexual and domestic violence
8. Use of illegal substances on campus
9. Alcohol abuse
10. IT infrastructure
11. Student misbehavior/code of conduct

Independent Liberal Arts College Risk Register (*Example 2*)

1. Cybersecurity
2. Student mental health
3. Incident preparedness
4. Emergencies during college-sponsored international travel
5. Student substance abuse
6. Adequacy of financial resources
7. Succession planning and transition plans
8. Title IX compliance
9. Exclusive campus culture
10. Non-Title IX compliance
11. Community relations

Public University System

1. Governance: Systemwide and institutional goals, roles, and methods
2. Student enrollment
3. Government support
4. Liquidity, debt, and reserves
5. Health care costs
6. Employee morale
7. Management turnover
8. Return on investment in new capital projects and programs
9. Legal/regulatory compliance
10. Information security
11. Disaster recovery and business continuity
12. Fraud and conflicts of interest

Institutionally Related Foundation Risk Register

1. Changing state legislation and regulation
2. Fiduciary: Investment of endowment, financial reporting, and disclosure requirements

3. Economic climate reduces donations
4. Failure to follow established procedures and policies separating foundation from university
5. Succession planning for leadership
6. IT and data security
7. Crisis response plans
8. Coordination and alignment with other groups supporting university (e.g. alumni association, boosters)

Source: The above samples are actual risk registers gathered from a variety of institutions of different sizes and types. While many risks are common among institutions, many differences also exist; these lists are designed to be copied, modified, and used to start Step 1 of the ERM process.

requires a quick assessment process; participants in the assessment should strive to move toward consensus.

Colleges and universities use an array of different tools for assessing risk, from simple heat maps and worksheets to complex modeling spreadsheets and scenarios. For example, the senior risk committee of an institution with limited resources, using a simple heat map (see Exhibit 3), can start by writing specific risks on sticky notes and placing the notes in the quadrant of a heat map to reflect the impact and probability of the risk. Placement of the sticky notes depends on administrator's answers to the questions: "How likely is it that this will occur on our campus?" and "How bad will it be if it does?" The goal of this exercise is to identify the risks that belong in the "high impact/high likelihood" quadrant and begin risk mitigation plans on these risks first.

Insight: Don't Overlook Small Programs with Over-sized Risks

Risk identification that looks only at big-budget or well-known programs runs the risk of missing nascent entrepreneurial efforts or small programs that could create oversized risks. One campus administrator recalled that the key strategic risks for the institution had been developed and reported to the board and committees. It seemed that all was well from an ERM standpoint. In a subsequent meeting with the education department, a small program that cost the campus very little money was mentioned. For years, the program had been operating off the radar screen of the central administration. The program served underprivileged youth from the community, partnering university students with the children. Because the program was so small and unnoticed, appropriate training, background checks, and other risk mitigation practices were not in place, leaving unsupervised students and staff working closely with vulnerable children.

Exhibit 3: Simple Heat Map

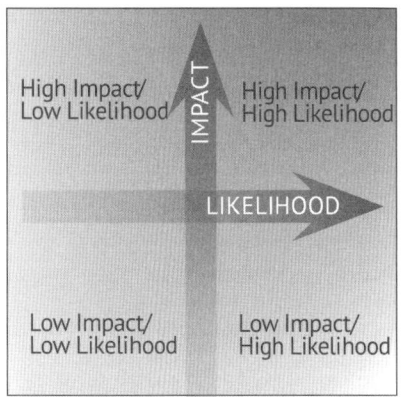

For institutions with more resources, a more complex risk assessment method involves the use of a scoring tool. (See Exhibit 4; for a more advanced risk scoring tool, see Exhibit 10.)[2]

By assigning risks an Impact and Likelihood score and then multiplying them, administrators can compute a total risk score (TRS) for each risk considered. The total risk score, however, should not be a substitute for the good judgment of the senior administration. While the TRS is a quantitative ranking, senior risk committee members should use their professional judgment to evaluate the ranking, reordering as appropriate and grouping the risks into high, medium, or low (or red, yellow, or green). This kind of ranking process helps institutions spend scarce resources on their greatest vulnerabilities, and not waste time and energy on risks that pose only minor threats to the institution.

The top five to 10 risks should be shared with the governing board and the appropriate board committee. The president and board chair should decide how the board will engage and conduct further inquiry

---

Insight: Overcoming the Availability Heuristic

People tend to rely on prominent examples rather than data when prioritizing risks, improperly using what psychologists call the availability heuristic. In our era of high-profile disaster media, objective risk assessment is essential to ensure that institutions spend their limited resources mitigating the right risks effectively.

In researching this updated edition, we spoke with multiple institutions where ERM grew out of a board-level concern about a specific, high-profile risk, such as an active shooter or a natural disaster. When starting ERM under these circumstances, it is especially important to assess competing risks honestly.

For example, one risk manager we spoke with had focused predominantly on active shooter preparedness since starting to work on ERM at the institution, reporting regularly to the board about that sole risk. When they had to evacuate a building due to a nearby fire, it became clear that the institution hadn't focused enough on fire preparedness. Even though active shooters were top of the mind for the board and senior leadership, fires were far more likely to occur and had the potential to be equally devastating. Balanced risk assessment ensures effective mitigation efforts.

Exhibit 4: Tool for Determining Total Risk Score (TRS)

RISK		1–2. Insignificant; Mild	3. Moderate	4–5. Significant; Catastrophic	SCORE
(Describe risk here.)	IMPACT	Minimal impact on annual operations, reputation or financial condition.	Moderate impact on annual operations, reputation, or financial condition. Could delay plans in place, affect short-term programs, and require moderate management effort; 1–6 months' recovery	Long-term and significant effect on annual operations, reputation, or financial condition. Affect ability to recruit students, faculty, financial support; material breach of confidence and reputation.	*(Assign number 1–5)*
					X
		1–2. Unlikely	3. More Likely	4–5. High Probability	
	LIKELI-HOOD	Unlikely to happen within a year and no immediate action is needed.	More than likely to occur within a year, and management should begin to mitigate.	High probability event/risk will occur within a year; immediate action plans needed.	*(Assign number 1–5)*
					=
				TOTAL RISK SCORE	

(Impact x Likelihood = TRS)

Using a Heat Map Smartly: One Public System's Approach

"Risk Assessment was somewhat arbitrary and capricious within our system. So the system's general counsel and internal auditor met with all of the presidents of the campuses in the system and identified the top 12 risks," reports the chancellor of a public system. "Working with my staff, we ranked each risk based on probability of the risk occurring and impact if it did. We shared our ranking with the presidents and a wider group. And, after some discussion, we agreed that getting the risks in the correct quadrant (of the heat map) was important, but we wanted to spend more time on the risk mitigation and risk planning, not arguing over the exact risk score."

into each risk. The second 10 to 20 risks should be assigned to department heads and deans with responsibility for developing mitigation plans and reporting regularly to the senior risk management committee.

RISK TOLERANCE AND RESIDUAL RISK

Part of the assessment process is understanding and articulating the institution's appetite for risk. How much risk is the institution willing to accept? When tied to specific objectives, this is sometimes called risk tolerance. A board can agree, for example, that an institution's finances can absorb a 10 percent decline in enrollment or a rise in interest rates of its variable rate bonds by 300 basis points. The board can ask for mitigation plans that address risks outside of that tolerance level.

It is unrealistic (and probably too costly) to have a plan to reduce the impact or likelihood of all risks to zero. The best risk management mitigation plans should strive to reduce the likelihood and impact to a level that would not disrupt the institution's plans and seriously damage its reputation. Residual risk is the risk that the institution is willing to accept after risk mitigation plans are in place. Residual risks usually reside in levels 1 and 2. (See Exhibit 6.) Legal counsel generally advises that it is not prudent to develop a risk tolerance score for health and safety risks, meaning that health and safety risks all require appropriate mitigation plans.

A goal of ERM is to have risk tolerance equal residual risk. The risk descriptions in Exhibit 6 can be used to rank scored risks into tolerance levels so that administrators can allocate resources to manage or

---

Insight: Identify the Upside of Risk

Sophisticated institutions don't limit the risks on their register to the downside. They identify speculative opportunities that, if approached effectively, could benefit the institution. Once institutions have identified and have a handle on the risks that keep senior leadership and the board up at night, it's time to expand the program to capture positive risks. What are the opportunities that will move your institution forward?

Several institutions place these risks on their own opportunity heat map, allowing ERM conversations to focus as much on capturing the upside of risk as mitigating the downside. For example, an institution might identify opportunities for increased enrollment, new programs, partnerships, or other strategic opportunities. By placing these on a heat map, the board and senior leadership can have productive conversations on how to prioritize opportunities based on their likelihood of success and probable impact on the institution.

Exhibit 5: Sample Heat Map of a State System

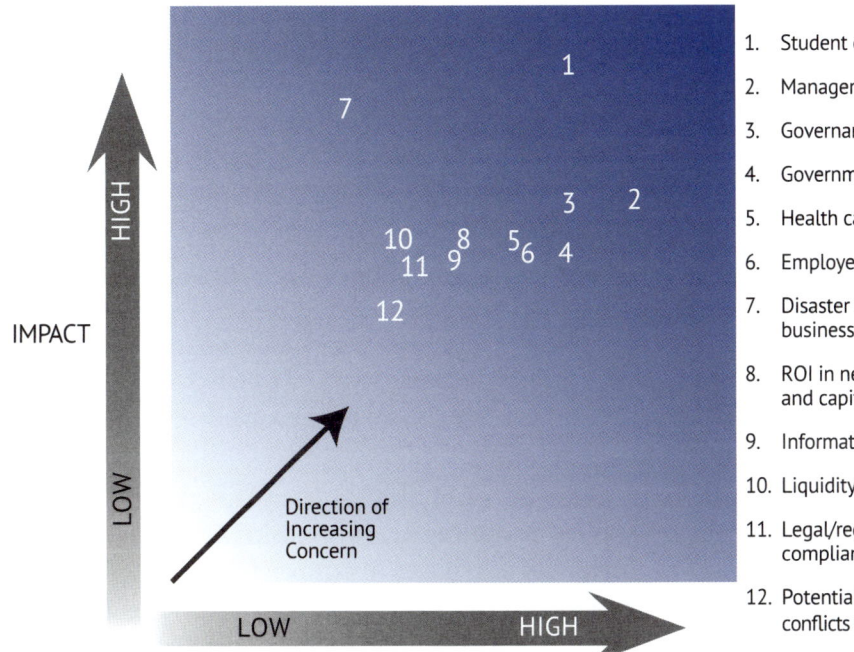

mitigate risks based on the institution's risk tolerance. Risk scores and tolerance levels should be reported to the board committees.

Step 3: Risk Mitigation—Developing Risk Plans

Risk mitigation is best described as problem solving. An event or trend has been identified that could either present great opportunities or seriously hinder the operations and plans of the institution. The challenge for the campus is: What course correction should be invoked to capitalize on or reduce the risk?

Textbook risk management definitions offer three options after risks are identified and assessed:

Exhibit 6: Levels of Risk Tolerance

Level 4 (Risk Score 16–25): Will not accept this risk. Risk treatment must be established immediately such that the residual risk is at level 3 or below. In general, these risks should be shared with the board as they will be strategic risks.

Level 3 (Risk Score 9–15): Will accept a risk at level 3 as long as it is reduced in the midterm through reasonable and practicable risk treatments.

Level 2 (Risk Score 5–8): Will accept a risk at level 2 as long as it is reduced in the long-term using low resource options. The risk should be analyzed to determine whether it is being overmanaged and where the control strategies could be relaxed in order to redeploy resources toward higher priorities.

Level 1 (Risk Score 1–4): Requires no additional risk treatment. The risk should be analyzed to determine whether it is being overmanaged and where control strategies can be relaxed in order to redeploy resources.

1. **Risk is transferred or shared** either through purchasing an insurance policy or signing a contract with a third party. Example: The university purchases insurance to replace buildings in the event of fire. (See Appendix C.)
2. **Risk is eliminated** because the program or risk is discontinued. Example: The president declines a grant to support a new research center because the risk of not securing long-term support after the five-year grant expires is too great.
3. **Risk is accepted but changes are made** to mitigate and reduce the risk. Example: Facing a sharply rising and unsustainable increase in the discount rate, the college implements plans to reduce its size to match student demand with available resources while it builds a new program to serve shifting student interests.

Administrators are rarely able to, or want to, eliminate risks by just staving them off. And the strategic risks identified at the senior level and shared with the board can rarely be transferred to an insurance company or shared with an outside vendor. Most of the strategic risks come from external forces, beyond the control of the institution, but they still must be addressed and managed. Mitigation plans should be developed to move risks from level 4 to level 3 or lower. Best practices for risk mitigation planning include establishing ownership and accountability for each risk, either at the senior administrator or department and dean level.

> **"Risk management is a process not a product."**
> —Director of risk management at a private research institution

Step 4: Monitoring and Risk Reports—Engaging the Board

Tracking and communicating the risks for board review is an often neglected but vital step in a sound ERM program. Monitoring and communicating risks answers the question of how well the institution is prepared to respond to issues and events that could derail its mission.

A board risk report should include two layers of documents:

1) To provide an at-a-glance portfolio view of the institution's top risks for the full board, the report should include a concise document summarizing the nature of each top risk, the campus owner, the risk score and tolerance level, the mitigation plan,

---

Insight: Learning from Peer Institutions

Higher education is distinctly good at sharing effective risk management practices. Whether you are managing a challenging risk or anticipating an emerging one, peer institutions are willing and able to help. We've heard that leaders in risk management, human resources, and other areas connect with regional peers to tackle similar risks and regulatory challenges. For example, many institutions seek advice from others in preparing for catastrophic events. Within a geographic region, institutions will work together to share resources in the event one of them faces a major disruption, from disruptive weather to an outbreak of disease to an act of violence.

One state system has formalized interinstitutional learning within the system. When encountering a new risk, the system office seeks a subject-matter expert within the system who trains on that risk. The subject-matter expert and his or her home institution becomes a "center of excellence." As other institutions in the system encounter the same risk, the system office directs them to the center of excellence for support. For example, one campus was among the first in the system to encounter the risks associated with on-campus drone operation by researchers. The drone expert on the campus became the go-to colleague for advice across the system as well as a popular speaker at conferences and events.

This information-sharing approach works beyond large university systems. Institutions not part of a formal system meet regionally with peers to discuss the emerging risks that many of them are facing and to share effective mitigation strategies for complex challenges. Professional associations and regional consortia for higher education connect peers on a regional and national level through conferences, regional meetings, live webinars, and listservs to enable institutions to share creative solutions to complex risks. While institutions in higher education may compete for the best students, risk management in higher education is a collaborative space.

and the risk score/tolerance level after the mitigation plan is in place. (See Exhibit 7.)

2) To provide a more detailed report on individual risks that informs the responsible board committee, the report should also include concise but more detailed accounts of each risk and its treatment plan, which should include a time line, status updates, and any relevant metrics. (See Exhibit 8.)

Board committee charters should clearly state the obligation to review and discuss—at least annually—risk mitigation plans presented

Exhibit 7: Sample Risk Management Report Cover Sheet for the Board

Risk Name	Risk Owner	Risk Description	Mitigation Summary	Current Risk Score	Future Risk Score
Enrollment	VP, Admissions and Financial Aid	Applicant pool, admit rate, and yields all producing negative trends. High school graduates in tristate region declining. Graduation rates below peer institutions.	• Increasing budget for recruitment • Developing ROI calculation for families • Increasing investment in career center	20	15
Controversial Events	VP, Student Affairs	Disruptive protests, demonstrations, speakers, or other unrest that can lead to reputational or physical harm	• Reviewing policies for controversial events • Training security and student affairs staff on their roles • Conducting table-top exercise for crises arising from events	15	8
Data Security	Chief Information Officer	Data breach leading to unauthorized disclosure of sensitive data. Loss of critical business and research data.	• Training end users on best practices • Implementing phishing tests • Purchasing back up servers	20	6

Exhibit 8: Sample Detailed Risk Management Report for the Board

Date:	January 1, 20XX
Name of Risk:	Enrollment
Risk Owner:	Vice President, Admissions and Financial Aid
Board Committee:	Student Affairs
Description of Risk:	Applicant pool, admit rate, and yields all producing negative trends. High school graduates in tristate region declining. Graduation rates below peer institutions.
Likelihood:	4 (Rate 1–5)
Impact:	5 (Rate 1–5)
Risk Score:	20 (Likelihood x Impact) Level 4
Risk Tolerance:	Level 3

Treatment:	**Treatment**	**Timeframe**	**Status**

	• Strengthen recruitment pipeline:
	  ◦ Increase budget for high school junior name search
	  ◦ Expand high school guidance counselor visits
	• Open admission office in city in new area
		End of fall semester	Complete

	• Focus admissions marketing on ROI:
	  ◦ Research and present reports on success of recent college graduates in securing gainful employment
	  ◦ Develop return on investment calculation to use in marketing to families of prospective students
		End of summer through next two years	In progress

	• Improve recent graduate career outcomes: ◦ Increase funding for career center to help place students in internships and jobs upon graduation	Next three years	In progress

Likelihood After Treatment:	2
Impact After Treatment:	3
Risk Score After Treatment:	6 (Likelihood x Impact) Level 2

Source: University of Alberta. Used with permission

by the administration. By providing annual reports on the risk mitigation strategies to the board and/or board committees, the committee is better positioned to hold the administration accountable and pinpoint gaps in identification of risks or plans for their mitigation.

ERM in Action

How ERM is put into practice varies, and it is often informed by the scale and scope of the enterprise. Comparing the process used by an individual university (University of Alberta) with that used by a statewide system (The University of Missouri System) helps illustrate this:

- **The University of Missouri System** assesses risks and assigns risk scores prior to risk mitigation plans and performs the same analysis after risk mitigation plans. The system also articulates its risk tolerance and continues to develop mitigation plans to move the risk score to be at or below the risk tolerance. The system office leads the process and involves campus presidents and senior staff in identifying, assessing, and mitigating the risks.
- **The University of Alberta** uses a continual loop focused on the university's top 10 institutional risks. The university uses internal and external subject matter experts inside and outside the university to identify risks. An internal ERM committee assesses the top risks and reports that assessment to the president's senior administrative committee before reporting to the board audit committee. The audit committee then reviews the reports and incorporates risks into the university's annual audit plan as needed. Other board committees also regularly review and monitor risk in their respective areas (such as finance, safety, and human resources) and report to the full board. Then the process begins again the following year. (See Exhibit 9.)

Exhibit 9: Sample Risk Management Process

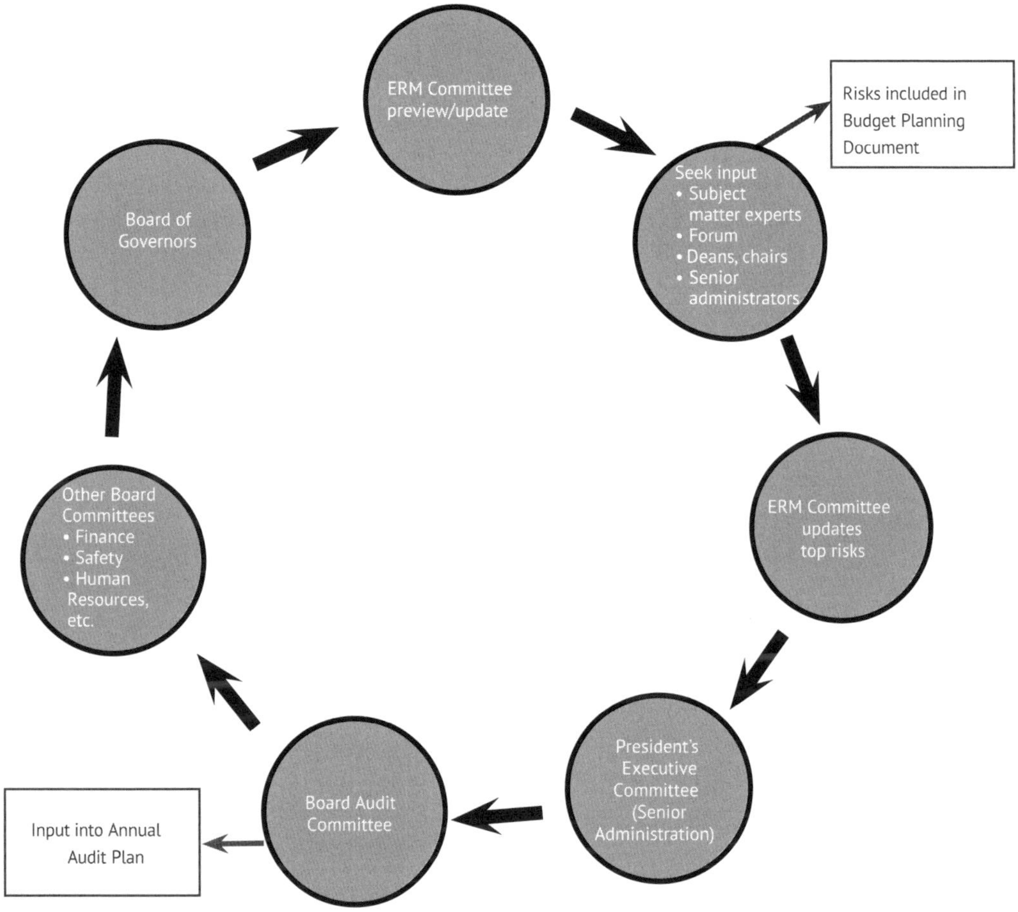

Exhibit 10: High-Maturity Risk Scoring Tool

Institutions that seek a higher level of precision when scoring risks may adopt a more detailed score card, such as the one below. This example, which pulls elements from several risk scoring tools in use at colleges and universities, retains the qualitative nature of the scoring tool in Exhibit 4 (page 17) while affording the ERM committee greater nuance in prioritizing risks. Institutions can modify risk scoring tools like this one to fit their risk prioritization needs—for example, by converting qualitative measures into quantitative ones.

How to Use the High-Maturity Risk Scoring Tool

First evaluate the impact of a risk across each row of the **Impact Scoring Tool**. Record the score for each row in the far right column. Some risks have a high impact in some rows and a low impact in others. For example, workplace discrimination can have a high impact on reputational effect and lawsuits, but a low impact on financial viability and safety. Then take the average of the four scores to determine the impact score.

After evaluating the impact, assess the likelihood of a risk's occurrence using the three rows of the **Likelihood Scoring Tool**. First consider how frequently the risk has occurred in the past. Then consider the likelihood that the risk will occur in the next year. Finally, evaluate the frequency of the risk if it occurs. In other words, if the risk occurs next year, is it likely to occur only one time, or does one occurrence portend future occurrences? Take the average of the three scores to determine the risk's likelihood score.

The risk of flooding exemplifies how the three likelihood dimensions might vary. The past frequency of floods on campus may be low, but forecasters predict a wet year next year. In addition, the campus drainage system is aging and needs repair. In this instance, the past frequency is low, but the chance of occurrence is high. If the drainage system fails, then the projected frequency will be medium or high since multiple flooding incidents could occur. If the drainage system were in good shape, the projected frequency would be low because it could handle most or all flooding incidents.

Impact Scoring Tool

	Low Impact 1–2	Medium Impact 3	High Impact 4–5	Score
Ability to Achieve Mission and Reputational Effect	Limited or no effect on achieving mission Inefficient work; some or limited rework Minimal reputational impact/negative publicity	May affect ability to achieve mission Extra work/rework; Loss of program(s) Moderate reputational impact/negative publicity	Unable to achieve mission Loss of program(s) Significant reputational impact/negative publicity	
Financial Viability of Institution	No or minor loss of assets or funds	Moderate financial loss Moderate loss of assets	Significant financial loss Large loss of assets	
Safety/Loss of Life	No or minor injury or illness	Moderate injury or illness	Loss of life Significant injuries or illness	
Lawsuits, Fines, and Penalties	No penalty, warning, or reprimand	Moderate fines and penalties	Criminal penalty, significant lawsuit(s), or liability	
Average Score				

Likelihood Scoring Tool

	Low Likelihood 1–2	Medium Likelihood 3	High Impact 4–5	Score
Past frequency	Has not occurred or has occurred very infrequently	Has occurred irregularly or occasionally	Has occurred regularly and frequently	
Chance of Occurrence	Unlikely to occur; low percentage chance of occurring	Somewhat likely to occur; moderate percentage chance of occurring	Likely to occur; high percentage chance of occurring	
Projected frequency	Zero to few projected occurrences in the next year	Few to several projected occurrences in the next year	Many projected occurrences in the next year	
Average Score				

Chapter 3
External and Internal Stakeholders in Risk Management

COLLEGE AND UNIVERSITY LEADERS ARE NOT ALONE in efforts to monitor risks and weigh their impacts on the future of the institution. Students and prospective students, families and alumni, legislators, regulators, accrediting commissions, bond rating agencies, bond holders, audit firms, bankers, employers, and the media—as well as every individual and entity with some stake or investment in an institution—are all watching to see whether the institution can survive and thrive as known and unknown risks occur at a dizzying speed. Each of these constituencies brings its own perspective and motivation to assess the institution's preparedness and resiliency.

External Stakeholders: Regulators, Auditors, Accrediting Commissions, Rating Agencies, and Banks

In particular, regulators, audit firms, accrediting commissions, and lenders (including bond holders, rating agencies, and banks) have direct and prescriptive responsibilities in assessing the institution's long-term viability and preparedness. The board and administration can learn from and tap into these external groups to support and enhance the risk management process.

REGULATORS

Higher education in the United States is heavily regulated. To ensure that institutions serve the interests of students and taxpayers, dozens of federal and state regulatory agencies, ranging from the U.S. Department of Education to the Federal Trade Commission, oversee institutions in connection with funding programs (including financial aid and research grants, as well as direct appropriations for public institutions), consumer protection laws, and other legal requirements.[1] State governments are increasingly involved in monitoring distance learning, and the National Collegiate Athletic Association requires a highly structured compliance framework for institutions participating in athletic conferences.

Penalties for noncompliance can be severe, including major fines, increased oversight, and even disqualification from funding programs. Because of the breadth of regulations in higher education, expertise in compliance is often spread throughout an institution. For example, facilities and student affairs are probably familiar with the Americans with Disabilities Act as they assist the community with questions of accessibility, while administrators overseeing the areas of facilities and environmental health and safety are most likely quite knowledgeable about the institution's Occupational Safety and Health Administration obligations.

A decentralized approach can work for many compliance issues. However, an enterprise approach to compliance management that includes input from experts across an institution can elevate compliance issues before regulators come knocking. Many institutions benefit from adopting an enterprise approach to compliance management to ensure they meet regulators' expectations. (For more information on the compliance risks, see chapter 6.)

AUDITORS

A cornerstone of a board's risk management and fiduciary responsibilities is an external review of the institution's financial statements and internal processes, one that is designed to ensure accuracy and completeness. A thorough review of management letters and accompanying reports, along with a confidential discussion between the independent auditors and the audit committee, supports the understanding and integrity of the representation of the institution's financial condition.

Insight: Audit Firms and Outside Consultants

Institutions working on enterprise risk management (ERM) programs have a range of options for outside help, including auditors, insurance brokers, and ERM specialists. Firms and independent consultants with expertise in higher education are using this experience to develop processes in risk identification, risk assessment, and reporting to boards. Using color-coded heat maps, metrics, and key performance indicators to help boards understand and track important risks, these consultants bring expertise and a broad range of perspectives to help senior administrators initiate and maintain an ERM process.

Here are some important considerations for engaging outside assistance:

Seek unbiased help. Following the corporate trend of ERM, audit firms may be engaged as both internal auditors and ERM consultants. However, conflict-of-interest standards dictate that different firms should be engaged to perform the financial audit and ERM consultation. Many insurance brokers also offer ERM consulting services. While an effective brokerage will understand the risks of its clients as well as anyone, consider whether guidance from an independent consultant might be preferred.

Make sure they know higher education. As discussed in chapter 4, heat maps and metrics don't guarantee effective risk management. Make sure consultants have experience working with higher education institutions. A corporate approach doesn't translate well to colleges or universities, where priorities can be multifaceted, shared governance is integrated into the culture, and planning involves a complex mix of qualitative and quantitative goals.

Use consultants to augment the institution's efforts rather than replace them. When leaders ask outside firms to develop an entire ERM program without input from internal stakeholders, that process is unlikely to take root. We have seen elaborate ERM assessments created by consultants languish because they were written in a vacuum. When administrators present the board with ERM plans from an outside consultant, the board should ask which internal stakeholders were involved in developing the plan, whether the plan lays out strategies that can work for the institution, and who the institutional owners are who will ensure continuity and integration within the institution's future operations.

Don't ignore in-house options. Many institutions—large and small, research and liberal arts, community colleges and foundations—use only internal resources when developing and implementing ERM. They advocate a homegrown approach to promote ownership of the process by senior administrators so as to take advantage of their institutional knowledge. Even if an institution seeks help from a consultant, senior administrators are going to be most effective in making the changes needed today, and they have credibility with institutional stakeholders that outsiders cannot match. Among the most effective college and university ERM program leaders interviewed for this book are a provost, a dean of students, and an executive director of an academic research center.

Whether the institution decides to retain outside consulting expertise or embark on an ERM program internally, it can rest assured that both are viable options.

ACCREDITING COMMISSIONS

As a risk management tool, the accreditation process illuminates the strengths and weaknesses in the planning processes and the ability of the institution to deliver on its promise of a quality education. The goals of accreditation are to: 1) ensure that the education provided by colleges and universities meets acceptable levels of quality and 2) help improve the quality through external review. The accreditation process focuses on evaluating an institution's ability to plan for academic success and student attainment as well as to measure the outcomes of the plan. In response to pressure, accreditors are concentrating more on risk management or how well the institution is able to respond to and recover from unplanned events.

> "If you want to launch ERM within an organization, you're best served to hire within because you want to find somebody that already has the relationships built."
>
> —Associate vice president for safety and risk services at a public flagship university

The accreditation process addresses risk management more in terms of concept than specific criteria. But how an institution thinks about, prepares for, and responds to risks is increasingly important. Another regional accreditor notes that, even though risk management is not an explicit focus of accreditors, "Board members need to understand that their obligations to risk management come through their three duties to their institution: care, loyalty, and obedience." To meet the expectations of accreditors, board members must develop strategies to counter the risks their institutions face.

Accreditors are particularly interested in college and university finances. Most risks directly or indirectly impact the institution's finances, and the recent uptick in closures and mergers has increased pressure to take adverse accreditation actions sooner to protect students. One authority at an accrediting commission noted that presidents and chief financial officers often understand the accreditation implications of a weak financial footing, but boards sometimes think they have more time to solve a financial crisis than an

> "Accrediting agencies are using the concept of risk management more than we explicitly talk about."
>
> —A regional accreditor

accreditor can allow. Financial instability is now the most common reason for accreditation action.[2]

Within written accreditation standards, specific references to risk management tend to focus on insured or financial risks and are more likely to be articulated in the standards governing the finances of an institution. Consider these standards:

- "In exercising its fiduciary responsibility, the governing board assures that senior officers identify, assess, and manage risk and ensure regulatory compliance."—*NECHE, Standard 3.11*
- "The institution ensures the integrity of its finances through prudent financial management and organization, a well-organized budget process, appropriate internal control mechanisms, risk assessment, and timely financial reporting to internal and external constituency groups, providing a basis for sound financial decision-making."—*NECHE, Standard 7.12*
- "The institution monitors its internal and external environments to identify current and emerging patterns, trends, and expectations. Through its governance system it uses those findings to assess its strategic position, define its future direction, and review and revise, as necessary, its mission, core themes, core theme objectives, goals or intended outcomes of its programs and services, and indicators of achievement."—*NWCCU, Standard 5.B.3*
- "The institution has sufficient cash flow and reserves to maintain stability, support strategies for appropriate risk management, and, when necessary, implement contingency plans to meet financial emergencies and unforeseen occurrences."—*ACCJC, Standard D.9*

Accrediting commissions are also increasing their focus on institutions' plans for new initiatives and their risks. Many institutions, particularly community colleges, have rapidly expanded campuses and workforces to accommodate new enrollments. Institutions that failed to account for the risk that growth would be temporary are now stretched thin. Accreditors expect boards and institutions to plan for a negative outlook in addition to a positive one.

Beyond financials, board members are often surprised to learn that accreditors are interested in governance. From the accrediting commission's perspective, the board is ultimately responsible for the sustainability of the institution and the quality of its instruction. Accreditors cited several examples of boards intensifying the risks their institutions face:

- Board members adjudicating their disagreements with each other and their administration in the media. (For more on this topic, see chapter 6 on reputational risks.);
- Factions on the board trickling down into the college's administration;
- Board members appealing to legislators to reduce funding to their college;
- Board member conflicts of interest between personal/business finances and the college's operations;
- Interference in shared governance; and
- Ambivalence to learning about their institution and the higher education landscape.

For accrediting commissions, governance includes actions state governments take involving public institutions and state- and system-coordinating bodies that are beyond the control of the board. Remember that accreditors serve as a quality control mechanism for the educational product.

Governance structures that sail through the accreditation process recognize the risks their institutions face and advocate for their institution to the government and the public. One president of an accreditation commission noted that she and her colleagues are willing to meet with boards who are unclear on their role in accreditation, and that they should contact their accrediting commission to clarify areas of confusion.

RATING AGENCIES, BANKS, AND BONDHOLDERS

The principles of risk management are integral to reviews that rating agencies and banks undertake as they evaluate an institution's ability to repay borrowed funds and interest. Banks, rating agencies, and, ultimately, bondholders evaluate the institution's ability to prepare for and respond to future external changes and shocks to the institution and economy. They also assess the institution's ability to respond to longer-term risks, including succession planning and shifting demographics within its traditional markets, as well as its capacity to develop and implement contingency plans.

The board and administration should also use the rating agency's or bank's report to identify emerging risks that may not be included on the institution's risk register. Checklists of risk management practices that rating agencies use to evaluate a higher education institution do not exist. However, rating agencies, as well as the broader financing community, increasingly expect institutions to have ERM principles in place. Such agencies as S&P Global and Moody's assess the institution's risks and risk management practices, evaluating how the administration and board prioritize risks, whether there is agreement on the top risks that the institution faces, and how actively top risks are mitigated. In response to high-profile scandals, boards and administrators are becoming more aware and concerned that emerging risks, as well as major reputational events, can materially impact an institution's financial strength, market position, and governance—for example, by leading to the departure (and even criminal prosecution) of key leadership, a drop in enrollment, or the reduction in gifts.

Moreover, a strong credit rating is not just important for access to credit. In an era when growing numbers of institutions face financial distress, creditworthiness can increasingly influence an institution's reputation among donors, regulators, and other stakeholders. By supporting better credit ratings, ERM protects an institution's broader strategic interests.

Rating agencies and investment banks continue to pay heightened attention to bondholder concerns for increased transparency relating to financial information, planning documents, and metrics. The Municipal Securities Rulemaking Board's website (emma.msrb.org) broadens the exposure of financial disclosures required by institutions issuing publicly traded debt. Such public and independent universities as Harvard University, Stanford University, Texas Tech University, the University of San Diego, and Vanderbilt University maintain websites to share

> "There is no perfect structure for ERM. Every campus is different. A large public university is going to need a different structure than a small private university. But it is certainly something that needs cross-functional participation and the engagement of staff, faculty, board, and even student leadership."
>
> –Vice president and senior credit officer at a credit ratings agency

Fundamentals of Risk Management

> **"Credit ratings aren't just about access to low-interest credit for many institutions. A downgrade from a top rating, even when taken intentionally, can damage our reputation among alumni and key partners."**
>
> –Chief risk officer at a private research university

relevant financial and planning documents with holders of their tax-exempt bonds. This trend will continue and intensify as transparency and risk management gain traction in all financial transactions.

Internal Stakeholders: The Board, Committees, and Task Forces

A clear understanding of the roles and responsibilities of all groups involved in developing a good risk management process will eliminate duplication of work and gaps in oversight as well as emphasize accountability.

THE ROLE OF SENIOR LEADERSHIP

The president/chancellor and senior administrators are responsible for implementing the ERM process by identifying, managing, and monitoring risks. The administration owns ERM and provides an organized process to identify risks to be shared with the governing board and committees. From the outset, senior administrators must allocate sufficient resources, including time and person hours, for ERM to succeed.

Insight: ERM Feeds Organizational Culture

A risk-aware culture embraces a way of working whereby employees at all levels collaborate to ensure that decisions and initiatives minimize the downside and maximize the upside of uncertainty. This culture brings strategic thinking to all levels of the organization, lifting employees above their departmental silos to consider the impact of decisions on the institution and all of its stakeholders. ERM can serve as one input to building a strong culture. To achieve a risk-aware culture, ERM must be present and meaningful for executive-level and director-level leadership. While that is more easily said than done, institutions can start by building accountability and collaboration for risk management. When influential leaders use the language of risk—for example, by asking about the uncertainties to an initiative and by recognizing collaborative risk mitigation efforts—other people on the campus see that this type of behavior and thought is valued. As they mimic that behavior, they not only develop risk-awareness but also help develop a stronger organizational culture.

Resource allocations vary by institution, but leaders will need to spend time identifying and assessing risks at regular intervals throughout the ERM cycle, as risk treatment and monitoring are ongoing activities that require attention throughout the year.

Once senior administrators have completed the initial ERM risk identification process, they should inform the board of the risks that have the greatest potential impact on the institution and the greatest likelihood of occurring. Boards should emphasize to administrators that ERM is never complete. It is a continuing effort that evolves and integrates into the institution as the years pass.

THE ROLE OF THE BOARD

Governing boards have the responsibility of setting the correct tone and demonstrating strong commitment to a robust risk management process but should refrain from actually developing the process or risk mitigation strategies. The full board's actions and words should encourage candor and transparency on risks. Boards should discourage the administration from bringing only positive issues forward and ignoring the gnarly, complex risks.

Insight: Discussing Risk with Non-Risk Managers

Administrators at many institutions are not accustomed to the vocabulary of risk management, and they are probably untrained in risk management. For them to understand the importance of ERM, boards and other ERM advocates may need to talk in terms they understand.

Some boards find that framing "risk" as "uncertainty" helps administrators conceptualize it. Every college or university leader must make decisions and act with imperfect knowledge of the future, and many are researchers who enjoy navigating ambiguity, so "uncertainty" comes naturally to many leaders.

Risk management then becomes the practice of reducing uncertainty. In other words, leaders are acting as risk managers when they envision the potential upside and downside of a decision or strategy and then act to maximize the upside and minimize the downside. ERM is a holistic, collaborative, or silo-busting framework to manage uncertainty—or to maximize the upside while minimizing the downside—for a team of experts guiding the institution through a perilous environment.

Insight: "Noses In, Fingers Out"

Frank Rhodes, the president emeritus of Cornell University, often referred to the board governance concept of "noses in and fingers out." That is also good advice for boards in how they approach risk management. The concept refers to the ability to sniff out risks and stay aware of trends while relying on the administration to provide appropriate and timely analysis and follow-through. The board's role in risk management should follow this guidance: Stay focused on fiduciary responsibilities and strategic direction, and rely on the administration for the data, reports, plans, and execution.

Insight: Three Models for Board Oversight of ERM

In researching this book, we identified three common models for board oversight of ERM:

- **Audit committee model.** The easiest answer for many institutions as to how the board should oversee risk management is to assign it to the audit committee. While this approach is popular and sometimes effective, there are several downsides. (For more, see *A Word About the Audit Committee* on page 101.) Among other things, this model may place too much emphasis on financial risks and fail to make risk oversight a responsibility shared by the entire board.
- **Dedicated risk committee model.** A more sophisticated approach is to establish a committee dedicated to risk oversight. Boards that use this approach often assign this committee responsibility for compliance, ethics, and other related functions as well as risk management. This model often maps the committee's responsibilities to those of the institution's risk management office, making oversight straightforward. However, it still fails to assign oversight of specific risks to the committees that oversee those functions.
- **Distributed model.** The most sophisticated model, which a number of institutional boards have implemented effectively, distributes oversight to each board committee for specific strategic risks that fall within its purview. Executed well, this model creates excellent accountability and recognizes the hard reality that risk ownership is a shared responsibility.

The authors of this book prefer the distributed oversight model. However, many institutions find success with the other models. It is important for each board to use the model that best fits its capabilities, as well as those of the institution.

BOARD COMMITTEES

Board committees should take responsibility for oversight of the most important strategic risks that fall within each committee's defined purview. (See Exhibit 11.)[3] For high-priority risks that do not fall neatly within a single committee's assigned role, and/or risks that transcend the charge of multiple committees, there are three routes to choose from:

- The **full board** addresses these risks.
- The **executive committee** performs the oversight role of risks that are not assigned to a standing committee and reports its work to the full board.
- A **task force** is appointed to monitor specific risks (such as a board task force on technology or diversity) and report its work to the full board.

For example, student mental health is often assigned to the student affairs/campus life committee. But the continued rise in mental health issues (including incidents of attempted suicide and suicide) combined with the impact that academic affairs, athletics, facilities, and other areas of institutional activity have on student well-being may prompt a task force of members of the student affairs, academic affairs, and finance committees to study this multifaceted risk. If a task force or the executive committee is appointed, it is important that members provide the full board with an analysis and review of these risks.

A Word About the Audit Committee

Boards are often tempted to assign responsibility for risk management to the audit committee alone, with a sigh of relief that now someone will be responsible for risk and the rest of the board can relax. The audit committee does a great job, the thinking goes, with reviewing the financial statements, checking on insurance coverage, meeting with the internal audit manager[4] (if the institution is large enough to have this function), and monitoring compliance issues—so why not give that committee the challenging job of overseeing institutional risk management?

Anecdotally, this approach appears to be the prevailing model for oversight of ERM, and it is similar to how many corporate boards

Exhibit 11: Sample Assignment of Risks to Board Committees

Board of Trustees Committee Oversight of Risks Report

Financial Risks

Risk Area	Responsible Management (Risk Owner)	Responsible Committee
Internal Controls	• University Controller	Audit
Finance Management	• Vice President for Finance and CFO	Finance
Budget Management	• Vice President for Planning and Budget	Finance
Endowment Management	• Chief Investment Officer • Vice President for Alumni Affairs and Development	Investment
Medical Billing Compliance	• Provost for Medical Affairs (Medical College) • Associate Dean, Billing Compliance (Medical College)	Audit
Financial Fraud	• University Auditor	Audit
Subsidiaries & Affiliates	• Subsidiary Management and Board of Directors • Vice President for Finance and CFO • Executive Vice Provost for Administration and Finance (Medical College)	Executive

Safety and Security Risks

Risk Area	Responsible Management	Responsible Committee
Patient Safety & Medical Malpractice	• Vice President for Student and Academic Services • Executive Director Health Services • Chief Medical Officer Physician Organization • Executive Vice Provost for Administration and Finance (Medical College)	Executive
Environmental Health & Safety	• Vice President for Human Resources • Senior Director Risk Management and Insurance (Medical Center)	Executive
Campus Crime & Code of Conduct Violation	• Chief of Campus Police • Judicial Administrator	Student Life
International Programs	• Vice Provost for International Relations • Senior Executive Vice Dean • Executive Vice Provost for Administration and Finance (Medical College)	Executive
IT Security & Disruption	• Chief Information Officer and Vice President • Chief Information Officer (Medical College)	Audit

Research Risks

Risk Area	Responsible Management	Responsible Committee
Research Subject Safety	• Senior Vice Provost for Research • Senior Executive Vice Dean (Medical College)	Audit
Integrity of Research Results	• Senior Vice Provost for Research • Dean of Faculty • Senior Executive Vice Dean (Medical College)	Audit
Allocation of Employees' Effort	• Senior Vice Provost for Research • Vice President Finance and CFO • Senior Executive Vice Dean (Medical College)	Audit
Research-Related Conflicts of Interest	• Senior Vice Provost for Research • Dean of Faculty • Deans • Senior Executive Vice Dean (Medical College)	Audit
Care of Animals	• Senior Vice Provost for Research • Senior Executive Vice Dean (Medical College)	Audit

Employment Risks

Risk Area	Responsible Management	Responsible Committee
Abuse of Authority	• Vice President for Human Resources • Senior Director Human Resources (Medical College)	Executive
Professional Misconduct	• Dean of Faculty • Vice President for Human Resources • Senior Director Human Resources (Medical College)	Executive
Governance-Related Conflicts of Interest	• University Counsel and Secretary of the Corporation	Executive
Discrimination	• Vice President for Human Resources • Senior Director Human Resources (Medical College)	Executive
Sexual Harassment	• Vice President for Human Resources • Senior Director Human Resources (Medical College)	Executive

Ancillary Activities

Risk Area	Responsible Management	Responsible Committee
Athletics Risks	• Vice President for Student and Academic Services • Director of Athletics and Physical Education	Student Life
Student Organizations, Fraternities & Sororities	• Vice President for Student and Academic Services • Dean of Students	Student Life

Corporate Officers = President, Provost, Provost for Medical Affairs, Vice President for Finance and CFO, University Counsel and Secretary of the Corporation

Adapted from Cornell University. Reprinted with permission.

function. Boards that use this approach must ensure, however, that the institution is able to understand, prepare for, and respond to the risks and opportunities that it faces beyond the financial ones. The purpose of a commercial business is to make money. Having risk management be the responsibility of the audit or finance committee aligns the financial priority of the business with its financial risks. But the business of higher education is teaching, learning, research, and service. While financial aspects are important—after all, there is no mission without margin—viewing risk management solely through the prism of finances creates a narrow lens through which the institution's strategic mission is not fully considered.

When overseeing cross-functional risk issues, each group assigned (board committee, the full board, a task force) should:

1. Review the risks the senior administration has identified. (See chapter 2, step 1.)
2. Ask questions on the process and scope of the risk identification process. (See Part II.)
3. Discuss and agree on the institution's risk tolerance for risks brought forward to the committees.
4. Review the risk mitigation plans or treatment that the administration has proposed.
5. Regularly monitor the administration's identification, assessment, and mitigation plans.

Which Committee Should Oversee Strategic, Yet Risky, New Initiatives?

Campus professionals and audit committee members in academic institutions and foundations where the board's risk management responsibilities reside in the audit or finance committee report some common themes and concerns. Most important is that institutions operating this way tend to monetize risks and may fail to address the strategic, reputational, and mission risks as effectively as they should.

Proposal: The alumni office and the career services staff proposed that the university consider offering additional courses to keep alumni current in their field and connected to campus. The administration believed that the institution remained on the top of alumni minds when it came to seeking professional development. An online learning program to serve alumni was proposed.

Dilemma: Administrators felt hard-pressed to handle an initiative to launch such an online learning program to reach alumni. Yet the project offered the potential to add to the bottom line and support the mission.

Decision: Assigning this initiative (and risks) to the academic affairs committee, rather than the audit committee, created deeper understanding and engagement among board members of the institution's programs and this initiative's relationship to other institutional priorities.

Risk Questions for the Academic Affairs Committee:

1. Has a formal market study been completed measuring interest in the idea and alternative options available to alumni?

2. Has the institution discussed partnering with other institutions or for-profit firms to develop online alumni courses?

3. Has legal counsel reviewed interstate regulations in offering online courses and other consumer-focused regulations?

Lesson: If the strategic direction of a new program or initiative is evaluated by a particular board committee, the attendant risks should reside with the same committee.

Chapter 4
Enterprise Risk Management Maturity

When the first edition of this book was published in 2013, many colleges and universities were just launching their enterprise risk management (ERM) programs. An assessment of the maturity and effectiveness of ERM was a distant challenge. Today, ERM varies in maturity at different institutions. Board members now sense an increasing severity of risks that their institutions face and are encouraging their administration to develop more-advanced ERM programs. They are posing new questions for their presidents and administrators:

- How do we identify the next big emerging risks?
- How do we maintain staff engagement in risk management?
- How do we incorporate the ERM process into our culture?
- How can ERM inform our strategy?
- How do we refresh our program after a few years of success (or even after a few years of challenges)?

Part II of this book will discuss many complex risks facing higher education. Readers may be unsure whether their institution is able to address those risks effectively. This chapter offers a framework for evaluating an institution's risk management capability. Where the institution is lacking, this chapter offers guidance on the characteristics and functions of high-performing ERM programs. As an ERM program matures, the institution will be better prepared to navigate the risk landscape.

Levels of ERM Maturity

Effective ERM programs in higher education elevate the risk management process over its outputs, emphasize cross-functional collaboration, and feed into culture and strategy. A mature risk management function must reflect those characteristics.

Before detailing the specific traits of the mature ERM programs in higher education, it is helpful to illustrate what **various levels of maturity** in ERM programs might look like at a college or university.

NO ERM PROGRAM

A college without an ERM program probably has a traditional risk management function, either as a stand-alone department or as part of another department, most often in the finance or legal division. Primary responsibilities for this function include insurance management, waivers, and contract management. There may be a dedicated risk manager, a full risk management team, or a staff member with responsibility for risk management and several other functions.

At this maturity level, risk managers have little authority to collaborate across campus, and many colleagues see risk management as a financial or business function. Departments across campus manage their own risks, often not realizing that many risks are shared across the institution. Risk mitigation is used to treat only symptoms of deeper problems or side effects of other initiatives; it is not incorporated into the institution as intentional risk management. The board rarely interacts with risk management staff except to discuss insurance.

LOW-MATURITY ERM

A low-maturity ERM program engages in some combination of risk identification, assessment, and treatment. ERM leaders or committees might end steps prematurely, fail to connect one step to the next, or omit steps entirely. One common low-maturity practice is to produce a risk assessment plan, or to hire a consultant to produce a risk assessment plan, only for it to languish unused. In other words, elements of ERM are present, but the institution is not taking tangible, repeatable action to manage risk.

ERM activities that require input from colleagues, such as identification and assessment, are vulnerable to strong personalities and bias.

The identification and treatment steps are particularly prone to recency bias in low-maturity ERM programs as leaders react to the latest event.

Administrative leadership participates in ERM only to meet a board or presidential mandate. As a result, risk treatment and accountability for risk management remains firmly with the formal risk management team. The risk management team tends to treat risks through risk transfer (i.e., buy insurance, enforce waivers, or sign contracts) or reactive, one-time mitigations that fail to address a risk properly over time.

Boards at institutions with a low-maturity program tend to deprioritize risk management. Risk reports are reviewed only by one committee or receive just a few minutes of attention each year. A lack of urgency on the board trickles down to the administration.

MEDIUM-MATURITY ERM

Medium-maturity ERM follows the four-step process discussed in chapter 2. This process repeats regularly and predictably, and involves most of the institution's executive leaders, communications professionals, and such key risk experts as security personnel. These leaders generally view ERM as a necessary process to protect the institution and perhaps themselves, and they assume ownership of the risks affecting their divisions.

Although the ERM process at this level sometimes identifies and treats risks before they occur, risk management continues to take a reactive stance to past crises and hot topics. ERM addresses risks to a department's or division's mission, but rarely cuts across functions or assembles cross-functional teams. The ERM leader, president, and board are confident that the ERM process manages downside risk effectively. The board receives regular risk management reports and expects campus leaders to mitigate risks.

HIGH-MATURITY ERM

All four steps of the ERM process are integrated into the institution's regular operations, and ERM staff meet at least as frequently as the board. The board and executive leaders review ERM outputs and use the ERM process when developing strategic plans to minimize the risks involved. The program identifies and assesses upside risks (i.e., opportunities) in addition to downside risks. Crucially, institutions with a high-maturity ERM program have refined their ERM processes over time to suit their culture and adapt to new needs.

The ERM process relies on methodologies that limit participants' biases, and it helps identify, assess, and treat the root causes of risks, which are often strategic or cross-functional. The process also includes a mechanism that enables stakeholders to elevate emerging risks to institutional leaders, who then begin treatment before the risk develops into an acute threat.

ERM helps the institution develop a risk-aware culture that informs decision making at the department and institution level. The ERM committee assigns risk owners to most or all risks, and risk owners consult risk management professionals as needed. The board and president hold risk owners and the ERM committee accountable by requesting regular reporting on mitigation progress and potential emerging risks. As a result, the board knows that staff are dealing with key risks and relies on data from the monitoring stage to keep a pulse on the institution's risks and strategy.

Exhibit 12: General Descriptions of Low-, Medium- and High-Maturity ERM Programs in Education

Low-Maturity	Medium-Maturity	High-Maturity
• ERM is reactive to the latest campus crisis or hot topic. • The ERM process is *ad hoc* and vulnerable to personalities or bias. • The risk management department is responsible for risk treatment. • Institutional leaders participate minimally or unenthusiastically. • Risk treatment focuses on fixing issues.	• ERM reacts to past crises while identifying risks to mitigate before they occur. • The ERM process follows the four main steps and repeats regularly. • Institutional leaders treat ERM as a necessary function to protect the institution. • Risk management is often undertaken by campus leaders at the department-level, but accountability could be better.	• ERM identifies emerging risks. • Risks to institutional strategies are considered before adoption. • The ERM process incorporates the four main steps and repeats regularly. • Risk management is the responsibility of ERM participants who are held accountable for risk treatment. • Institutional leaders develop a risk-aware culture. • ERM manages risks to the institution's mission across silos.

False Indicators of Maturity

Some board members and institutional leaders have noticed that their ERM programs are not producing desired outcomes despite complex tools or the faithful re-creation of a model that worked elsewhere. While ERM programs may appear deceivingly mature for any number of reasons, the following indicators commonly mask a program's efficacy. We urge boards to focus on action and process rather than written documents. To ensure that ERM influences the institution's direction, boards should ask:

- What concrete actions has the institution taken to address the risks assessed as priorities?
- How are leaders collaborating on institution-level risks?
- How do stakeholders identify and plan for emerging risks, and what are some of the emerging risks the ERM committee is investigating?
- What is the institution able to do or prepare for now that it was not able to before ERM was instituted?

The following three ERM program attributes are often mistaken for maturity:

1. **Too much emphasis on complex tools**. Many institutions, particularly large research universities, implemented complex ERM tools and software in recent years. These tools can visualize risk assessments, plan and record risk treatments, and create dynamic reporting dashboards. While an institution may input robust data into ERM tools or software, a weak process for collaboratively discussing and acting on risk limits effectiveness and disguises what actually may be a low-maturity program.

    Example: One large research university hired two staff members to lead ERM. After establishing a committee, they developed a complex software system to facilitate the ERM process. The quantity and detail of the data the system collected was impressive, and the board appreciated the reports they were able to generate. However, the board noticed that the ERM function had become perfunctory after a couple of years. Colleagues across the campus struggled to engage in the software's risk management language and processes. As a result, risk owners decided that ERM was not worth their time, and they rarely participated in risk mitigation.

To overcome this challenge, the ERM staff dramatically simplified their colleagues' access to the software system, keeping the technical aspects on the back end for their access only.

2. **Nominal participation on an ERM committee**. Boards may assume that the existence of a committee consisting of an enterprise risk manager and everyone on the cabinet is sufficient for an effective ERM program. It is easy to suppose that because staff are assigned to a task, it will be prioritized. However, the existence of an ERM committee does not guarantee attention to risk management or action to mitigate risks. Without dedication from participants and the board, ERM will have limited success. In other words, it's the commitment, not the committee that signals a high-maturity program.

    Example: One community college enterprise risk manager assembled an ERM committee consisting of the president's cabinet. Unfortunately for the enterprise risk manager, the cabinet was too focused on managing their divisions to commit to the ERM program. After one year with little success, the enterprise risk manager dissolved the committee with the intent to reconvene it from the bottom up. The enterprise risk manager sought new participants focusing on their interest in improving the college, aptitude for strategic thinking, and reputation among their colleagues rather than functional or executive representation. This new committee of risk champions varied in seniority and formal leadership roles. They were able to identify institutional risks and use their influence on campus to mitigate risks and advance risk management in a way that the cabinet did not.

3. **Excessive focus on ERM standards**, Risk management guidelines, such as those developed by the Committee of Sponsoring Organizations of the Treadway Commission (COSO) or the International Standards Organization (ISO) 31000, can provide a foundation for a strong ERM program. However, institutions sometimes get lost in faithfully adhering to outside guidelines rather than building an ERM program that is appropriate for the institution's culture. Board members should not assume that their institution's ERM program is mature simply because the risk manager claims to follow an established standard. Instead, look to the outcomes of the ERM process to determine its maturity.

    Example: Two public flagships with high-maturity ERM programs demonstrate how an institution can develop an effective program with and without outside guidelines. One university built its program using a combination of COSO and the Australia New Zealand Risk Management Standard. That program has been effective in managing risks on its own campus and has even been asked to support risk management at other institutions in the state. The second university's chief financial officer quipped that "COSO makes your head hurt," and that he would never be able to simplify it enough for his colleagues to participate. Instead he built his ERM program using the first edition of this book as his model. Like the first university, his program developed into one that the board trusts to manage risks with little additional oversight, and he has collaborated with other institutions in his state to build out their ERM programs.

Characteristics of ERM Maturity

Although there is no single path to a high-maturity ERM program, there are patterns that classify maturity across four main qualitative variables: "ERM scope," "ERM centralization," "ERM process," and "campus risk management culture." Each variable is made up of a few subcomponents. Such variables and their subcomponents are outlined in exhibit 13.

To use this education-specific maturity model, developed by United Educators, assess your institution's ERM program for each variable and subcomponent and select the level that best matches your program. Areas in which your program rates the lowest suggest the greatest areas for improvement. Use the variable maturity levels as general targets for the long-term growth of your ERM program and the subcomponent maturity levels as discreet goals for short-term improvements.

Remember that the purpose of ERM is to strategically mitigate institutional risks and seize opportunities, not to point to a model to claim that your institution has a highly scored program. As you read about specific risks in Part II, think back to this chapter and exhibit 13. Growth along which variable of ERM maturity is going to help your institution address a given risk? What low-hanging fruit exists on which to develop your risk management function? Which aspect of risk management is in most need of a refresh? This model serves as an aspirational ideal for risk management. The closer your institution can get to achieving this ideal, the likelier your institution is to withstand the risks outlined in Part II.

Exhibit 13: Characteristics of ERM Maturity in Higher Education

Topic		No ERM	Low Maturity	Medium Maturity	High Maturity
ERM Scope		Risk management is a transactional function.	ERM is a "pet project" for one or more administrative or board leaders.	ERM is recognized as a tool to manage risk across the institution.	ERM is integrated into institutional strategy/strategic planning and drives risk treatment activities.
	Purpose Statement	If a traditional risk management purpose statement exists, it does not mention ERM.	ERM exists, but its purpose is undefined or unclear.	ERM has a defined purpose, but goals are vague and activities are siloed.	ERM purpose is clear and drives ERM leaders to take action toward explicit risk management goals.
	Strategic Planning	Risk management has no voice in strategic decision-making.	ERM reacts to strategic decisions after they are made.	Leaders refer to ERM data and reports as an input when making strategic decisions.	Leaders discuss options with ERM as part of strategic decision making.
	Budget and Risk	The risk management function requests budget allocations specifically for risk management.	ERM does not influence budget allocations.	Leaders informally refer to ERM needs when deciding on budget allocations.	There is a process that uses ERM's assessment outputs and treatment needs to inform budget allocations.
	Reactive vs Proactive Planning	Risk management responds to incidents and mitigates risks after they occur.	ERM evaluates new risks after decisions are made.	ERM sometimes plans for risks in the immediate and near future.	ERM consistently plans proactively and scans for emerging and long-term risks.
ERM Centralization		Responsibility for risk management is held by one department or employee with little input from others.	ERM exists, but remains a niche with little influence.	ERM is established, but relevance is limited to selected functional areas.	ERM is a central business process that the board or president rely on to manage institutional risks.

Topic		No ERM	Low Maturity	Medium Maturity	High Maturity
	Accountability	There is no executive or board support for risk management beyond traditional RM functions.	ERM is an *ad hoc* function with no accountability or resources from the president or board.	President or board mandates leaders' participation in ERM but does not hold them accountable for results.	President or board mandates leadership participation in ERM and regularly holds leaders accountable for ERM participation and results.
	Connection to Board	Traditional RM activities are siloed in a risk management department, function, or employee with little to no connection to the board.	ERM reports to audit committee of board in an informative role (i.e., no actions are taken explicitly because of ERM).	ERM reports to one or more board committees who use that information in their role as institutional leaders.	Multiple board committees or the full board hold president accountable for managing institutional risks through ERM over time.
ERM Process		Risk management beyond traditional RM is an *ad hoc* activity.	ERM process is developed for a static point in time and with unclear roles for participants and a focus on minor issues.	ERM participants understand their role in the ERM process and use their expertise to address department-level risks.	ERM processes include a feedback loop that enables treated risks to fall in priority and places urgency on treating institutional risks.
	Risk Identification	Risks are not formally identified; employees and campus leaders implicitly know the risks to their functions.	Identified risks focus on small problems or break-fix issues rather than institutional risks.	Identified risks primarily affect the people or functions represented in the ERM process instead of the entire institution.	Risk identification uncovers the root causes of risks that cut across institutional silos.

Exhibit 13: Characteristics of ERM Maturity in Higher Education
(continued)

Topic		No ERM	Low Maturity	Medium Maturity	High Maturity
	Risk Assessment	Risks are not prioritized.	Risk prioritization is *ad hoc*, based on gut feeling or political considerations.	Risks are prioritized using quantitative or qualitative measurements that lack an established scale.	Risks are prioritized using quantitative or qualitative measurements that follow an established scale.
	Risk Treatment	There is no organized risk treatment planning or coordinated treatment.	Risk treatment is *ad hoc* and fails to treat top risks effectively due to a lack of planning, collaboration, or accountability.	ERM develops risk treatment plans that stakeholders follow, but activity is mostly uncoordinated or occurs in departmental silos.	Top risk treatment plans clearly define cross-functional treatment activities that are reviewed and updated as treatments reduce the likelihood or impact of risks.
	Risk Monitoring	Risk management outcomes are not reported beyond the risk management supervisor.	Risk management activities and risks are reported inconsistently or upon request.	Risks and risk treatments are consistently reported and updated.	ERM outcomes are measured through quantitative or qualitative metrics and are actively reported.
ERM Culture		Leaders see risk management as a transactional function that buys insurance.	Risk management is a service provider.	Risk management is a necessary, if burdensome, process to protect the institution.	Risk management is seen as a framework to enable more effective problem solving and strategic and operational decisionmaking.

Topic		No ERM	Low Maturity	Medium Maturity	High Maturity
	Commitment	Risk management's buy-in is limited to traditional risk management functions.	One or a few board members or institutional leaders think ERM is important to have but assign little priority to it.	Board and president are committed to ERM as a means to protect the institution.	Board and president rely on ERM for input into strategic decisions.
	Risk-Informed Operations	Campus leaders, directors, and managers consider risk indirectly, if at all, when making daily operational decisions.	Some ERM participants informally think about the risks to their operational decisions.	ERM participants consider risk when making operational decisions, though not necessarily with a consistent methodology.	Campus leaders, directors, and managers consider the risks to operational decisions in the context of the institution's risk profile.
	Communication	Risk management communications are rare and dictated by pressing risk management needs.	ERM participants use inconsistent language to describe risks and the risk management process.	Groups of ERM participants use consistent language to discuss risks and risk management, but there is no internal consensus on how to talk about risk.	Relevant employees, including staff not on the ERM committee, use consistent risk terminology to discuss risks and deliberate over strategic decisions.
	Collaboration	Risk management activities are exclusively implemented by the traditional RM function or in silos.	Collaboration on risk management exists on paper only.	Some risks are managed collaboratively but others remain in silos.	Leadership collaborates across divisions to address top risks.
	Risk Ownership	Risk ownership is the *de facto* duty of traditional risk management.	Risks are owned by no one at all or only willing department leaders across operations.	Ownership of some risks is assigned to institutional leaders with limited accountability.	All institutional risks have appropriate leadership owners.

Adapted from *Higher Ed: Use a Maturity Tool to Advance the ERM Process*, United Educators, 2020.

PART II | Risk from the Board's Perspective

> "Boards in every industry are being more closely scrutinized for their role in protecting companies from risk and fraud. Higher education is no exception.... Regulatory bodies expect all boards to practice strong oversight and good governance. As a result, there is much pressure on today's college and university boards to forgo the traditional roles of college boards of trustees in favor of transitioning to the same roles and responsibilities as boards in other industries."
> –BoardEffect publication from August 2018[1]

As outlined in Part I: Fundamentals of Risk Management, the ERM process, led by senior administrators, identifies and addresses for the board the top risks confronting the institution. Part II attempts to educate boards and arm them with questions to explore common risks to:

- effective governance,
- strategic direction,
- institutional resources, and
- the student experience.

This section culminates with a discussion on reputational risk and providing boards with practices to advance their institution's reputation.

The purpose of these chapters is to provide background information on a variety of risk areas prevalent in higher education and to enable the full board and specific board committees to explore these risks more deeply. The risks that are raised in the following chapters closely track the scope of the board and specific committees.

Not all of these risks will be on the risk register of every institution. Some may have been omitted by the senior administration when compiling the risk register, and others may not be applicable. The complexities of large research universities present different risks compared to small liberal arts colleges. Multi-campus public university systems face different risks than single-campus community colleges. Depending on their structure and scope, institutionally related foundations face their own unique set of risks, some of which may echo those identified here.

The board and its committees can use the conversation-starting questions in the following chapters to identify risks the administration may have omitted in its review and to support their understanding of the risk mitigation plans. The authors included a new section on warning signs at the end of each of the following chapters to further assist board members with their inquiries. Because many aspects of the higher education environment are changing at breakneck speed, neither the risks nor the questions are complete or comprehensive. Board members have an obligation to stay current on emerging issues and ask probing questions on those and other issues.

Chapter 5
Risks to Effective Governance

EFFECTIVE GOVERNANCE DOES NOT COME EASILY. Boards must be particularly attentive to the work required to establish and maintain strong governance practices. Both the executive committee and governance committee are tasked with responsibilities in this domain.

Executive Committee

Most boards of independent institutions and related foundations have an executive committee, as do a growing number of public institutions and systems boards. The principal purpose of an executive committee is to act on behalf of the board between meetings, as needed, and to assume specific responsibilities not otherwise assigned to standing or *ad hoc* committees. The executive committee's work generally falls within five broad categories:

1. Significant matters dictated by the calendar of events that cannot wait for a board meeting;
2. Processes that the committee has specifically been charged with facilitating, such as presidential compensation or oversight of strategic planning;
3. Matters referred to the committee by the board, chair, or president for study and possible resolution, such as community relations or public policy;
4. Issues generated by the committee itself or that intersect with the work of other committees and require cross-functional coordination, such as risk assessment or brand management; and

5. Routine or relatively inconsequential matters requiring pro forma action by the committee to conserve the board's time, such as approving board meeting agendas.[1]

The executive committee can play a role in helping the audit committee identify gaps in the board's risk management oversight. If the committee includes chairs of other standing committees and rotating at-large members, the executive committee can assess gaps in the risk identification work that the senior administration and standing committees have done. Standing committees of the board are best positioned to evaluate the risks senior administrators identify that are specifically related to their respective committee charters. However, some risks to an institution (such as those described in the chapters that follow) may overlap several committees or fall beyond the purview of specific committees. In those instances, the executive committee may lead the board in examining those risks and coordinating input from multiple committees.

In addition, an executive committee usually has responsibility for two areas of risk: 1) its own committee scope and 2) talent management and succession planning. (See the discussion on human capital in chapter 7, "Risks to Institutional Resources.")

EXECUTIVE COMMITTEE SCOPE

To open the dialogue, executive committee members should ask themselves:

1. **Boundaries**. Are we overstepping the boundaries delineated in the bylaws?

> "Executive committees that shift into activities reserved exclusively for the full board, and fail to communicate to the board, risk alienating the board and eroding a culture of strong governance essential to a strong and effective board. An executive committee that understands its appropriate role and has a transparent discussion of these questions will turn a risky situation into a force of positive governance."
>
> —Richard D. Legon, former AGB president and chief executive officer, in *The Executive Committee*

2. **Information sharing.** What information can and should we share with the full board and when?
3. **Agenda.** Is the board chair fully engaged in setting the executive committee's agenda?
4. **Chair responsibility.** Does the chair assume responsibility for informing other board members of the executive committee's agenda, priorities, and current work?

The greatest risk the executive committee will encounter, as a committee, is an expansion of its activities and authority, which compromises the engagement and authority of the full board. The executive committee should resist the temptation to take on risk assessment activities. Instead, when possible, it should delegate them to other standing or *ad hoc* committees.

In reviewing the work of the multiple committees, the executive committee is well positioned to identify gaps of both risk and opportunities that may not otherwise be uncovered. With the benefit of such a discussion by the executive committee, the committees and administration can then bring a more thoughtful analysis to the full board for consideration.

Consider this example. A university recognized the importance of increasing its online learning presence and made it a strategic priority. But the administration also knew that its technology readiness was a challenge, so the executive committee tasked other standing committees with examining different aspects of this issue, as follows:

Standing Committee	Risks of increasing online learning presence
Student Affairs	Diverse student body arriving on campus with disparity of devices prompts consideration of including technology funding in financial aid packages.
Academic Affairs	Investments are needed in training and equipment for faculty to offer online and hybrid courses. Review compliance with Americans with Disabilities Act.
Finance Committee	Budgeted full-time enrollments may decline as more students bring credits from nationally available online courses to institution; online learning portals need significant upgrades and budget support.
Full Board	Security issues need to be addressed to accommodate broader usage.

Conclusion: A discussion of these risks revealed the opportunity to partner with other colleges and universities through a consortium to share development costs for courses, which then could be offered to students from all institutions.

Governance Committee

The governance committee (sometimes known as the committee on trustees or the nominating committee) serves a unique role in board performance and in setting the tone for risk management. The risks that fall within the purview of the governance committee include:

- Board recruitment and development;
- Board performance assessment;
- Conflict-of-interest and code-of-conduct oversight; and
- Board policies and procedures, including institutional bylaws.

This is not a complete list; new risks will emerge over time at each institution. But governance committees should understand that these board issues can pose risks to the institution. Each governance committee should identify risks related to board functioning and then ensure that mitigation plans are developed and followed.

BOARD RECRUITMENT AND DEVELOPMENT

To open the dialogue the governance committee should ask itself:

- **Board composition needs**. Does the committee maintain a thorough list of skills, experience, and perspectives needed to enhance the board and use this list to identify candidates?
- **Board expectations**. Does the committee maintain and share with prospective nominees a clear description of the role and responsibilities of board members, including attendance and gift expectations?
- **Orientation and mentoring**. Does the board provide a comprehensive orientation and assign mentors to new board members?
- **Ongoing board education**. Does the committee identify strengths and areas of current board knowledge and, with the

president and board professional, identify needed board education and training programs in response?

In the current environment, board recruitment and development include concerns that can pose risks for boards of colleges, universities, systems, and foundations. Those risk factors include board member independence (and conflicts of interest), board member attendance, board knowledge and information sharing, and full board participation in decision making.

Some boards, most often those of independent colleges and universities and of related foundations, are self-perpetuating and not dependent on elections or appointment of members. They have the responsibility to identify and cultivate a strong and engaged board. Developing clear criteria to identify and cultivate prospective board members should be a high priority for the governance committee. In practice, this means developing a matrix of skills and experience needed and recognizing special talents and expertise that may enhance the ability of the board to perform its duties. For example, if the institution is trying to achieve a more national presence, the governance committee should identify candidates from a geographically diverse area.

Whether the board is self-perpetuating, elected, or appointed, comprehensive board orientation and mentorship programs encourage a quick assimilation of the board's culture. An exemplary orientation process includes a balance between education on fiduciary responsibilities and an understanding of how the institution works. When combined with a mentoring program, a strong orientation creates a safe space in which new board members can ask questions and existing board members can offer private guidance on the roles and responsibilities of board members.

Orientation should be carried through into ongoing board education, and time should be allotted at regular board meetings to examine the big issues affecting higher education, the institution, and the board's work. Not properly onboarding and educating board members can hinder the effectiveness of the board. New, and sometimes returning, board members may distract the board by moving into territory that is not within the purview of the board or by focusing on less relevant issues at the expense of institutional priorities.[2]

BOARD PERFORMANCE ASSESSMENTS

To start the dialogue, the governance committee should ask itself:

- **Board and committee evaluations**. Does the committee complete and review board and committee evaluations? How often?
- **Board member self-assessments**. Does the committee complete and review individual board member self-assessments?
- **Board strengths and weaknesses**. Does the committee identify strengths and areas for development of the board and establish appropriate board education activities in response?

Regular board assessments—of the full board, committees, and individuals—provide the governance committee with insights on board engagement, satisfaction, and effectiveness. Boards that fail to regularly assess individual members, committees, and full board performance increase the risk of perpetuating ineffective governance processes, ongoing conflicts, or dysfunctional deliberations. A well-functioning board cannot eliminate institutional risks, but it can increase the odds that they will be identified and managed appropriately. An institution is only as good as its board. Strong boards are more able to attract, retain, and support a strong president. And they help the institution fulfill its mission and implement its plans. Board assessments are important undertakings for the governance committee because they enable it to identify and address potential problems. The governance committee should create opportunities for board members to evaluate their contribution to the board and the institution, and for board committees[3] and the full board to evaluate their work and adherence to their respective charters. Well-tested assessment instruments exist for assessing individual, committee, and board performance. Committee and board assessments should be done periodically—best practice is every three years—and reviewed by the governance committee. Individual board members should complete their self-assessments before reappointment to the board.

CONFLICTS OF INTEREST AND CODE OF CONDUCT

To open the dialogue the governance committee should ask:

- **Conflicts of interest**. Does the board have a conflict-of-interest policy? Does it require annual disclosure? Is it followed consistently?

- **Code of conduct**. Does the institution have a code of conduct? Do board members adhere to it?

All board members must understand and follow the institution's conflict-of-interest policy and code of conduct; nonadherence presents particular risks to the institution. Oversight and enforcement of these policies—as they relate to the board—often fall under the jurisdiction of the governance committee (or sometimes the executive or audit committee).

A conflict-of-interest policy spells out the responsibility of board members to act in an unbiased manner that is in the best interests of the institution without regard to personal interest or gain. (See Exhibit 14.) The policy should prescribe, to board members and officers, the institution's commitment to avoid both actual conflicts of interests and the appearance of such conflicts. Because of the transactional nature of matters that come before them, investment and facilities committees should pay special attention to potential or perceived conflicts with their members.

Opinions differ on whether a board (or committee) member may have any business relationship with an institution. The institution, through the governance committee and the board, should decide what, if any, business relationships can exist and identify when compelling reasons or extraordinary circumstances may allow for certain business relationships. Regardless, in all cases, the business relationship should be fully disclosed to the board. (See Exhibit 15 for guiding principles: *AGB Statement on External Influences on Universities and Colleges*.)

Best practice is for all board and committee members (if committees have non-board members serving on them) to complete annual statements disclosing any existing or possible conflicts of interest. The governance committee should review these statements and respond as needed. Periodically, the governance committee should review and recommend for full board approval updated conflict-of-interest policies for the board, faculty, and administrators. It should also oversee the implementation of the policy and receive reports on its completion.[4]

In addition to a conflict-of-interest policy, the committee should maintain and annually share a code-of-conduct policy that clearly articulates expectations of each board member.

Exhibit 14: AGB Conflict-of-Interest Principles

1. Each board must bear ultimate responsibility for the terms and administration of its conflict-of-interest policy. Although institutional officers, staff, and legal counsel can assist in administration of the policy, boards should be sensitive to the risk that the judgment of such persons may be impaired by their roles relative to the board's.

2. We believe that the following standard properly gauges whether a board member's actual or apparent conflict of interest should be permissible, with or without (as the situation warrants) institutional management of the conflict: (a) If reasonable observers, having knowledge of all the relevant circumstances, would conclude that the board member has an actual or apparent conflict of interest in a matter related to the institution, the board member should have no role for the institution in the matter. (b) If, however, involvement by the board member would bring such compelling benefit to the institution that the board should consider whether to approve involvement, any decision to approve involvement should be subject to carefully defined conditions that assure both propriety and the appearance of propriety.

3. (a) When a board member is barred from voting on a matter due to actual or apparent conflict of interest, ordinarily the board member should not participate in or attend board discussion of the matter, even if to do so would be legally permissible. (b) If, however, the board determines that it would significantly serve the interests of the board to have the conflicted board member explain the issue or answer questions, the board, if legally free to do so, may consider whether to invite the board member for that limited purpose. Any resulting invitation should be recorded in the minutes of the meeting.

4. A board should not confine its conflict-of-interest policy to financial conflicts, but should instead extend that policy to all kinds of interests that may (a) lead a board member to advance an initiative that is incompatible with the board member's fiduciary duty to the institution, or (b) entail steps by the board member to achieve personal gain, or gain to family, friends, or associates, by apparent use of the board member's role at the institution.

5. Board members should be required to disclose promptly all situations that involve actual or apparent conflicts of interest related to the institution as the situations become known to them. To facilitate board members' identification of such conflicts, institutions should take affirmative steps at least annually to inform their board members of major institutional relationships and transactions so as to maximize awareness of possible conflicts.

6. Board members should be required to disclose not less often than annually interests known by them to entail potential conflicts of interest.

7. At institutions that receive substantial federal research funding, financial thresholds for mandatory disclosure of board members' conflicts of interest should not be higher than the thresholds then in effect that regulate conflicts of interest by faculty engaged in federally sponsored research. Boards of institutions that do not receive substantial federal research funding should take into account the federal sponsorship-related thresholds in determining thresholds for mandatory disclosure of board member conflicts of interest.

8. Interests of a board member's dependent children, and of members of a board member's immediate household, should be disclosed and regulated by the conflict-of-interest policy applicable to board members in the same manner as are conflicts of the board member.

9. Institutional policy on board member conflicts of interest should extend to the activities of board committees and should apply to all committee members, including those who are not board members.

10. Boards should consider whether to adopt conflict-of-interest policies that specifically address board members' parallel or "side-by-side" investments in which the institution has a financial interest.

11. Boards should also consider whether to adopt especially rigorous conflict-of-interest provisions applicable to members of the board investment committee.

12. To the extent that the foregoing recommendations exceed but are not inconsistent with state law requirements applicable to members of public college and public university boards, such boards should voluntarily adopt the recommendations.

Source: *AGB Board of Directors' Statement on Conflict of Interest with Guidelines on Compelling Benefit* (April 2013)
For AGB's full statement on conflict of interest, see www.AGB.org.

Exhibit 15: AGB Guiding Principles on External Influences on Universities and Colleges

Boards must police themselves in assuring the highest level of ethical behavior among their members, including avoiding any board member assuming the role as an advocate for a special interest in the outcome of a board's decision.

Governing boards must:

1. Preserve institutional independence and autonomy by:
   - Keeping the mission as a beacon;
   - Ensuring that philanthropy does not inappropriately influence institutional independence and autonomy or skew academic programs or mission; and
   - Ensuring that institutional policies governing corporate-sponsored research and partnerships with the private sector are clear, up to date, and periodically reviewed.

2. Demonstrate board independence to govern as established in charter, state law, or constitution by:
   - Ensuring the full board governs as a collective, corporate body, taking into consideration the need for individual members to apply their individual consciences and judgments;
   - Individual board members committing to the duties of care, loyalty, and obedience as essential fiduciary responsibilities; and
   - Basing the selection or appointment of board members on merit and their ability to fulfill the responsibilities of the position.

3. Keep academic freedom central and be the standard bearer for the due-process protection of faculty, staff, and students.

4. Assure institutional accountability to the public interest by:
   - Serving as a bridge to the external community;
   - Informing, advocating, and communicating on behalf of the institution; and
   - Exhibiting exemplary public behavior.

Source: AGB Statement on External Influences on Universities and Colleges (2012).
(See full statement at: www.AGB.org)

BYLAWS, POLICIES, AND PROCEDURES

To open the dialogue the governance committee should ask:

- **Bylaws**. When were the bylaws last reviewed? Do they incorporate any legal or regulatory changes? Do they reflect how the board currently operates?
- **Policies**. Is the board manual current and up to date? Do all board members have a copy or electronic access to it?

Bylaws provide a roadmap for good governance. They outline the duties of board members and officers, procedures for holding meetings, elections processes, conflict-of-interest and indemnification policies, and other essential corporate governance matters. To be effective, they must be current. Bylaws are governed by state law and should be reviewed by legal counsel every five years to ensure that they reflect both changes in laws and significant changes in how the board conducts its business.

The bylaws become very important when something goes wrong, either internally or from an external source. While board members might not regularly reference them, if the institution is involved in a lawsuit, the bylaws become a foundational document for guiding the board through the conflict.[5]

The board's policies and procedures, which clarify the components and implementation of its legal fiduciary obligations, are also the responsibility of the governance committee. More specifically, a policy manual or handbook should be in place to guide the work of the board and its committees. The governance committee's role in risk management begins with reviewing board-level policies and procedures (or making sure the appropriate committee reviews them) on a regular basis to ensure that they are up to date and that the board follows them.

INSTITUTIONALLY RELATED FOUNDATIONS

In addition to assuring that good governance is in place, boards also need to understand the limits of their governing duties. Not all matters related to the institutions they serve require a board's oversight.

Since the middle of the 20th century, institutionally related foundations have supported a "margin of excellence" at public colleges and universities by generating financial support that supplements tuition and state funding. They are tax-exempt, charitable organizations that may accept tax-deductible contributions to support the institution pursuant to Internal Revenue Code sections 170(b)(l)(A)(iv) and 501 (c)(3). Over the years, the mission of related foundations has expanded to include certain duties that the public universities cannot perform under state law, such as accepting charitable contributions. In practice, foundations enable public universities to access private funds for research, scholarships, and other activities areas.[6]

Varying widely from institution to institution, foundation responsibilities may include, but are not limited to, management of the endowment, real estate, and intellectual property; donor and alumni record-keeping; and purchasing—all pursued in support of the mission and goals of the respective public college or university. In today's increasingly competitive world, foundations allow public institutions to better compete with independent colleges and universities that have endowments. Experts in higher education anticipate that foundations supporting public institutions—from community colleges to comprehensive research universities—will gain in importance as public support of higher education continues to decline.

This section addresses issues distinct to foundations that support public institutions; other sections in the book address risks that are common to most boards and managed through committees (such as investment, governance, and development). Risks specific to foundation boards include:

- State laws and regulations, including freedom of information;
- Board membership and conflicts of interest; and
- Administrative support and shared services.

To open the dialogue foundation board members should ask:

- **Delineation of roles**. Are the functions of the foundation and institution clearly delineated and understood by board members and staff of both?
- **Separation of operations**. Are policies and procedures separating the operations of the foundation and institution developed with guidance of legal counsel? Are they strictly adhered to?
- **Open-records laws**. Does the foundation comply with state requirements for open records? Where possible, does it protect the confidentiality of donors?

Foundation-Institution Relations

Establishing clear distinctions on the roles and responsibilities of the foundation staff and board members and adherence to a memorandum of understanding between the university and the foundation are best practices. Although state laws vary greatly, most foundations will not be able to accept any state funding if they want to operate independently. A new foundation will be particularly challenged as it begins operations, reimbursing the university for any services it provides to the foundation and maintaining financial independence without endowment support.

The greatest risk for a foundation is the reputational risk to the institution it supports that comes with a breach of public trust. It's crucial that the foundation board monitor the university's adherence to gift-use policies and to following the donor's intent of the gift.

Open-Records Laws

The scrutiny of foundation policies and practices from the press and public has increased in recent years. High-profile cases of alleged misuse of funds and court rulings imposing state open-records standards on related foundations raise the risks that a foundation will not be able to achieve its mission in support of the institution, including maintaining anonymity for donors that request it.

Foundations that rely on the college or university for resources—such as information technology (including data storage), office space and facilities,

---

Foundations and Open-Records Laws

The Student Press Law Center lists the following factors as influential in successfully litigating the applicability of a state's open-records laws to a related foundation:

1. Whether the foundation shares the same directors with the university;
2. Whether it uses university employees;
3. Whether it uses university property or resources;
4. Whether it receives state funds; and
5. Whether it is responsible for managing university assets.

The center notes in its tip sheet, "Unfortunately, courts ranked the relative importance of each factor differently, and one judge's analysis may not prevail in a neighboring jurisdiction."

Source: "Tip Sheet: Access to University Foundation Records." Student Press Law Center, 2010. For more information, see www.splc.org.

human resources (for example, shared staff), and accounting functions should understand the structure of their relationship, the autonomy of the foundation, and relevant state laws. Because this is a complex and evolving area, the foundation board should use legal counsel and association resources to stay abreast of changes in state regulations and court rulings that may necessitate changes in how the institution and foundation operate in support of their respective missions.

Governance Warning Signs and Board Actions

The board can get a sense of whether additional coordination or internal oversight around board governance issues are needed by considering the following warning signs:

Board Inquiry	Board Governance Warning Sign	Possible Board Actions
Does each board committee have a clear scope, including which risks that committee is responsible for overseeing?	Risks are not tied to committees, or it is unclear which risks are overseen by which committee.	Assign a board committee to each of the institution's ERM plan risks in addition to the administrator assigned to oversee the risk.
Are board members trained regularly and has the board engaged in succession planning?	New board members do not receive training on the board's scope, purpose, and responsibilities. Current board members are not regularly trained on best practices and emerging risks. When board members leave, their responsibilities are not documented.	Develop training for new board members, ongoing training for current board members, and document responsibilities and practices for each committee.
Does the institution implement, follow, and audit conflicts of interest, code of conduct, and performance assessments for all board members?	There are no clear policies involving conflicts of interest, conduct, or performance assessments. There are known conflicts of interest or issues involving board conduct or performance.	Develop and audit the implementation of conflicts of interest, code of conduct, performance assessments.

Chapter 6
Risks to Strategic Direction (and Shared Risks)

STANDING COMMITTEES PLAY AN IMPORTANT ROLE IN working with senior administrators to assess the risks and responses facing the institution. Some risks do not fit neatly within the charter and purview of the standing committees and can be the work of the full board. While the executive committee or the audit committee can address some of those risks, for reasons that AGB's *The Executive Committee* describes, the full board—sometimes facilitated through ad hoc committees or task forces—is the ideal place for discussion of shared risks that cross functional boundaries.

Risks that ultimately fall within the purview of the full board include:

- Strategic planning;
- Mergers, acquisitions, and closures;
- Compliance;
- Crisis response and business continuity;
- Catastrophic weather and climate change;
- Reputation and brand (for a discussion of reputational risk, see chapter 9, "Advancing Reputation");
- Campus unrest and controversial events; and
- Community relations.

Strategic Planning

To open the dialogue the full board should ask:

- **Market position.** What is the institution's position in the market? Do internal or external dynamics threaten that position?
- **Constituents.** Who are the institution's core enrollment demographic groups? Are there demographic shifts that affect the institution's relationship within those demographic groups? How are their needs and expectations changing, and how will the institution respond?
- **Metrics.** Has the institution identified the appropriate metrics and tracking tools, beyond financial ratios, to provide timely and accurate reports on performance against its plans?
- **Data quality.** Does the board have confidence in the quality of the data and ongoing metrics and reports?
- **New initiatives.** Is a sound business plan in place for evaluating new programs, regulatory requirements, and other special initiatives? Do these plans take into account revenue and expense assumptions and identify key risk factors?

The power and value of a strategic plan, which articulates the institution's aspirations and priorities, should not be underestimated. Discussions with accrediting commissions reveal that an institution's planning process is an important criterion, explicitly in specific standards and implicitly in the tone and focus of the accreditation process. The accreditation process not only gauges academic quality; it also assesses whether the institution will continue to be in business for the next five to 10 years and graduate students as promised. A well-constructed, thoroughly tested, and clearly displayed strategic plan helps to answer that question.

The presence of so many stakeholders and a constantly evolving legal and financial landscape make risk unavoidable in strategic planning. In fact, the purpose of a strategic plan is to take the right mix of risks to better achieve the institution's mission. A collaborative risk analysis can help the institution ensure the success of its strategic plan. Clarity on strategic risks helps an institution select ambitious objectives while maintaining confidence that it is taking the right steps to enhance its position in the market.

A risk-aware approach helps avoid the decision paralysis that causes many institutions to draft risk-averse, consensus-driven strategic

> **"Planning is the one area that generates major governance problems, most often manifested as the absence of planning."**
>
> —Former president at a regional accreditor

plans. One former executive vice president of a private research institution, says that presidents who have guided their institutions to success often have risk top of mind. He notes, "They are not paralyzed by risk. They and their teams become artful managers who manage through risk."

Enterprise risk management (ERM) should extend strategic thought throughout the life of a strategic plan. "Does the institution adequately plan and monitor its performance against that plan?" is an important risk management question for boards to ask of senior leadership. Ralph Wolff, a former president of the Western Association of Schools and Colleges, notes that institutions are called upon to assess their "changing ecology," which includes changing demographics, competition, external funding, and elasticity of demand for education. In this environment, the institution must monitor the success of its strategic plan and adapt to new risks as necessary. In turn, boards must assess the rigor and thoroughness of the institution's interpretation of and response to this changing ecology.

Plans are just that: plans. As circumstances change, the strategic plan and institutional priorities may also evolve. From its vantage point, the board should encourage administrators to identify programs and services that the institution can phase out or eliminate to make room for new initiatives to adapt to the changing landscape. New programs and partnerships are often incorporated into a strategic plan, and the board should insist that an ERM analysis be completed for major new programs and ventures.[1]

MERGERS, ACQUISITIONS, AND CLOSURES

Merger and acquisition activity increased in the years after the recession, as some institutions, typically small private colleges in the Northeast and Midwest, realized they could not survive financially. Consolidation is likely to continue as the population of traditional-age students declines. In fact, 12 percent of college business officers report that their senior administration held serious internal discussions about merging with another college or university in the 2018–2019 year.[2]

Risks pertaining to mergers, acquisitions, and closures are far too plentiful to enumerate here. Suffice it to say that both sides to the transaction must consider critical risks. For the weaker institution, waiting too long to explore a merger or closure is the primary risk.

Boards should frame mergers as a strategy to ensure the institution's mission continues, even if the institution itself is no longer financially viable. When an institution waits too long, it cannot negotiate from a position of strength, potentially compromising the continuation of its mission. Worse, a merger may not even be possible, leaving closure as the only option.

The acquiring institution also has many risks, from acquired institution's deferred maintenance backlog to securing state and accreditor approval. While an acquisition can greatly expand capacity, it also increases operating expenditures as the institution takes on new staff, buildings, and programs. If the institution does not have a plan to secure revenue from the increased capacity, the merger could put it in in a precarious financial position resulting from an expansion beyond core strengths.

For both the acquired and acquiring institutions, stakeholders become a major risk to a merger's success. Establishing buy-in from key constituencies—especially students, faculty, staff, and alumni—is vital. Opposition to a merger is inevitable, but a clear articulation of how the merger helps achieve the mission that stakeholders care deeply about, while protecting the institution's traditions and history, can mitigate the strength of stakeholder opposition.

Mergers are equally financial and emotional affairs. Boards at institutions on both sides of a merger should keep their emotions in check as they consider what is best for their stakeholders today and in the future. An honest approach to asking questions about the institution's long-term viability early on in the process can mean the difference between a successful merger and a sudden closure.[3]

> **"Higher education mergers are often seen as a sign of personal and institutional defeat, to be avoided at all costs. Yet the truth is that waiting until the last possible moment, when the institution is in full tail spin, is the true sign of failure. The time to be watching for strategic partnerships or opportunities for merger or acquisition—specifically those opportunities that make the institution stronger, not weaker—is always now."**
>
> —Chief officer and founding president of a public research institution and medical center[4]

Institutional Compliance

The board is ultimately responsible for ensuring that the institution manages compliance risks responsibly. To open the dialogue the board can ask leaders questions including:

- **Compliance obligations.** Is the institution meeting its compliance obligations?
- **Management of compliance.** Who manages compliance—is it an individual position or department, or is compliance scattered across the institution?
- **Internal compliance processes.** Who ensures that the institution is in compliance? Does that position or department have authority to mandate corrective actions by individual departments?
- **Compliance policies and training.** What policies does the institution have, where are they stored, how frequently are they updated and by whom, and how are stakeholders trained on existing policies?

Higher education is a highly regulated sector, with federal and state legislatures continuing to look for ways to monitor activities and outcomes. Although not at the level of financial institutions and utilities, higher education faces a labyrinth of rules and regulations that must be followed. Noncompliance can lead to fines, liabilities, and reputational risk.

Compliance requirements vary according to the size, complexity, and mission of the institution. However, all institutions must comply with a core set of employment, financial, safety, and environmental regulations. The size and scope of an institution's athletic programs, research agenda, and international programs are key differentiators in compliance obligations. A variety of useful resources are available online.[5]

Compliance is a risk category. Institutions should evaluate and respond to compliance risks using a framework similar to the broader ERM structure. Senior administrators are responsible for developing the structure of the compliance program. They should report regularly to the audit committee on the structure of the program, as well as on any compliance violations that may be reported to federal or state agencies and therefore become public. The audit committee typically plays a central role in understanding an institution's compliance obligations and ensuring that the institution has policies and processes in place to effectively meet these obligations. Because compliance relates to nearly every function on a college campus, other board committees may also monitor compliance specific to the functional areas they oversee.

The reality of the sheer number of regulations requires institutions to make informed judgment calls aimed at determining top compliance priorities and those that should be tackled before less-pressing issues. Institutions must focus initially on regulations that have the greatest potential to provide safety. Then institutions can evaluate compliance through a thoughtful assessment process, analyzing which regulations bring the greatest financial cost for noncompliance and which regulations bring the greatest reputational costs.

Compliance encompasses more than local, state, and federal rules. Inaccurate reporting to the National Collegiate Athletic Association, *U.S. News & World Report*, and other external parties creates reputational and financial risk. False reporting of information during an accreditation review can jeopardize accreditation. While misrepresenting admissions or other data to the external media may not carry the same consequences, fines, and penalties, reputational damage can be significant, and processes should be in place to avoid intentional and unintentional misreporting of data. New programs and initiatives bring both new opportunities and new compliance issues. While the appropriate board committee will review the risks associated with a new program, the audit committee should have a process in place to ensure that any new compliance issues are also addressed.

Reporting Structures: Who Oversees Compliance?

Much like the internal audit office and the general counsel's office, an institutional compliance office must be viewed as an impartial entity looking out for the institution's best interests rather than the interests of a department or individual leader.

At some institutions, the compliance office reports to the chief financial officer, the general counsel, the risk management personnel, or ERM personnel with no direct line to the president. In other cases, the compliance office reports directly to the president to ensure that all areas have appropriate oversight. More institutions are shifting the compliance office to report directly to the president to avoid conflicts of interest and create an additional resource for all stakeholders. This structure allows the compliance office to audit the compliance practices of all areas, including the chief financial officer or the general counsel, which may not be possible when the compliance office reports to these areas.

At institutions with decentralized compliance models, it can be unclear who is responsible for ensuring institutional compliance when there are no coordinated efforts and multiple positions or departments may manage a single compliance risk. In this case, the institution may not be reviewing the policies and practices of departments responsible for individual compliance efforts.

Ultimately, boards should consider reporting structures for the compliance office or position responsible for overseeing institutional compliance. Boards should inquire regularly about if and how the institution is auditing departmental compliance, and what compliance risks may need additional resources or oversight.

Insight: Using Compliance Programs to Kick-Start ERM

When compliance, finance, or auditing lead the charge for an ERM program, the focus may initially be to capture legal or regulatory issues. However, a successful compliance program can assist leaders with buy-in for ERM across all risk areas.

Instead of tackling ERM for all areas at once, one institution started by developing an institutional compliance program. The program grew to include 30 cross-functional units as leaders requested to have a voice in the compliance program.

Much like traditional risk management, stakeholders often view compliance as the "office of no." Another institution's office of compliance uses a carrot approach by partnering with departments to find common solutions. The compliance officer sees himself as a "compliance concierge" instead of a "compliance cop" in working with various areas to solve problems rather than policing them. Given the program's success, the institution is now looking to expand the program into an institutionwide ERM program in partnership with risk management. While compliance will not lead the ERM charge, the success of a centralized compliance program created the buy-in necessary to launch an enterprise model at a larger scale.

Compliance Is Not Risk Management. Boards should not confuse compliance with risk management. Merely complying with regulations and legal obligations does not mean that the institution has managed a risk effectively.

Boards must help the institution push past a compliance lens to get to the deeper, strategic issues. Instead of focusing on never-ending lists of regulations and legal requirements, the board's role is to set the tone for the institution's compliance program. It must ensure that the institution has the resources to adequately consider compliance as a whole, rather than in silos without coordination or through internal auditing by a single entity.

Crisis Response and Business Continuity

To open the dialogue the board may ask:

- **Crisis response plan.** Does the campus have a crisis response plan, and is it regularly tested and revised? Does it include a communications plan?
- **Board communications.** Do board members understand their collective and individual roles in a crisis? Are procedures in place to keep them informed during a crisis?
- **Leadership contingency plan.** Is a plan in place to respond if a crisis is directed at the president, a board member, or the board chair?
- **Data recovery.** Does the crisis response plan include an evaluation of technology needs to support recovery of data and restoration of all services? Does it include evaluation of campus research to support protection and recovery?

> "Over the last decade, most financial institutions have taken appropriate steps and made critical investments in response to increased regulatory compliance requirements. Efforts to address compliance requirements alone, however, do not necessarily prepare institutions to deal with the diversity of risks they face on a continual basis. Leading institutions have gone beyond addressing compliance needs and have more fully integrated risk management processes into business activities, IT and operations, and treasury and finance functions."
>
> —"Risk Management—Moving Beyond Compliance," *Risk & Compliance*[6]

- **Business continuity plan**. After the immediate crisis has passed, does the institution have a plan to resume instruction and research if it does not have access to some of its core operating assets, such as the physical plant, cash, faculty, staff, or IT infrastructure? Do departments have continuity plans in the event that a crisis disproportionately affects their operations?

Hazing, alcohol abuse, sports scandals, sexual assault, shootings, high-profile tenure decisions, disputes over academic freedom (and academics speaking freely on social media), quarreling boards and presidents, and board member misconduct begin the list of high-profile campus crises that plague higher education institutions. But external events beyond the institution, such as a flood, earthquake, or hurricane can also become crises.[7] So can, if left unheeded, societal trends of shifting demographics, declining state support, and competition from new education providers. A trend is not a crisis, until it is.

Campus leaders should recognize that crises are not predictable but inevitable. A crisis is an unplanned event that has the potential to endanger community members or the institution's facilities. A crisis can quickly turn into a reputation event, costing the institution hard-earned goodwill from its stakeholders. (For a further discussion, see chapter 9, "Advancing Reputation.")

It is easy for institutional leaders to think that they are immune from the headline-grabbing, mission-weakening crises that afflict other campuses, but history proves otherwise. Whether the institution is large or small, rural, suburban, or urban, crises do not discriminate. A "cool head, warm heart"SM philosophy is a principled approach for responding to a crisis. In short, it includes responding to families and the community in a caring manner while adhering to established policies and practices that limit liability and speed recovery.

Many academic institutions spend a disproportional amount of time identifying the risks that could derail or delay their plans and mission. Similarly, institutions spend significant time and energy developing crisis response plans but very little of it testing the plans. If that is the case, boards should encourage flipping the planning and practicing equation. (See page 10, "Insight: Invert the 80/20 rule.") While the institution cannot predict what the crisis will be or when it will occur, the leadership should practice how to respond to a wide range of possible risks. Like training a muscle, practicing crisis response—through a tabletop drill or mock exercise involving community participants when possible—develops the skills and relationships that your leaders will call on when the inevitable occurs, even if they never prepared for that specific crisis.

The complexity and intensity of some of the most prominent scandals to hit higher education require expertise in response that is well beyond any campus.[8] As a faculty member notes, "No campus is prepared for the media spotlight that accompanies a crisis of the size and scope that occurred at Duke University or Penn State. Even the most experienced campus public relations staff need outside help." The need for immediate responses—via multiple channels—and the viral potential of events and any additional missteps call for specialized expertise beyond the experience and talent of internal staff. Having an external communications firm or consultant familiar with the institution, its culture, and its circumstances can provide much-needed additional support for managing the messages in the midst of a crisis.

The board can play a role before and during a crisis, but unless the crisis focuses on the president directly, that role will be limited. Before a crisis, the board should ensure that a plan is in place and require that it is regularly tested. During a crisis, the board and president must maintain alignment on the response, with the board offering to support the president and senior administrative team as appropriate for the crisis.

After the immediate crisis is over, it is time to get back to business. Unfortunately, that can be challenging when the crisis disrupts critical campus functions. Physical emergencies—such as a violent crime on campus or a natural disaster—may make parts of campus inaccessible or

Insight: Preparing for A Global Pandemic

The rapid and global spread of a new strain of the coronavirus (COVID-19) in early 2020 provided an opportunity for institutions to test crisis response and business continuity plans. As the coronavirus outbreak spread across the United States, institutions were faced with unprecedented decisions to prevent virus transmission. The pandemic impacted core academic and business activities, as institutions canceled on-campus activities and shifted to remote classes and telework. Many institutions also canceled large events and discontinued extracurricular programs such as athletics and study abroad. As this guide is being published, institutions continue implementing innovative social distancing actions to maintain business continuity during the ongoing pandemic. ERM can help evaluate medium-term and long-term responses to the pandemic including increased investment in on-line learning, technology, and potential mergers and acquisitions.

prevent some employees from returning to work. For example, at one institution, campus leaders who responded to a violent crime were surprised that they could not access their administrative or IT buildings until after an investigation was complete.

At a minimum, campuses should have a plan in place for how to return to instruction and research following a disruptive event. This plan should address how the institution will reopen if:

- Part or all of the campus is closed or inaccessible;
- The administration is largely incapacitated;
- Significant portions of faculty are unable to teach;
- Liquid cash is unavailable;
- IT infrastructure is offline or damaged.

Some campuses create plans for combinations of the scenarios above, while others also require their colleges or academic departments to create unit-level continuity plans. Some plans rely on the administrations, faculty, staff, and campuses of neighboring institutions to overcome continuity challenges. The board should encourage the administration to develop and role play such plans.

> **Insight: Know Where the Crisis Management "A Team" Resides**
>
> In hindsight, campus leaders who have lived through headline-grabbing events often acknowledge that stumbles were made immediately after the crisis while the campus team tried to respond and hire a public relations firm with relevant higher education experience—all within hours after the crisis hit. One president commented, "We tried to respond ourselves to the crisis for the first 24 hours, got the B team from a PR firm for the next 36 hours, and then finally identified the A team. But we were three days into the crisis with much damage done before we were truly ready to respond."

Catastrophic Weather and Climate Change

The increase in catastrophic weather events over the past several years demonstrates the need for institutions everywhere to prepare for a changing climate. To open the dialogue the board may ask:

- **Emergency plans**. Does the institution have emergency policies in place to keep students, faculty, and staff safe, and to protect the institution's physical property?
- **Continuity and recovery plan**. Does our continuity planning address how to respond during a weather emergency, and how the institution will get back up and running?

- **Satellite campuses and study abroad.** If the institution has remote or overseas campuses, has it also developed plans appropriate to these alternate locations?
- **Lending a hand and receiving a hand.** If a disaster strikes nearby, is the institution prepared to fill the need for facilities and supplies to support relief efforts? Does the institution know where to turn if resources are inaccessible in a weather crisis?
- **Geographic and economic impact.** What are the likely long-term impacts of climate change to the institution?

Institutions must be able to respond to the impact of catastrophic weather and other natural disasters. While institutions once needed only to focus on being prepared for extreme weather common to their geographic region, they now have to adopt a general posture of preparedness. From fires and floods to hurricanes and landslides, institutions must be prepared for extreme weather events.

Generally, there are two kinds of extreme weather events: those for which there is advance notice and those that occur without warning. For foreseeable events like wildfires and hurricanes, institutions have time to mobilize. In contrast, for sudden events like floods and tornadoes, the only way to mitigate the risk of these events is to prepare beforehand.

Institutions should have emergency plans for all types of weather events that might affect them. It is also important to conduct tabletop exercises to prepare staff for emergencies, as well as to identify gaps in policies and procedures.

Over the longer term, institutions should expect disruptive weather events to become increasingly frequent and severe as the effects of climate change become more pronounced. That trend will harm the institution financially: property and flood insurance are likely to become more expensive, and facilities will be more difficult to maintain. For some regions, climate change is likely to cause long-term negative economic damage. Boards and senior administrators should consider how climate change will affect the institution's operations in both the short term and the long term.

Brand

To open the dialogue the full board may ask administrators:

- **Core beliefs**. Does the branding strategy truly represent the mission, values, and core beliefs of the institution?
- **Brand audit**. Has an institutional brand audit (conducted either with internal or external experts) been completed within the last five years to ensure clarity and consistency of the brand?
- **Rebranding**. If there is a strategy to rebrand the institution, does the campus community, including alumni, support the aspirational brand?

Although many in higher education may have been slow to embrace brand management, most institutions now recognize it is an integral part of a strategic plan and risk management strategy. Quantifying what happens to an institution if the brand is damaged is a challenge. But recognizing that every brand is vulnerable is an important first step.

A brand audit can help an institution understand if its brand is effective for achieving the institution's objectives. Particularly for admission and fundraising, brands are an essential element of an institution's strategy. For attracting students, the brand must be aligned with the authentic student experience. Otherwise, prospective students and families may avoid the institution in favor of others with more coherent brands. As the institution and the external environment evolve, institutions should conduct audits and may need to rebrand periodically to remain authentic.

Campus Unrest and Demonstrations

To open the dialogue the board should ask administrators:

- **Campus climate**. What is the political climate on campus, and how are students and faculty members likely to respond to controversial events?
- **Speech and facility use policies**. Does the institution have a campus speech policy? What about policies about where and when public events can occur, and who can host them?

- **Security and preparedness.** Does the institution have a security plan for controversial events? Has the institution practiced the plan? How much advance notice does the institution need to execute its plan?
- **Event management.** Is there an interdepartmental team prepared to oversee controversial events?

Over the past several years, campus protests have become increasingly controversial and divisive events, some bordering on violent. From large public universities to small colleges, every institution must prepare for such events, which can lead to unrest led by outsiders or members of the institution's community. Boards need to understand the institution's approach to this issue.

Managing controversial events starts with understanding campus climate. Senior leaders, including student affairs and faculty leaders, should be informed about the political climate at the institution, as well as likely reactions to controversial events and outside speakers.

Many institutions adopt campus speech policies, attempting to balance a commitment to free expression with creating a safe and inclusive campus environment. Every institution has a distinct set of core values on these issues, and it is important for any policies addressing campus speech to reflect those values. Related policies outlining permissible use of facilities, both by students and faculty as well as outsiders, are also important. Many institutions, for example, choose to allow only recognized campus organizations to invite and sponsor guest speakers. Public institutions need to ensure that their policies meet applicable legal requirements, including First Amendment considerations.

It is also important to have an effective security plan for any controversial events. Such a plan identifies the circumstances under which security officers will act and encourages security outreach to student groups before any events. To manage the actual events, senior leadership should establish an interdepartmental team tasked with overseeing event preparations and response. Institutions should also consider the added (and potentially unexpected) cost of security for an event, which can run as high as six or seven figures.

Community Relations

To open the dialogue the board may ask administrators:

- **Community impact**. Does the institution provide a clear and current description of the economic and social benefits that its programs bring to the community?
- **Community engagement**. Are multiple levels and individuals within the administration involved in community activities and programs? Are those involvements included in the description of economic and social benefits?
- **Communication**. Are channels of communication open between campus planning activities and local neighbors and planning commissions?

Community relations, often referred to as town/gown relations, are as old as campuses themselves. Wherever it is located, each campus exists as part of a larger community, be it urban, suburban, or rural. And towns and cities develop around institutions of higher education. This symbiotic relationship can carry risks for colleges and universities when not given the appropriate thought and attention. Campuses bring significant economic benefits to their communities and, often, added costs for emergency response and event management. Because higher education institutions may not pay corporate, real estate, and other taxes, hosting a college or university may also be seen as reducing tax revenue for the municipality.

It is especially true of independent colleges and universities that economic pressures on local jurisdictions, as well as perceptions of excessively high tuitions and inequality, have reopened issues related to tax-exempt status. At the local level, many municipalities have implemented "in lieu of taxes" payments as an effort to grow revenue and pay some of the costs of hosting a large private university. At the national level, the Tax Cuts and Jobs Act of 2017 included a tax on endowment returns at some of the wealthiest universities. While this tax affects only a handful of institutions, there is concern that this could be just the first of several taxes that an increasingly skeptical public may levy.

With higher education's tax-exempt status facing more questions than at any point in recent history, institutions must emphasize the benefits they provide the local community. Some of the ways that academic institutions support their surrounding communities include conducting research on economic development and incubating small businesses. They also bring additional revenues through tourism and student, faculty, and staff spending in the community. These efforts serve as a strong counterargument to increasing calls for tax or in-lieu-of-tax payments.

Developing and implementing a strong, cohesive community relations program is the administration's responsibility, but the board has a role in supporting community outreach and engagement initiatives and asking questions that reflect the importance of the relationship. To preempt views by some community members and elected officials that the institution is a resource drain rather than a vibrant part of the local economy, boards can encourage the institution to take a strategic and active role in working with business leaders to find ways to support regional and state economic development. Institutions can identify opportunities that will best leverage campus resources, including faculty subject-matter experts, facilities, and students to support economic development efforts of the community. Boards can ensure that the proposed initiatives support and reinforce the institution's strategic plan. Local board members, in particular, can play an important role in communicating and advocating on the institution's behalf.

Strategic Direction, Shared Risk Warning Signs, and Board Actions

The board can get a sense of whether additional coordination or internal oversight around strategic planning are needed by considering the following warning signs:

Board Inquiry	Strategic Risk Warning Sign	Possible Board Actions
Does the institution's strategic plan set forth a distinct, achievable vision for the future?	The strategic plan is muddled and would require resources beyond the institution's capacity to succeed.	Clarify and prioritize strategic plan goals and enforce accountability for achieving them in the short term. For the long term, begin pre-planning the next strategic planning cycle.

Risks to Strategic Direction (and Shared Risks)

Board Inquiry	Strategic Risk Warning Sign	Possible Board Actions
Does the institution adequately plan and monitor its performance against its strategic plan?	The institution does not plan or assess its performance related to the strategic plan. The strategic plan goals are not measurable.	Consider requiring the president or administration to report on status of strategic plan initiatives to the board.
Does the institution include risk management in strategic planning?	Strategic planning does not consider risks to achieving objectives.	Committees tasked with strategic planning should identify, assess, and plan for risks to the execution of strategic objectives.
Does the compliance program lack oversight?	Compliance is scattered across the institution with no clear management.	Recommend that the institution assign responsibility to a single administrator or department for: • inventorying compliance requirements across all departments and • overseeing the status of compliance efforts.
Has the institution established crisis response and business continuity protocols?	The institution has established a crisis management and response plan, but it has not reviewed or updated the plan for several years.	Require that the institution regularly update its crisis response and business continuity protocols based on lessons learned from prior activations of the plan and practice drills.
Does the administration regularly practice response to a variety of crises and catastrophic weather events?	The administration has not practiced crisis response before existing crises and catastrophic weather events.	Mandate that the administration conduct regular tabletop exercises for a variety of crisis scenarios and catastrophic weather events.

RISK MANAGEMENT

Chapter 7
Risks to Institutional Resources

BOARDS ARE TASKED WITH ENSURING THAT INSTITUTIONS have adequate resources in place, including financial, human capital, facilities, and information technology resources. Given the breadth of these resource areas, no single committee can oversee all of them. Instead, various board committees oversee aspects of financial planning, strategic employment practices, maintenance and master planning, and information and cybersecurity strategy.

Risks in these resource categories are constantly changing, and boards must continue to ask how the institution is adapting to global changes and trends that affect higher education. While administrators are tasked with operational aspects of managing these resources, board members will look at resource risks strategically and hold the administration accountable for having programs in place to advance the institution's mission and objectives.

Financial Risks

Boards are responsible for the future of their institution, which includes effective financial and strategic oversight; balanced operating budgets and funding for deferred maintenance; prudent investment policies, adequate liquidity, and serviceable long-term debt; and strong fundraising and advancement efforts. Given the magnitude of these responsibilities, the board relies on several committees—including finance, audit, investment, and development—to facilitate this work.

FINANCE COMMITTEE

The finance committee provides guidance and oversight to an institution's financial and business operations. It ensures that the institution has a long-term plan that is continually updated and monitors ongoing financial health. The combination of the business experiences of many board members and the intense financial pressures felt by virtually all educational institutions have expanded the role of the finance committee. The risks that fall within the purview of the finance committee include:

- Budgeting and planning;
- Revenue;
- Financial strength; and
- Debt.

This is not a complete list; new risks will emerge over time. And some of these risks may not be relevant to every institution. But a board's finance committee should understand that these areas can pose risk to the institution and then use that knowledge to ensure that potential gaps in risk identification are revealed and comprehensive mitigation plans are adhered to. The finance committee should receive annual risk reports from senior administrators that indicate the owner(s) of the top risks and describe progress toward mitigation plans. In turn, with guidance from the finance committee and administrators, the full board should understand and discuss the most significant risks.[1]

Insight: Good Risk Management Links Mission and Margin

The greatest risk for a board is that the institution does not have the necessary resources to achieve its mission and accomplish its strategic plan. Enter the finance committee and its focus on financial strength and sustainability. Risk management can provide a vital link between mission and margin by helping all those involved understand the risk to mission if the financial resources or reputation are seriously degraded.

Budgeting and Planning

To open the dialogue, the finance committee should ask administrators about:

- **Mission.** Do the annual and multiyear budgets reflect the values and mission of the institution?
- **Assumptions.** Are the assumptions used in developing the budget realistic—neither too conservative nor too aggressive?
- **Stress tests.** Are multiyear plans and assumptions stress-tested to illuminate areas of weaknesses and vulnerability?

- **Transparency**. Is there openness and transparency in the development and dissemination of the budget to the appropriate campus communities?
- **Incentives**. Does the budget promote revenue growth or cost cutting in a manner consistent with the institution's ethical standards and reputation?

An institution's strategic and annual plans capture the spirit and vision of an institution's future, and the budget is the financial translation of those plans. Plans and budgets require rigor, focus, and transparency to be effective governance tools. The finance committee has the responsibility to test whether the annual budget reflects the institution's priorities and the president's goals. It must periodically challenge the institution to identify programs or services that should be eliminated or phased out to make room for new initiatives that better align with current goals.

The finance committee's role is to make sure that the budgeting process considers both upside and downside risks. Some institutions budget so conservatively that they miss opportunities to make strategic investments in areas that will help the institution succeed and thrive over the long term. For example, a new program in the career center could strain current staff resources, but it may help students gain meaningful employment and contribute to long-term goals related to admissions. Other institutions have been too optimistic and burdened themselves with long-term expenses for short-term gains. For example, many community colleges and regional colleges saw an enrollment—and revenue—bump in the first years following the recession as adults returned to school. To accommodate new demand, institutions spent on new buildings and faculty, only to see enrollments recede to prerecession norms in a few years.

Budgets are the codification of the institution's priorities. Institutions that prioritize innovation and entrepreneurial activities may design their budget model to allocate funding and new revenue in a way that incentivizes margin-seeking activity at the department level. In brief, such models reward departments that earn additional revenue (e.g., through enrollments, research grants, partnerships) with a larger budget. However, when poorly designed or taken to an extreme, the risk of misconduct on the part of poorly supervised employees—fraud, corruption, and embezzlement, for example—increases.

Finance committees also focus on a constellation of competing forces: net tuition revenue, cost containment, the quality of the

Insight: Stress-test to Illuminate Areas of Vulnerability

An important part of a budgeting process includes stress-testing the plans and projections. In many ways, this is similar to emergency response planning, just with different scenarios and players. While it is unlikely that reality will exactly match any hypothetical scenario, practicing builds the skills, patience, and fortitude to respond to financial adversity.

The finance committee might ask, for example, what if:

- Enrollment is 15 percent lower than anticipated?
- Annual gifts decline by 20 percent?
- Faculty members retire at a slower (or faster) rate?
- The state cuts appropriations by 30 percent or leaves community college funding to local jurisdictions?
- The federal government issues a tax on all endowment revenues, and the local government taxes all property not used for instruction?
- The university suddenly has to spend a large portion of its cash reserves?

---

education, and student expectations. Setting annual tuition rates is one of the most difficult functions of a finance committee because it requires balancing the burden on students with financial aid and other institutional expenses.[2]

Revenue

Economic recessions threaten most institutions' primary revenue streams: tuition, fees, and aid; state and local appropriations; federal research grants; fundraising; and endowment returns. Most institutions also earn revenue from auxiliary functions, such as summer camps and space rentals, which can decline during economic recessions.

Primary sources of revenue can decline following a recession, and many institutions are not prepared. Tuition revenue in past recessions varied substantially across the country, growing for some institutions, as newly unemployed Americans returned to college, and shrinking for others, as higher education became an even more distant possibility for students and prospective students. Students supported by tuition reimbursement programs, for instance, may drop out if pressure on their employers' benefits package mounts.

A post-recession recovery can lead to increases in some revenue sources. State and local appropriations climb, endowments earn greater returns, the federal government reinvests in research, and donors increase their giving. The gains, however, rarely return to pre-recession levels, and institutions experience them differently. These changes highlight the fragility of revenue and the need to be prepared for economic swings.

Board members may find it helpful to think about the risks to each source of revenue independently. Due to their relative importance, risks to tuition, fees, and financial aid, as well as state and local appropriations, are discussed below. The following sections provide a starting point for discussion among board members. Note that risks are far more numerous than those discussed here and will continue to evolve over time.

Tuition, Fees, and Financial Aid

Most private institutions and an increasing number of public institutions are highly dependent on their net tuition revenue: revenue from tuition, fees, and external financial aid less internal financial aid and discounts. Risks to enrollment revenue is perhaps the most universal major risk in higher education: in a recent United Educators survey, 70 percent of institutions cited it as one of their top risks. In a broad sense, tuition revenue risks are risks to the institution's ability to attract, support, enroll, retain, and graduate students who will benefit from its particular academic and extracurricular programs.

Two primary forces influence net tuition revenue: 1) tuition prices, which includes tuition discounts, and 2) student enrollments. Enrollments can be broken down into enrolling new students, which may include launching programs to reach new segments of prospective students, and retaining existing students. As the ever-increasing average tuition discount rate shows, these forces are interdependent, making tuition revenue a delicate balance of risks that is distinct to each institution.

To address its particular set of tuition revenue risks, each institution needs to generate and meet market demand for its programs as well as adapt to upcoming changes. To open the dialogue the finance committee can ask administrators about:

- **Demographic shifts**. Does the institution have a plan in place to adapt to shifts in demographics?
- **Discount rate**. Is the institution able to enroll its target class size without exceeding its budgeted discount rate?
- **Analytics**. Do reports and analyses track the efficiency and effectiveness of admissions and retention strategies?

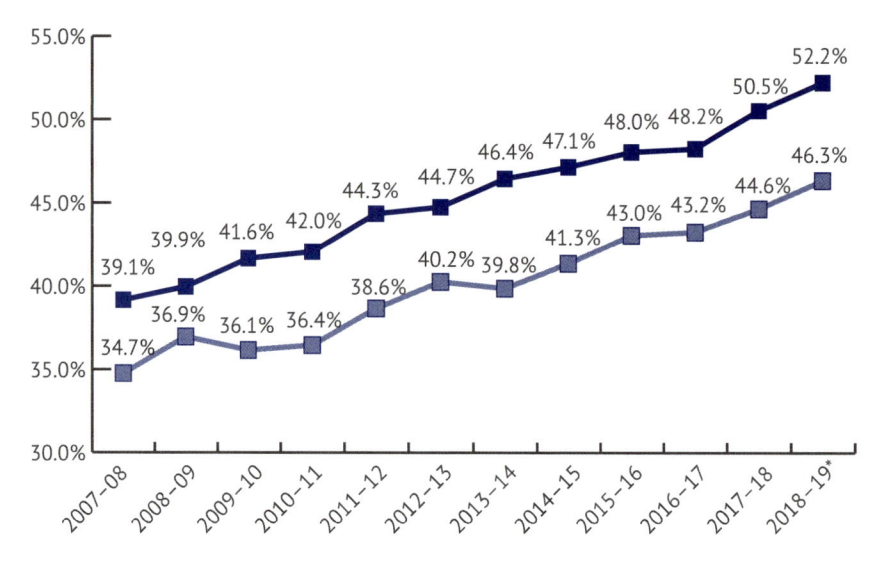

[Figure: line chart showing Average Institutional Tuition Discount Rate by Student Category, 2007-08 through 2018-19*]

First-time, Full-time Freshmen: 39.1%, 39.9%, 41.6%, 42.0%, 44.3%, 44.7%, 46.4%, 47.1%, 48.0%, 48.2%, 50.5%, 52.2%

All undergraduates: 34.7%, 36.9%, 36.1%, 36.4%, 38.6%, 40.2%, 39.8%, 41.3%, 43.0%, 43.2%, 44.6%, 46.3%

Source: NACUBO Tuition Discounting Survey, 2007 to 2018; Data are as of the Fall of each academic year.
* Preliminary estimates.

Figure 1: Average Institutional Tuition Discount Rate by Student Category
Source: https://www.nacubo.org/research/2018/nacubo-tuition-discounting-study

- **Retention**. Are there opportunities to improve retention that could help achieve the institution's mission while growing tuition revenue?
- **International enrollments and immigration policies**. Is the institution overexposed to shifts in enrollment from a single country or region?
- **Contingency planning**. What will the institution do if it misses its enrollment target by 10 percent? What if there is an external event (economic recession, pandemic, natural catastrophe, terrorist attack, or policy change) that negatively impacts the budget?

An impending drop in the traditional college-age population, particularly in the Northeast and Midwest, will force many institutions to look beyond their traditional markets to identify the next generation of students.[3] Expect competitors to try to attract students in your institution's typical markets. For example, regional universities may seek students nationally, and four-year universities may recruit students who typically attend community colleges. Others will shift to serve older student demographics or start online continuing education and certification programs.

These strategies are not without their own risks. Launching new programs and opening new markets requires startup funding; serving new student demographics, such as older students, may stretch existing student services to a point at which they cannot adequately serve any students without additional investments. Significant investments are needed to build online learning programs, either through partnering with a third party or building the systems and support to deliver the programs within the institution. Students and families are increasingly more likely to negotiate for increased financial aid, placing increased pressure on net tuition revenue. All of these risks increase recruitment costs for universities without a commensurate growth in net tuition revenue.

To help the institution understand its current student profile and protect existing recruitment strengths, the finance and academic affairs committees should encourage long-term analysis of admissions trends, creative recruitment strategies, and an effective response to unmet tuition targets.

Institutions expend tremendous effort and expense to attract students but often significantly less to retain them through graduation. Retention and graduation rates are starting to attract more attention, both from state and federal regulators and from chief financial officers looking to increase revenues. A student who returns the next semester is a student who pays a tuition bill, after all.

In partnership with the student affairs committee, the finance committee should review reports of retention rates and analyze the reasons students do not persist to degree completion. The institution may identify opportunities to retain students—and their tuition dollars—and improve graduation rates for less expense than it takes to recruit new students.

Operationally, the admissions process has changed dramatically since the time when most board members applied to college. The common application, entrance exams, multiple applications, social media and portals, and negotiating for financial aid are now fixtures in the admissions landscape.

To ensure that prospective students are treated appropriately and ethically, admissions procedures need to be established and followed closely, even within a holistic admissions framework. As a board

Insight: Looking Abroad for Enrollments? Prepare to Compete

In the past, many institutions turned to other countries for full-paying students as a strategy to insulate themselves from domestic fluctuations. What was once an effective strategy is now a source of risk: an increasingly competitive international market amplifies the dangers of a competitive domestic market. An effective international recruitment strategy must account for a fiercely competitive market, and understand that there is no guarantee of a substantial margin on international student enrollments.

member, ask about the exceptions to the normal admissions process, such as athletics, arts, legacy status, and nonprofit partnerships, and the policies that inform the institution's response to fraudulent admissions and financial aid activity. Even if operational risks such as these typically fall outside the purview of a finance committee, committee members should be aware that stress on all parties in the admissions process, including institutions striving to enroll the ideal class, makes that process ripe for such risks.

State and Local Appropriations

At a general level, state and local appropriations refer to funding allocated to public institutions, often through a combination of base funding and per-student funding. Unsurprisingly, changes to state and local allocations are often correlated with the economic situation of the jurisdiction.

Many state legislatures perceive higher education to be the easiest area to cut in an economic downturn. Higher education competes for its state allocations with the state's other responsibilities: health care, corrections, transportation, K-12 education, and social services. Health care has dominated state spending priorities since 2008, leaving other funding recipients to fight over whatever remains.

To manage the risk to appropriation revenue, boards in states with funding models that reward specific state priorities (e.g., employment outcomes or graduation rates) should ensure that their administration establishes a budget that honestly assesses the institution's ability to achieve state targets.

Financial Strength

To open the dialogue the finance committee should ask about:

- **Ratios**. Does the institution calculate and report appropriate ratios for monitoring its financial health and viability?
- **Trends**. What trends do the ratios reveal?
- **The long view**. Does the administration provide long-term cost and revenue projections to inform the board of challenges that the institution is likely to encounter in the future?

Insight: Risks from Grants

When finances are tight, institutions often turn to grants to provide startup funding for new initiatives that will hopefully lead to more revenue or reduced costs. However, grant programs often stipulate reporting obligations, contributions from the institution, or a commitment to support a program after the grant expires. Grant-funded programs that operate at a loss raise difficult questions for boards and administrations.

Boards should encourage the administration to conduct a risk analysis that weighs the upside and the downside before applying for the grant. Ideally, the risk assessment should advise the institution on whether to accept the grant and how to maximize the program's financial and strategic success.

Financial sustainability and protection of the institution's assets is at the foundation of the board's responsibility. The greatest risk to any institution is that essential resources will no longer be available. Recovery from the 2008 recession has had a mixed effect on colleges and universities. The higher education price index continues to outpace the consumer price index, a phenomenon that began in the early 1980s, and some institutions have a particularly small margin for error.[4]

Key financial indicators at most institutions show a mix of positive and negative signals that offer both relief and alarm. Conflicting indicators demonstrate the importance of financial risk analysis so the board knows where to turn to mitigate the most significant risks to the institution's financial strength.

Whether financial risks arise from a sudden recession or a gradual population shift, colleges and universities that are not highly selective or do not have strong balance sheets are in the riskiest position. They lack the ability to pass on tuition increases, do not have adequate unrestricted endowments to provide a cushion, and, in many cases, are in a competitive race to discount tuition, add facilities (often using debt), and increase services.

The finance committee can benefit from looking at metrics[5] and early warning signs to examine the relationship between

> "Because boards have the ultimate fiduciary responsibility, one would think they would raise serious concerns each time an increase in tuition well above the rate of inflation was brought to them for approval. Trustees should advocate, expect, and demand greater efficiencies and pilot programs that constrain escalating costs without compromising quality."
>
> —Davis Educational Foundation

financial health and mission accomplishment. For example, the following ratios, which are part of the composite financial index (CFI), can reveal answers to strategic finance questions about the:

- **Primary Reserve Ratio.** Are resources sufficient and flexible enough to support the mission?
- **Viability Ratio.** Are debt resources managed strategically to advance the mission?
- **Return on Net Assets Ratio.** Do asset performance and management support the institution's strategic direction?
- **Net Operating Revenues Ratio.** Do operating results indicate the institution is living within available resources?[6]

Debt

To open the dialogue the finance committee should ask administrators about:

- **Debt service.** Can the institution service its debt over the entire term of the commitment? Are all proforma financials stress-tested?
- **Reserves.** Does the institution have the appropriate controls on the debt-service reserve fund to ensure its stability and liquidity?
- **Transparency.** Is there appropriate transparency and communication with rating agencies and bond holders?[7] Does the institution adhere to the standards and rules promulgated by the rating and regulatory agencies?
- **Covenants.** Does the institution track and regularly report adherence to bond covenants? Has a process been established to seek a waiver in a timely manner if covenants have the potential to be breeched?

In addition to constricted access to borrowing, many colleges and universities are finding a heightened interest by banks and bondholders to add covenants to bond and loan contracts that further restrict the flexibility institutions have to operate. Despite the distance from the global financial crisis, borrowing money to support operations and capital projects remains risky. Boards must question whether the college or university is living beyond its means, and the finance committee should take the lead in those conversations.

AUDIT COMMITTEE

The audit committee is the institution's first line of defense when considering financial reporting, internal control, compliance, and risk management. To fulfill this role on fiduciary matters requires membership on the audit committee to be more technically focused and bring deep subject-matter expertise to bear around financial and compliance issues. Some smaller colleges, universities, and foundations combine the responsibilities of the audit committee and finance committee. This is becoming increasingly difficult, given the complexities and scope of both committees. The risks that fall within the purview of the audit committee[8] include:

- External financial audit and IRS Form 990;
- Compliance and external reporting (for a discussion of compliance risks, see chapter 6, "Risks to Strategic Direction");
- Accountability policies (conflicts of interest, fraud reporting and whistle-blower protection, and records retention);
- Insurance and risk transfer (can be covered in finance committee); and
- Internal controls and risk management coordination.

External Audit and IRS Form 990
To open the dialogue audit committees should ask about:

- **External auditors**. Does the audit committee annually meet with external auditors, with and without the president and administrators?
- **Areas for special review**. Working with administration and external auditors, does the audit committee periodically identify areas for special review?
- **Form 990**. For independent institutions and foundations, does the entire board receive and review the annual IRS Form 990?

External and independent annual financial audits are the first stop for audit committees. The audit committee has the responsibility to thoroughly review and understand the external auditor's presentation, including additional required letters and management reports. As noted in chapter 3, "External and Internal Stakeholders in Risk Management," institutions can engage audit firms that have deep experience in higher education to assist risk identification and assessment or to evaluate the quality and thoroughness of the institution's internal accounting processes.

Because independent institutions and related foundations are nonprofit corporations, their entire board must receive the IRS Form 990, which is, in reality, part tax return and part governance checklist. It asks questions about how the institution and board conducts its business. The form is public information and is easily accessible at www.guidestar.org. While neither the board nor any individual committee is required to approve the Form 990, the IRS asks whether the board received it before its submission. Best practice is for the audit committee to use the completed form to review core governance practices and policies outlined in its questions.

The Form 990 also articulates specific disclosure requirements for conflicts of interest for actions and business relationships within the campus community, including those of family members. That has implications not just for the board but also well beyond it. For example, institutions with a research program should consider developing an institutional conflict-of-interest statement and process to address ownership and support of commercial products generated from institutionally funded research.[9]

Accountability Policies

To open the dialogue audit committee members should ask administrators:

- **Conflicts of interest.** Does the institution have a clear, well-written conflict-of-interest policy for board members, faculty, staff, and vendors?
- **Fraud reporting and whistleblower protection.** Are processes in place that address how to monitor and respond to whistleblowers and other reports of misconduct or ethics violations?
- **Records retention.** Does the institution have a process to handle digital and physical documents in the event of pending litigation?

Among the countless policies and procedures at institutions of higher education, some rise to the level of board oversight because of federal law and public perception. Several of them—including conflicts of interest, fraud reporting and whistle-blower protection, and records retention—garnered renewed attention with the Sarbanes-Oxley Act of 2002, which brought increased scrutiny to corporate governance and board oversight.

The board has two core functions related to addressing conflicts of interest. The first is to ensure that a strong conflict-of-interest policy exists and is followed by all individual board members. The second is to ensure that the institution has and regularly monitors adherence to a conflict-of-interest policy that applies to staff, faculty, and vendors; that the policy outlines steps for responding to any conflicts; and that it is implemented rigorously and consistently throughout the institution. For example, institutions with a research program should consider developing a conflict-of-interest statement and process to address ownership and support of commercial products generated from research. Furthermore, for independent institutions and related foundations, the IRS Form 990 articulates specific disclosure requirements for conflicts involving the transactions and business relationships of the campus community (including those of family members).

Unfortunately, fraud is a fact of life in for-profit businesses, nonprofit enterprises, and government entities. A 2018 Association of Certified Fraud Examiners study reports that 6 percent of worldwide fraud occurs in the higher education sector and 9 percent occurs in the health care sector. The report reveals that 68 percent of fraud cases were discovered by tips, internal audit, or routine reviews by management.[10] Whistleblowers and tip lines reveal not just instances of financial fraud but other misconduct, such as sexual assault, discrimination, harassment, and conflict of interest violations. Prevention programs include three parts:

1. Education and awareness;
2. Reporting and intake process; and
3. Investigation of reports.

Depending on the size of the institution and board structure, the audit committee may be involved in fraud reporting. Third-party vendors provide whistle-blower hotlines to receive and record anonymous

> "One significant provision in Sarbanes-Oxley, applicable to nonprofit and for-profit institutions alike, makes it a felony to take adverse employment action against any person 'for providing to a law-enforcement officer any truthful information relating to the commission or possible commission of any Federal offense.'"
>
> —Vice president and general counsel at a public research university[11]

allegations of wrongdoing. While the cost of whistle-blower tip lines is relatively modest, other alternatives exist. Smaller institutions may appoint an individual or team (for example, outside legal counsel, the audit committee chair, or other responsible individuals) to receive tips via an anonymous email reporting site. At medium-sized institutions, the audit committee chair may receive a report of all tips submitted. At large institutions, the general counsel may submit a summary of the anonymous tips to the audit committee. Although the administration is responsible for developing and implementing a process for investigation, the audit committee should also periodically review that process.

In the past, a record retention policy focused on: 1) protection against unplanned destruction of records due to flood, fire, or other accident or employee misconduct and 2) the ability to respond to document production for litigation or public records requests. Today, the retaining, discarding, and managing of records is significantly more complex. Beyond the data security implications of record retention, electronic discovery has grown to be a significant litigation expense with terabytes of data from networks in the cloud, on home computer hard drives, in voice mail and text messages, and on social media—all possibly subject to legal discovery in a lawsuit. The institution's record retention policies should address the variety of records maintained by the institution, how they are maintained and archived, and the ability to respond promptly to potential lawsuits and other legitimate information requests.[12]

Insurance and Risk Transfer

To open the dialogue audit committee members should ask senior administrators, typically the chief financial officer and general counsel, about:

- **Risk transfer.** Does the institution transfer appropriate risks through insurance? Should the institution transfer the financial aspects of niche risks, such as data breaches, or should it accept the risk?
- **Coverage.** Does the audit committee, at least every five years, review the insurance program's scope and a list of insurance coverage purchased, including limits, exclusions, and deductibles?
- **Contracts.** Does the institution have a process to review third-party contracts to ensure they contain appropriate risk transfer, indemnification, and hold-harmless terms and conditions?

An institution faces more risks that are uninsurable than are insurable, but purchasing insurance is a viable strategy to reduce exposure to specific losses. Responsibility for insurance and risk transfer often resides in the audit committee, but some institutions assign it to the finance committee, which may be in a better position to understand the financial consequences of insurance decisions.

The audit committee is well-suited to assess the risk appetite of the institution, determining how much financial risk can be tolerated given the institution's financial health, liquidity, and other obligations. The audit committee is also best positioned to evaluate the administration's recommendations on how much risk should be shared or transferred—either through purchasing insurance coverage or through contracts with third parties. Institutions contract with outside vendors to provide myriad services, ranging from food service to child care and from summer sports camps to foreign campus operations. Each of these contracts presents an opportunity to evaluate the appropriate level of risk for the institution to retain or to transfer to the third party through a well-written contract.

The audit committee's role in the insurance review is to:

1. Monitor the quality of the insurance companies that the institution selects, ensuring that each company is financially strong and able to meet its obligations to pay covered claims. This is particularly important for insurance claims that might take many years to resolve. For example, a sexual molestation allegation against an employee could take 10 to 20 years to surface and conclude.
2. Evaluate the limits of coverage purchased. For example, to determine adequate property insurance coverage, the board should know whether all campus facilities are covered in the event of a fire, flood, or other event or if the committee is comfortable (as many institutions are) obtaining coverage for "probable maximum loss"—thereby not having full replacement coverage for the entire facilities inventory.
3. Evaluate the deductible or self-insured retention, accepting the institution's responsibility to pay this amount prior to the insurance coverage.

These roles focus on articulating, either explicitly or implicitly, the institution's financial risk tolerance for a specific set of risks that may occur. While every institution will consider purchasing certain core lines of insurance, the range of coverages increases significantly based on the complexity, size, and location(s) of the institution:

- A small liberal arts college with one campus and no graduate programs might be well served with only core coverages, while a large, comprehensive university with active research and teaching programs throughout the world could purchase upwards of 40 different types of insurance policies. (See Appendix C.)
- Public institutions located in a state with strong immunities may purchase only liability insurance to cover claims that fall outside the state immunity protections, including violations of federal laws, cases brought against the institution in another state or country, or cases brought in a way to circumvent the immunity laws.
- University systems and large universities with medical centers may establish and manage captive insurance companies to handle large deductibles or self-insured retentions and to self-finance risks that are not well suited to third-party insurance providers.
- Some public institutions can participate in state funding pools that manage claims and cover all losses or enforce charge-back mechanisms. Increasingly, however, public higher education systems are exploring ways to separate from state pools in order to provide more specialized insurance coverage and institutional control over claims.

Contracting fundamentals have always been important in higher education. In the current climate of increased interest in partnerships with other institutions, service providers, and public and private entities, the need for strong agreements resulting from sound contracting practices is imperative. No two partnerships call for the same contract, but the institution should have a defined system for contract negotiation and management, and the board should inquire whether the following elements are present:

- Guidelines on risk tolerance—what risks can be accepted and what risks must be transferred to the partner whenever possible;
- A clear protocol for contract review, including whether contracts should be reviewed by legal counsel, risk management, finance, or others;

- Guidelines on who has contracting authority;
- Model forms for routine contracts; and
- A known system for storing and recalling signed contracts.

For complex partnerships, a contract can require extensive negotiations for the parties to get to a mutually beneficial legal agreement. For example, the chief financial officer at a private university that partnered with a public university to launch a new school described the contracting process as a "months-long effort with multiple versions of contracts, each starting with different assumptions that guided us to the right agreement." In these instances, the institution should set parameters for the nonnegotiable and negotiable elements of each contract. The board may wish to have input on the boundaries of negotiations for major partnerships, such as a public-private partnership with a development company to construct new buildings or a partnership with another institution to launch new academic programs.

For smaller partnerships, such as one with a startup providing a tech solution, the institution should not assume that the partner has given much thought to its contract or how it will fulfill its obligations. If the contract contains sensitive elements, such as how the partner will secure confidential data, insist that the partner meets the institution's standards to minimize risk. This may seem excessive for smaller partnerships, but an ounce of risk mitigation upfront could protect the institution later if the partner suffers a data breach or an employee of the partner intentionally harms the company.

Regardless of a contract's scope or complexity, to transfer risk effectively institutions must require indemnification and hold-harmless terms that clearly outline the responsibility of each party for liabilities that may arise during the course of contract performance.

> "We partnered with a development company to build a new academic building. The developers, building management company, and the university signed the contract, but the students got stuck in the middle. Students have complained to the board of regents that repairs take too long, but [repair schedules are] in the contract, and there's nothing the university can do. We should have looked at it better, but we learned a lesson: in a public-private partnership, spend as much effort as possible on the contract!"
>
> —Risk manager at a public research university

Internal Controls and Risk Management Coordination

The audit committee performs two core functions related to risk management throughout the institution: monitoring internal controls and coordinating board committees' risk management processes. To open the dialogue audit committee members can ask administrators:

- **Internal audit**. Does the institution have and adhere to stringent internal financial controls?
- **Committee risk reports**. Will the committee receive annual reports on risks reviewed by each standing committee and the full board?

The audit committee monitors the institution's internal controls, risk management and compliance processes, and specific risks that are assigned to it. Its role is similar to the oversight role of internal audit. The Institute of Internal Auditors describes the purpose of the internal audit function as "objective assurance and insight on the effectiveness and efficiency of governance, risk management, and internal control processes." To support its integrity and autonomy, the administration's internal audit function often reports to the board's audit committee. That ensures that the policies and procedures approved by the administration and board are followed.

Most large institutions and many medium-sized institutions have internal audit staff that develop, implement, and monitor internal policies and procedures to improve organizational performance and cost efficiencies. Small to medium institutions may not have internal audit functions or the scope and size of such functions may be limited. Those institutions may outsource internal audit tasks to a firm with special expertise in higher education. If outsourced, the firm should not be the same one that performs the annual external financial audit. It is important for the board to emphasize the need for candor and openness in the risk identification and assessment process completed by the senior administrators who serve as the risk owners.

In addition to reviewing adherence to institutional risk management policies and processes, internal auditors perform oversight of other processes within an institution. Coordination between the internal auditors and risk managers on their respective annual agendas and projects can leverage resources, supporting the administration's broad risk management agenda. But because of the need to separate duties, it is not appropriate for the internal audit department to lead an ERM initiative. However, the internal auditors and other institutional risk managers should participate in ERM, lending expertise and support throughout the review and analysis.

In the same spirit of internal auditors who work across the organization, the board audit committee can perform a vital role in ensuring appropriate risk management engagement and oversight by the full board. The audit committee should gather and monitor the risk management processes of the standing committees and the full board.

INVESTMENT COMMITTEE

Risks that fall within the purview of the investment committee include:

- Conflicts of interest;
- Investment portfolio; and
- Liquidity.

This is not a complete list as new risks emerge over time. Investment committees should understand that these areas in particular can pose risks to the institution and use that knowledge to ensure that potential gaps in risk identification are revealed and comprehensive mitigation plans are adhered to. Of course, risk management is at the core of every investment portfolio and integral to achieving the goals of an investment policy. Investing is a continual trade-off of risk and reward. Long before ERM and strategic risk management, investment committees understood volatility, standard deviation, counterparty risk, and other risk and reward calculations that make up the investors' lexicon.

An investment committee also faces other risks linked to its charter and processes. For starters, the investment committee must establish and adhere to an investment policy, articulate the risk appetite, establish asset allocation, and in most instances, hire, monitor, and dismiss investment managers. Establishing good policies and processes is extremely important for an investment committee.

Investment Committee Composition

To open the dialogue the investment committee should ask administrators:

- **Committee composition.** Do committee members have financial and investment experience? Is the committee the right size?

- **Conflicts of interest.** Are conflict-of-interest policies governing investment committee members clear? Are they enforced?

Committee composition is a key consideration. Some of the greatest risks for the investment committee are groupthink and its opposite: allowing one individual or a subset of the committee members to drive a decision or point of view, subrogating the committee's policies and sidestepping a thorough analysis. Rightsizing the committee to between five and eight voting members helps support active participation and attendance at all meetings. The size of the endowment or the institution's budget should not influence the size of the investment committee; rather expertise and experience should determine committee membership. Limiting attendance at investment meetings to only voting members can reduce the amount of external influence and sideline quarterbacking that often accompanies guest attendance.[13]

The charter and composition of investment committees open the door for challenges to ambiguous conflict-of-interest policies. Investment committees benefit from access to distinct and specialized expertise. To tap into skills and knowledge from the broader alumni or local community, they may include committee members who are not board members. Regardless, board and committee risk management policies, including conflict-of-interest policies, should extend to all committee members.

Opinions differ as to whether the institution should allow investments with a money manager who serves on the investment committee. AGB's publication *The Investment Committee* (AGB Press, 2011) describes the two approaches: 1) to take advantage of the unique expertise and allow the investment with disclosure or 2) to not allow institutional investments in funds managed by committee members. The investment committee and full board should discuss the advantages and risks of these alternatives, share the discussion and conclusion with the broader campus community, and regularly evaluate if the policy continues to meet the institution's needs. Over time, the skills, investment performance, and ability to consistently add value can change for money managers, so investment committees should thoroughly review all managers, including those who serve on the committee.

Investments Policy and Performance

To open the dialogue investment committee members should ask about:

- **Policy**. Does the committee review the investment policy and philosophy annually?
- **Adherence**. Does it review adherence to the investment policy at every meeting? Are deviations to the policy, including asset allocation directives and diversification, acknowledged?
- **Liquidity**. Is a liquidity policy in place that supports the institution's operating needs and potential call on capital for committed investments? Is it followed?
- **Investment composition**. Does the investment portfolio include assets that face reputational risks from student and alumni interests, such as divestment from fossil fuels, or undue financial risks, such as shifts in global trade?
- **Information sharing**. Does the committee regularly report investment performance to the full board?

The investment committee is responsible for periodically reviewing and revising, as needed, the investment or endowment policy. Generally, an endowment policy has four goals:

1. Provide current institutional support;
2. Provide future institutional support;
3. Maintain sustainable payout levels; and
4. Ensure predictability of distributions.

In evaluating its endowment policy, the investment committee should consider a variety of risks related to invested assets. (See Exhibit 16.) Beyond the inherent risks associated with investing, many institutions are creating additional strategic investment risk through their endowment strategy by consistently planning for greater returns than they earn. Every year in the decade following the recession (2009–2018), 10-year investment returns failed to meet 10-year return objectives.[14]

DEVELOPMENT COMMITTEE

Ensuring the future of an institution also means planning and executing successful fundraising campaigns to support annual operations and long-term plans. A development committee and, in the case of some public universities, the foundation board provide broad oversight of the institution's fundraising and friend-raising programs. The scope and corresponding risks that fall within the purview of the development committee include:

- Comprehensive campaigns;
- Gift policies;
- Board member philanthropy; and
- Support for advancement, fundraising, and marketing.

This is not a complete list; new risks will emerge over time, and some of these risks may not be relevant to every institution. But for the vast majority of independent colleges and universities and related foundations, development committees should understand that these areas pose potential risk and use that knowledge to ensure that any gaps in risk identification are revealed and comprehensive mitigation plans are adhered to.

Some of the risks noted above are among the top concerns in higher education today. For example, the viability of a comprehensive campaign often heads the list for many institutions. Every higher education institution and foundation should have a fundraising or development

Exhibit 16: Commonfund's Risk Factors

Investment Risk—Covers all aspects of market risk as well as the returns associated with any investment. This risk also assesses the potential gain distribution to ensure that any investment opportunity offers the potential for a consistent, risk adjusted return over time.

Operational Risk—Risk of loss resulting from human error or failed internal processes or systems, or from external events.

Credit/Counterparty Risk—Any risk associated with exposure to dealing with certain counterparties. Typically includes an assessment of creditworthiness of one's trading counterparties using market indicators such as long-term and short-term credit ratings, spreads, and trading indicators. Also includes any action to mitigate potential exposure to these counterparties (for example, collateral management).

Liquidity Risk—Decomposition of the investment portfolio by immediate cash requirements, liquid strategies, and illiquid strategies.

Regulatory Risk—Risk of loss through penalty or changing procedures due to a rapidly changing regulatory and compliance environment.

Reputational Risk—Investment risks that do not result in direct financial consequences, but rather expose the institution to negative effects on its reputation or its ability to pursue its mission.

For more information, visit www.commonfund.org.

plan that includes both annual and multiyear fundraising plans. The scope of the goals will determine the resources needed to be successful.

The development committee should understand the variety of risks related to fundraising, discuss them with administrators, and report their recommendations and conclusions to the full board.[15] The development committee should expect to see annual risk reports from the president or executive director and chief development officer designating the owner(s) of the top fundraising risks and progress toward the mitigation of those risks.

Comprehensive Campaigns

To open the conversations development committee members should ask about:

- **Strategic alignment**. Is the case for launching a comprehensive campaign clear and aligned with the strategic plan of the institution?
- **Trustee commitment**. Are current and prospective trustees personally committed to contributing a substantial gift, their time, and their connections to the campaign?
- **Resources**. Does the institution have sufficient professional staff, training for volunteers, and infrastructure to support the multiyear effort?
- **Budget**. Is there a realistic budget, including funds to support the annual operations of the campaign?
- **Integrity**. Are strong policies and procedures in place to ensure integrity in the acceptance, naming opportunities, and accounting for all gifts?
- **Gift policy**. Are policies and procedures in place to ensure that the institution uses gifts for their intended purposes?
- **Progress reports**. Does the board receive regular reports on the progress of the campaign, including the net present value and face value of all gifts, including deferred gifts?

Comprehensive campaigns are big business. They are complex and multiyear undertakings. They depend on an army of staff, volunteers, and consultants. They require specialized software, extensive travel, event planning, and sophisticated recordkeeping that can tax even the largest, most complex university. Board members perform a critical role in the planning and execution of comprehensive campaigns. They not only approve the strategic and fundraising plans, but they are also the foundation—through their contributions and ability to open doors—of every successful comprehensive campaign.

Successful comprehensive campaigns align mission, strategic plans, and annual operating needs. Although the primary motivation for any campaign is to raise money to support strategic and operating plans, successful ones can also enhance the institution's reputation, raise visibility, boost morale, and elevate its mission and vision. They can also help the institution identify and reconnect with alumni, local businesses, and even prospective students. But a campaign launched before an institution is ready can cause significant damage and turn those positives into negatives.[16]

Development committees should be alert to some of the most common campaign risks, which often stem from poor planning at the early stages, including in the following six areas:

1. **Case statement**: Comprehensive campaigns begin with a strong case. The president often takes the lead in articulating the case and describing the vision for the future of the institution. The development committee then scrutinizes, discusses, and ultimately recommends its approval to the full board. At this initial stage, the greatest risk is a weak case. Failing to clearly articulate the rationale for asking donors to dig deep into personal resources to support the institution can doom a campaign.
2. **Campaign readiness**: After building a case—which should involve extensive discussions with a wide range of constituents—the development committee must assess the campaign-readiness of the institution. Often, an outside consulting firm will conduct a campaign-readiness or feasibility study. The results should not be ignored. A common risk is a desire by the administration or the board to proceed before addressing any challenges or weaknesses identified in the study.
3. **Development infrastructure**: Comprehensive campaigns are expensive and require steady resources to be successful. Development committees are responsible for ensuring that the institution has allocated adequate resources to launch and sustain the campaign. Benchmarks are available to compare proposed budgets and assess the adequacy of resources. The most notable risk in this area is a lack of appreciation for the additional costs of a campaign and underinvestment in staffing and related expenses.

4. **Campaign costs**: Before starting the campaign, the development committee needs to decide how the institution will pay for the campaign costs. Will expenses come from unrestricted gifts, the institution's operating budget, as a tax or portion of every gift collected, or (if an institution is fortunate) from a donor through a designated gift? Careful attention should be paid to clearly disclose to all prospective donors whether a portion of a gift will be used to support campaign operations.
5. **Donor fatigue**: As most board members are probably aware, campaigns often rely on leadership gifts from a few wealthy donors. Institutions of higher education are competing with all other charitable interests for those few donors, who are being asked frequently for gifts. Medium-sized and small-sized donors face similar pressures, and recent graduates are often more interested in giving to cause-related nonprofits than their *alma mater*. Each campaign runs the risk of not reaching an adequate number of donors, and successive campaigns, if not carefully managed, can amplify the risk of donor fatigue.
6. **Volunteer training**: Successful capital campaigns rely on a cadre of volunteers to solicit gifts. Training and support for those volunteers is vital to ensure the integrity of the message, appropriate follow-through, and ongoing positive relations with this important constituency. As volunteers themselves, development committee members are well positioned to evaluate the readiness and needs of other volunteers to support the campaign effort.

Once a comprehensive campaign is under way, many of the development committee's responsibilities parallel those of its ongoing oversight responsibilities (for example, gift-acceptance policies, compliance with donor intent, and ethical fundraising practices), described as follows.

Gift-Related Policies

The development committee, in collaboration with senior administrators, is responsible for ensuring that the college, university, or foundation has and follows appropriate policies and practices in terms of donor intent, internal gift acceptance and recordkeeping, and fundraising ethics.

Several high-profile lawsuits, which alleged that institutions did not follow donor intent on gift uses, put this issue in newspaper headlines and board meeting agendas. Ensuring compliance with donor intent requires institutionwide coordination and communication. On the front end, the development committee and the administration should ensure that policies and procedures are in place for communicating donor intent. Then the administration (through the development office) is responsible for: 1) recording the donor's intent and the institution's agreement on the specific use of the gift, 2) communicating donor intent to the relevant departments, and 3) monitoring ongoing compliance with those intentions. Through the internal audit function or periodic review by external auditors, the administration and development committee can monitor adherence to gift use policies.

The development committee is also responsible for protecting the institution's tax-exempt status when it comes to fundraising and gift acceptance. It should ensure compliance with federal and state laws related to charitable contributions, as well as state fundraising registration requirements. Looking internally, the development committee should ensure that gift-acceptance policies have been established and are followed (especially for non-cash gifts, such as real estate and securities). It should ensure equal treatment in crediting gifts, and that institutional naming policies are followed. It should assure donor confidentiality when requested and allowed. (Public institutions and related foundations may have specific challenges in assuring confidentiality, as discussed in the next section on foundations.)

Last but not least, the development committee should pay attention to fundraising integrity. It should encourage and support a culture of ethical fundraising. It should ensure solicitation and acceptance of gifts that are appropriate for the mission of the institution. It should also seek ways to prevent development staff and the president from benefiting personally through commissions, personal gifts, or other benefits. For example, the institution should encourage donors to consult with their personal tax and legal advisors, and it should involve its own legal counsel in major (and planned) gift agreements and pledges.

Human Capital

Higher education is a people business. More than 65 percent of most institutions' operating budgets are compensation expenses. There is no doubt that the talent, skills, and diversity of perspectives that administrators, faculty, and staff possess collectively are among the institution's most valuable assets. As such, the board must focus attention on the human capital needed to operate the institution and deliver academic

Insight: Evaluate Major Gifts for Reputational Risks

Colleges and universities teach their students how to ask questions and how to critique an idea or organization. The institution and its donors are not immune from inquiring students, alumni, and faculty.

Several institutions have accepted gifts—often launching a program, establishing a center, or granting naming rights in return—that have angered campus stakeholders. In some cases, the institution has returned the gift to alleviate public pressure, though "undoing" an old gift is not always feasible, depending on the conditions attached to the gift. Public anger may be delayed by many years, even until long after the donor dies. Generally, such instances occur when the donor is judged to have gained his or her wealth in violation of the ethics of the modern era.

In cases in which stakeholders perceive the source of a gift as unethical or politically motivated, the gift causes reputational damage that harms an ongoing campaign. What seemed to be a generous gift and boon to the institution at the time turns into a liability to be managed into the future.

Major gifts are risks in their own right—their long-term costs and benefits are uncertain. (This is especially true for non-cash gifts, which carry financial risks, such as the future value of securities and real estate, as well as the reputational risks mentioned above.) Institutions should set a policy to vet major gifts for potential reputational harm, defining what amounts, sources, and designations to investigate further. Once the policy is defined, consider whether donors may be perceived to have acted unethically in earning their wealth and whether there are political intentions to their gifts. Despite the temptation to accept every large gift, discretion is required to manage reputational risks.

---

programs, campus life experiences, and support services required by the institution's mission and strategic objectives. At the same time, the board must understand that its focus on the institution's human assets is not an invitation to oversee the human resources function or manage specific employment decisions, which clearly fall within the province of the administration. The full board can evaluate human capital needs and plans, although the executive committee often oversees those issues, particularly with regard to decisions specific to the president's performance and compensation.

The risks that come within the purview of the board or its executive committee relate to:

- Executive compensation and performance;
- Succession planning;
- Employee hiring and retention;

- Compensation and pay equity; and
- Diversity and inclusion.

This is not a complete list; new risks will emerge over time, and some of these risks may not be relevant to every college or university. The board and its executive committee should understand issues that pose the greatest risk to the institution, help identify potential gaps in risk identification, and ensure that mitigation plans are developed and implemented. The committee should work closely with the administration and receive annual reports that designate the owner of the risk and document progress on mitigation plans. (See page 23, Exhibit 8 for a sample report, and page 191, Appendix A, for a sample human capital risk register.)

EXECUTIVE PERFORMANCE AND SUCCESSION PLANNING

The president and senior administrators are crucial to the success of the institution, its strategic direction, and its operations; therefore, the board should pay special attention to the institution's leaders. The executive committee often takes the lead with talent management and succession planning related to leadership.

To open the dialogue executive committee members should ask about:

- **President evaluation.** Is a thorough annual evaluation process in place for the president's performance?
- **Executive compensation.** Are the results of the president's evaluation and compensation package shared with the full board?
- **Talent and retention.** Does the institution have appropriate plans in place to attract and retain senior administrators?
- **Succession.** Are succession plans in place for replacing senior administrators in the event of an emergency and/or over a longer time period?

A departing chancellor of a major public university opined that "[t]he toughest job In the nation is the one of an academic- or health-institution president." Presidents are experiencing increasing challenges: lack of financial resources, mounting demands for prompt and quantifiable outcomes, and increased political and media scrutiny. Not surprisingly, the average tenure of college presidents is at a record low of 6.5 years, according to the American Council on Education.[17]

While the full board's responsibility is hiring, evaluating, and dismissing the president, nurturing and supporting the president's success is key to mitigating the risk of a failed presidency. Bolstering the president and his or her efforts to attract and retain high-caliber senior administrators is important to the institution's long-term health and vitality, as well. The committee should also support the efforts of senior administrators to develop and train all faculty and staff, with special emphasis on supervisors.

The financial pressures and complexity of academic institutions impose new challenges on the ability to attract and retain high-quality, engaged campus administrators and leaders. The executive committee may also serve as the compensation committee, meeting with an external compensation expert to assess comparability of the president's compensation, soliciting ongoing feedback on the president's performance, and, through the board chair, delivering the annual performance review and compensation decisions to the president and the full board.

EMPLOYEE HIRING AND RETENTION

Good hiring decisions and long-term retention are cost-effective for institutions when considering the expense (including the loss of institutional knowledge) of faculty and staff separations and recruitment. A board focused on its institution's human capital will want to understand institutional retention and turnover trends, the number of open positions and any recruiting challenges, and trends in employment claims trends—all of which may signal deeper workplace culture issues that potentially impede the institution's ability to advance its mission and programs.

Colleges and universities consistently report hundreds of employment claims to United Educators every year, which reflect hasty (and ultimately poor) hiring decisions, terminations that occur without appropriate documentation of performance problems, and workplace discrimination and harassment. Clear workplace policies and procedures related to performance evaluation, codes

> **"Performance management—the ongoing communication between a supervisor and employee to advance the organization's strategic objectives—is the responsibility of every supervisor, not the human resources department."**
>
> —*Reviewing Your School's Performance Management System*, United Educators

Insight: Location as a Risk to Recruitment and Retention

Rural institutions report that their location can affect employee recruitment and retention. A leader at a multicampus institution observed struggles to attract and retain talent due in part to lack of proximity to a major city and unreliable internet that added to the sense of isolation. Leadership invested in technological solutions to ensure that faculty and staff had the ability to connect and collaborate with other institutions, scholars, and professional colleagues to advance their work. Understanding the issues that lie beneath recruitment and retention challenges is important and may require cross-functional solutions rather than relying on traditional HR recruiting practices.

While increases in faculty and staff retirements play a role in employee turnover, 75 percent of turnover is preventable.[18] A poor institutional culture and lack of opportunities for employee development are consistently cited as major sources of turnover. In higher education, 71 percent of employees report that they would stay at their current institution if they had greater opportunities for professional development, and 86 percent report having no clear performance objectives or formal development plan.[19] Boards should inquire about the institution's approach to employment practices, such as performance management, supervisory training, employee training and development, and documentation of employee progress and misconduct.

of conduct, affirmative action, nondiscrimination, and harassment prevention all help define workplace expectations and culture. Boards have a keen interest in ensuring that the institution develops a reputation as a good and fair employer, which is critical in recruiting and retaining the talent and skill required to meet institutional goals. To this end, the board can ask the administration about:

- **Policies**. Has the institution adopted an employee code of conduct and clear policies addressing nondiscrimination and harassment so as to establish a respectful culture and behavioral expectations for the workplace? How does the institution ensure that those policies are followed and applied consistently for all employees?
- **Performance management**. Are job descriptions in place for all positions? Does the institution have clear policies and procedures for addressing poor performance and employee misconduct?
- **Formal evaluations and ongoing feedback**. Do all employees subject receive regular written evaluations? Are all supervisors and leaders subject to regular evaluations, as well?
- **Documentation and supervisor training**. What systems are in place to ensure that the institution maintains accurate employee

records? Are supervisors regularly trained and assessed on documentation of employee conduct and performance?
- **Climate surveys**. Does the institution conduct regular employee climate surveys to understand workplace issues and to get ahead of claims and turnover?

COMPENSATION AND PAY EQUITY

According to the Society for Human Resource Management (SHRM), compensation (salary and benefits) is among the top factors affecting employee satisfaction. While economic downturns restrain employee mobility, an increasingly robust economy provides more employment options. In either case, institutions should strive to provide fair and competitive compensation, which means they must understand how their compensation packages compare to higher education peers and employers in their geographic region to attract and retain talent.

Pay inequity is also an issue requiring attention and a concerted effort to overcome. States and employee organizations increasingly monitor pay equity to ensure that institutions are not paying any population disproportionately as a result of gender, race, or ethnic background. Higher education is not immune to less than favorable trends. A 2018 CUPA-HR study showed that female administrators earn 81 cents on the dollar compared to male counterparts. Similarly, the ethnicity pay gap is even greater, with men and women of color earning 72 and 67 cents on the dollar, respectively.[20] These troubling statistics mean that higher education has room to improve.

Human resources and the legal team may lead efforts on these fronts, and the board can play a role as well by assessing the fairness of the institution's compensation practices across all employee demographics. Boards should ask administrators to provide annual reviews of compensation budgets and spending, pay equity studies, as well as the cost of employment claims. They must also ask their administration about the strategies they are implementing to get ahead of compensation trends, including gauging the competitiveness of salaries and other forms of compensation, and their effect on recruitment and retention of talent.[21]

The cost of benefits is rising. As changes to benefits are considered to control budget spending, boards should be aware of the impact these decisions could have on the institution's talent recruitment and retention strategies. As an industry, higher education is perceived to offer better benefits than other industries. However, increased financial pressures have forced many institutions to reexamine benefits and their costs. Many institutions have shifted from traditional health plans to high-deductible health plans, which now offer reduced dental, vision, and long-term care plans, and scrutinize employee and dependent tuition assistance programs. Additionally, recent higher education employee legal challenges to 403(b) retirement plan administration have spurred more active institutional oversight of those plans.

DIVERSITY AND INCLUSION

The quality and vibrancy of the education community depends on highly skilled and engaged faculty and staff. Higher education institutions also recognize that a diversity of perspectives, backgrounds, experiences, and talents enriches an institution's mission of education, research, and service. Increasingly, boards and their institutions are setting objectives for increased diversity and inclusion as a means

---

Insight: Workplace Harassment and Discrimination

Reports of workplace discrimination and harassment submitted to United Educators suggest that this inappropriate behavior is all too common across higher education campuses. Between 2014 and 2018, 90 percent of all colleges and universities insured under United Educators' educators legal liability (ELL) policy reported more than 3,000 charges of employment discrimination (i.e., nearly 60 percent of all ELL claims). These claims resulted in significant costs, including $66.5 million in legal defense and settlement costs as well as the disruption and divisiveness that often comes when litigating such highly charged matters. Despite these trends, "top risk" surveys suggest that college and university leaders may not appreciate the excessive number and costs associated with discrimination and harassment challenges in higher education. In three consecutive annual surveys conducted by United Educators, leaders failed to prioritize employee discrimination and harassment as a "top of mind" risk.

A rash of discrimination claims at an institution can suggest that disrespectful and unacceptable behavior persists that will undermine the work aimed at improving campus diversity and inclusion. A board that has made a commitment to diversity should periodically review the institution's experience with incidents and legal claims of discrimination to determine whether trends exist suggesting that a particular department, administrator or supervisor, or demographic is implicated. Boards can remind the administration that in addition to putting programs in place to advance the goal of diversity and inclusion, it must also address the incidents and behaviors that undercut the institution's ability to meet those goals.

to educational excellence. To attract a more diverse student body, institutions must provide a diverse workforce, embracing diversity and inclusion goals for leadership, faculty, and staff positions to create a positive and robust learning community across cultures, political and religious affiliations, legally protected classifications (gender, race, age, disability), and educational scholarship, learning styles and values.[22]

To achieve diversity and inclusion goals, the board should first examine its own composition and that of leadership, and then seek to understand the steps the administration has taken to attract diverse talent, create a respectful and accepting culture, and ensure that equitable opportunities are available to all. As a baseline, the board should also explore the policies and programs in place that secure fair and equal treatment required under federal and state antidiscrimination laws. Questions that the board can ask include:

- Has the institution articulated a commitment to diversity and inclusion in a formal statement or policy? Is the statement backed up with staff and resources to advance diversity goals?
- Is the institution's board and leadership diverse and committed to increasing diversity across the faculty and staff?
- What strategies does the institution employ to attract, mentor, and retain minorities and women?
- Does the institution provide workplace accommodations that ensure the accessibility of its physical and digital spaces to employees with different abilities?
- Has the institution established nondiscrimination and harassment prevention policies and does it train supervisors and staff on them regularly?

Facilities and Campus Safety

The facilities committee, working with the institution's facilities staff, has five primary areas of responsibility:

1. Guiding long-range physical planning, including buildings, grounds, and infrastructure;
2. Monitoring the state of the institution's physical plant, budgets, and expenses;

3. Evaluating facility needs, prioritizing capital projects, exploring funding scenarios, and monitoring major project milestones;
4. Developing capital-asset preservation and renewal plans, including monitoring deferred and preventative maintenance and modernization plans; and
5. Ensuring compliance with all federal, state, local, and campus rules and regulations, including safety, the Americans with Disabilities Act, conflicts of interest, and the like.[23]

The risks that fall within the purview of the facilities committee include:

- Accessibility compliance;
- Auto/fleet condition/maintenance;
- Campus master plan;
- Current maintenance support;
- Deferred maintenance and life safety projects;
- Effectiveness of project management and cost control;
- Energy supply;
- Environmental health and safety;
- Space utilization; and
- Total cost of capital projects.

This is not a complete list; new risks will inevitably emerge, and some risks may not be relevant to all colleges, universities, and systems. The facilities committee is tasked with understanding the areas that pose greatest risk to the institution, helping to identify potential gaps in risk identification, and ensuring that mitigation plans are developed and followed. The committee should work closely with senior members of the administration and receive annual reports that designate the owner of the risk and document progress on mitigation plans. (See page 191, Appendix A, for sample facilities committee risk register.)

The following discussions focus on some of the most common, challenging, and significant risks related to facilities management and oversight, including:

- Campus master plan;
- Deferred maintenance and life safety projects; and
- Total cost of capital projects, including space utilization.

The following pages are intended to offer insights to members of the board so that they are better prepared to explore the risks and contribute to productive conversations with administrators. The facilities committee should expect to see annual risk reports from senior administrators that designate the owner(s) of the top risks and document progress toward mitigation plans.

CAMPUS MASTER PLAN

To open the dialogue facilities committee members can ask administrators about:

- **Strategic alignment**. Is the campus master plan aligned with the current strategic direction and priorities of the institution?
- **Campus master plan**. Does the campus master plan address changing student needs, new technology, and evolving learning (classroom) opportunities? Was it developed with broad-based input from all campus constituents?

Boards and facilities committees are responsible for approving campus master plans. In some jurisdictions, local zoning or planning commissions may also have a role in approving a plan. There are risks not only for institutions without a campus master plan but also for those that move forward with a poorly developed plan or take shortcuts in its implementation. On the one hand, campus planning can tap into the specialized expertise of board and committee members in engineering, architecture, and real estate development, for example. On the other, few businesses have a time horizon of perpetuity, and board and committee members often have limited experience in the nature of and need for campus plans that encompass a 10-to-25-year horizon. To further complicate the challenges, campus needs and physical facilities may be on the verge of significant change.

Most master plans include a thorough analysis of the current state of the campus and its environment, planning priorities for the institution, an established framework for planning and decision-making, and guidelines for implementation. Well-done campus master plans are grounded in two critical components: 1) a deep understanding of the campus strategic plan and institutional priorities, and 2) broad input from all campus constituents. The facilities committee may facilitate the process of developing the plan, but the entire board and campus community must be appropriately engaged.

Deferred Maintenance and Life Safety Projects

To open the dialogue facilities committee members should ask about:

- **Inventory.** Does the campus maintain a comprehensive inventory of its facilities?
- **Deferred maintenance.** Does the committee review major maintenance projects that have been deferred due to reduced funding, phasing, or programmatic purposes?
- **Classification.** Is the list of major maintenance projects classified by type of project (safety/security, space renewal, programmatic change)? Can these classifications help ensure that the institution addresses the right balance of maintenance projects?
- **Safety prioritized.** Are life safety projects afforded the highest priority on recapitalization lists?
- **Energy strategy.** Does the campus have a comprehensive energy supply-and-demand strategy?

The decades have not been kind to college and university campuses. A building boom in the latter part of the 20th century was followed by an economic downturn in the first decade of the 21st century, creating a figurative and literal hole in facilities that may take years to fill. As net tuition revenue and state support declined, many campuses diverted money supporting preventative maintenance to fund other operating expenses, adding to the backlog of deferred maintenance projects. While campuses wrestled with the decrease in funding, campus buildings and infrastructure continued to deteriorate and program needs changed, creating new demands for facilities renewal.

The facilities committee plays a role in supporting a comprehensive inventory review of all campus facilities, including a breakdown of major building components, such as heating, ventilation, and air conditioning (HVAC) systems, roofs, and major electrical systems. The inventory provides a structure to assess the backlog of deferred maintenance

---

Insight: Important Facilities Changes Afoot

For decades, there have been predictions that technological innovations would dramatically change the traditional campus. Yet, decades have passed without college and university campuses looking significantly different. How will libraries evolve to accommodate increased need for spaces to collaborate and for experiential learning rather than spaces for physical books? Will the competitive race to build bigger and better student and athletic centers abate? Will parking garages be repurposed as demand declines? At the risk of making one more unfounded prediction: Important changes are afoot in energy use and learning strategies. These changes may finally reshape campus facilities in dramatic new ways.

and a roadmap for planning recapitalization projects. The facilities committee should use the inventory during the annual budgeting process to advocate for funding.

The committee should pay special attention to maintenance projects that address life safety risks, including adding fire suppression sprinklers to residence halls, improving lighting in stairways, resurfacing parking lots on a regular schedule, and using daily campus accident reports to investigate areas that generate increased pedestrian and vehicular accidents.

Institutions should not forget institution-owned, off-campus facilities as part of this inventory since the institution is responsible for breakdowns and accidents on those properties. A 2017 article[24] by United Educators highlights the importance of inventorying all properties on and off campus, consolidating responsibility for oversight and record-keeping related to maintenance and insurance policies, conducting periodic on-site reviews to address and correct hazards, and developing a deferred maintenance plan, budget, and schedule. For off-campus properties in particular, institutions may consider engaging property management companies with overall maintenance responsibilities.

Total Cost of Capital Projects

To open the dialogue facilities committee members should ask about:

- **Total life cycle cost**. Does the facilities committee (and full board) review the total life cycle cost of the project, including ongoing operating costs?
- **Capital renewal account**. Does the institution have a policy to fund a capital renewal account in its operating budget? Is the institution committed to eliminating the deferred maintenance backlog?
- **Capital project record**. Does the campus have a history of on-time and on-budget completion of major capital projects?
- **Space utilization**. Does the institution maintain a space utilization plan? Is it reviewed when new construction, recapitalization, or leasing proposals are considered?

Boards often approve too many campus capital projects without a complete understanding of the total cost or life cycle cost. The inability to adequately maintain campus facilities poses life safety, accreditation, enrollment, and reputational risks to an institution. E. Lander

Medlin, the executive vice president of the Association of Physical Plan Administrators, notes that the initial cost of a new building (planning, design, and construction) is typically only 30 percent of the total cost of operating a building over its useful life. That means 70 percent of the total cost is in ongoing operations, energy, and capital renewal.

Facilities committees, in reviewing and approving major capital projects, should evaluate the total cost of the project, including energy costs (in some cases, new facilities will actually reduce energy needs), maintenance, and ongoing renewal costs. Additional parking, enhanced utility infrastructure, increased staff, and new contracts for upkeep should all be factored into the total cost of a project.

Space Utilization

Utilization of existing space on a campus takes on greater importance as the total cost of operating a new building steadily increases. Experts estimate that space utilization is, on average, approximately 50 percent for most campuses. As campuses evaluate the total cost of building new facilities or leasing additional space, the facilities committee should understand that alternatives for space utilization can offer options that support long-term financial sustainability.

Improving utilization of campus space is often a politically charged and unpopular discussion, but the financial risks of burdening a campus with new facilities (that add to operating budgets, fundraising needs, and debt loads) necessitate that attention be paid to this often-neglected area of facilities planning.

A commitment from the board to long-range facilities stewardship is a best practice for facilities risk management, and the facilities committee bears responsibility for leading this charge.

Information Technology

To open the dialogue the full board may ask administrators about:

- **Information technology (IT) strategy.** Does the institution have an information technology strategy? Does it reflect the institution's core values and strategic plan?
- **Protection.** Do agreements with partners properly protect intellectual property rights and other institutional values (such as privacy and nondiscrimination)?

- **Privacy**. Do IT staff members regularly assess changes in privacy and other federal and state compliance areas?
- **Cybersecurity**. Does the institution perform regular IT security risk assessments and report findings to the board?
- **Regulatory risk**. Is the institution ready for emerging data privacy regulations from the European Union and elsewhere?
- **Data sharing**. Does the institution have a consistent approach to contracting with cloud vendors? Is the institution clear on who owns data stored with those vendors and who will bear the cost in the event of a breach?
- **Accessibility**. Does the institution have an electronic information technology (EIT) accessibility policy? Are the institution's websites accessible to individuals using assistive technologies?
- **Missed opportunities**. Is the institution taking enough risk with its IT strategies? Are there opportunities to enhance the educational experience that have not been considered?

Over the past 20 years, information technology has evolved from being an operational support function for financial reporting and student records to becoming an integral part of teaching, research, and service. Data and cyber assets should be counted as one of four major assets (human, facilities, financial, and cyber) under the board's fiduciary responsibilities for institutional assets. The risks of loss or diminution of any of these assets is an important part of the institution's risk management strategy.

Institutions benefit from having IT experts serve on their boards. They bring a wealth of experience and knowledge of trends in a rapidly changing industry. While IT issues in higher education and commercial businesses are often similar, the differences are also substantial, and boards need to recognize the differences as well as the commonalities. The culture of higher education is one of transparency, openness, and collaboration. Businesses can operate secure and closed systems, while colleges, universities, and foundations serve broad communities from students, alumni, and donors to researchers and faculty. Small to midsized academic institutions have correspondingly smaller staffs, with members who are often generalists without the level of specialization or access to the top vendors that people who work in large corporate (and some large research university) IT departments have. Boards that understand these contexts and issues of scale are best positioned to help their institutions identify, assess, and mitigate IT risk.[25]

CYBERSECURITY

Cybersecurity poses a prominent risk for institutions of higher education. The nature of open networks, extensive systems, "creative" users, and sensitive data can generate the temptation to engage in mischievous and/or criminal actions. Unlike other industries, the openness of higher education networks means that a compromise in one place can impact the whole enterprise. Educational institutions have increasingly become targets of cyberattackers, who seek access to everything from email accounts and human resources records to medical information and research data. And the recovery, legal advice, and forensics work required to respond to a data breach are extremely expensive.

For cyber risks, the 80/20 rule is that institutions should allocate 80 percent of their resources to developing and testing cybersecurity systems (including on-campus and mobile computing) and 20 percent of their resources to responding to the significantly reduced risk of a major breach.

The board should ensure that policies are established and updated periodically, that testing is regularly conducted and reviewed, and that appropriate resources are invested in the security of computer systems and data. With the rise in prevalence of phishing and malware attacks, institutions should also train all employees with access to sensitive data–including human resources, finance, and other administrators—as well as research faculty on how to detect and avoid such scams.

DATA COLLECTION, INTEGRITY, AND ANALYSIS

Within the IT function the emphasis on decision making is shifting from technology to information. IT discussions in higher education now include not just hardware and software considerations but also more intangible issues, such as privacy and instructional learning methodology.

Data analytics supports academic missions and also increases institutional risks. The trend toward collecting and analyzing information on potential students, current students, and alumni offers tremendous opportunities and significant risks. Identifying what data to collect, how to analyze them, what privacy and transparency policies should be in place, and whether the campus is prepared to use the analysis are the risks and opportunities of the new frontier of data analytics. The board should confirm that the institution has a privacy policy on the collection and use of such data and that the policy is made readily available.

Insight: Data Analytics Support Missions but Raise Privacy and Data Security Risks

The power of data analytics that is sweeping the business world has the potential to change student health services, academic advising, and alumni relations. Many campuses collect data on a student's class attendance, number of meals eaten in the dining hall, library visits, and attendance at sporting events. Campus administrators can analyze such data and, using predictive modeling techniques, potentially identify students with substance abuse problems, those most likely to drop out, and/or those likely to become loyal and generous alumni. Questions that the board should ask and that should be answered include:

- Does the institution have a data analytics strategy?
- Is the institution collecting the right data?
- Is the institution willing to act on the data for the good of the institution?
- What is the institution's policy on data privacy?

Emerging Risk: New Regulations

From data collected through admissions applications and student and employee records to information from alumni and donors, institutions frequently collect and retain information about individuals related to the institution. Because institutions are typically decentralized, without a single strategy that governs all data, many institutions struggle to fully grasp how much data are retained and how and where they are stored.

With the passage of the General Data Protection Regulation (GDPR) and California Consumer Privacy Act (CCPA), organizations with data on consumers are facing a new kind of compliance regime requiring a strategic, end-to-end approach to data privacy that allows consumers to delete that data or take them with them to another provider.

For now, these regulators are not focused on higher education. European Union regulators are focused on marketers, and the CCPA law generally does not apply to nonprofit organizations. However, the day may come when these sorts of laws are commonplace, and institutions should be prepared. To comply with this new type of law, institutions must track their data on students and other consumers, knowing everywhere that data go and where they came from to begin with. Some institutions are drafting privacy policies that are more stringent than existing privacy regulations. This ensures that they are prepared for future regulations while also building a reputation for protecting their students, faculty, staff, and community.

One type of data potentially impacted by these new regulations involves admission and recruiting information. If someone from the

European Union or California asked an institution to delete admissions data on them, how would the institution respond?

DATA SHARING AND CLOUD VENDORS

Institutions must be vigilant when contracting with cloud vendors to preserve appropriate rights to institutional data. Many vendors want their customers' data because that allows them to provide value to all those customers through better analytics and benchmarking.

Institutions should contract with cloud vendors in a centralized manner, with all contracts vetted by IT and legal counsel. Industry standard language may not apply to higher education, so institutions should negotiate contracts that allow them to comply with the Family Educational Rights and Privacy Act and other applicable rules.

It is also important to vet the data security practices of vendors. That includes reviewing their practices for security data in transit over the internet as well as data at rest on their servers and in backups. Institutions should also request audits of the physical security of the vendor's infrastructure, as well as the security of their application.

It is also important to understand, in the event of a breach, whether the vendor is required to notify the institution and who is responsible to pay breach notification costs and other related expenses.

WEB ACCESSIBILITY

In recent years, Electronic Information Technology (EIT) accessibility has become an important topic as regulators and plaintiffs' attorneys have pursued institutions with outdated and inaccessible websites. Federal law—specifically, Section 504 of the Rehabilitation Act as well as the Americans with Disabilities Act—requires institutions to provide students with disabilities, and in some instances the general public, with access to electronic information. Many states have related requirements that apply to colleges and universities, some only to publics but others to all institutions in the state.

To succeed at EIT accessibility, institutions should adopt an accessibility policy and implementation plan. Designating an EIT accessibility coordinator and creating guidelines for faculty and staff to ensure web-based content is accessible is also key.

Vendor contracts should guarantee that EIT products meet these same accessibility requirements. Vendors should provide a voluntary product accessibility template (VPAT) for their products, identifying the level of support those products have for federal accessibility requirements. Legal counsel should vet contracts with EIT vendors to ensure that those vendors are obligated to remedy any accessibility shortcomings that arise and also, ideally, to have the vendor indemnify the institution in the event of a lawsuit or regulatory action involving the product. Multiple institutions should also consider procuring their products as a group to have more leverage with vendors over accessibility support.

Institutional Resources Warning Signs and Board Actions

The board can get a sense of whether additional coordination or internal oversight around financial issues are needed by considering the following warning signs:

Board Inquiry	Resource Warning Sign	Possible Board Actions
Are tuition increases resulting in greater net tuition revenue?	Tuition increases are offset by an increasing discount rate.	Understand drivers for increased tuition discounting. Set a discount target and require the administration to adhere to it.
Are investments in capital bringing adequate returns?	Property, plant, and equipment (PP&E) asset is increasing faster than revenue.	Study how property can be sold or repurposed to generate new revenue.
Is the institution operating at a margin or a deficit?	The institution has run an operating deficit annually or almost every year in the last few years.	Require the administration to develop realistic (meet or beat) budgets and instill discipline to adhere to the budget. Stress-test against likely scenarios that could cause deviations from the budget, including lessons learned from past years.

Board Inquiry	Resource Warning Sign	Possible Board Actions
Which of the institution's revenues are increasing the fastest?	The institution is increasingly tuition dependent.	Direct the administration to analyze the institution's assets for other revenue sources. Encourage scenario planning so the institution is prepared if net tuition revenue targets are not met.
Has the board established performance objectives for the president that are evaluated on an annual basis?	The president is not advancing the institution's strategic plan as promptly as the board would expect.	Provide feedback for a written evaluation of the president that the board chair will prepare and deliver.
Does the campus have a strategy to address the needs of the physical plant, including capital projects and deferred maintenance?	The institution has unplanned expenses involving maintenance or does not have strategies to address long-term physical plant maintenance.	Consider asking the institution to develop strategies involving capital projects, space utilization, and deferred maintenance.
Does the institution have policies in place for: • Cybersecurity and information security; • Data governance; and • Privacy.	The institution does not have a data governance policy that establishes practices for data security and privacy.	Ask the institution to develop policies, practices, and tools for inventory data storage, sharing, and security practices.

Chapter 8
Risks to the Student Experience

WHILE AUDIT, GOVERNANCE, AND EXECUTIVE COMMITTEES ARE common to all boards, institutions also maintain board committees that provide oversight of the core student experience: academics and campus life.

These academic affairs and student life committees guide and support the mission of the institution—teaching, research, and service—and ensure an overall positive student experience. It is not the role of the committees to manage these functions, but it is their responsibility to understand, question, and ultimately support the direction set by the institution's strategic plan and implemented through its annual operations. Committee oversight requires strong knowledge of potential risks.

Academic Affairs Committee

The academic affairs committee is one of the busiest intersections of shared governance. On behalf of the governing board, the academic affairs committee bears the primary responsibility for defining, overseeing, and modifying the policies that fulfill a college or university's academic mission. This includes what students learn and how well they learn it; the effectiveness of teaching and learning; faculty selection, recognition, and development; how to assess and reward teaching excellence; efficient and sensible organization of departments, divisions, and colleges within larger institutions; academic standards and requirements; and the appropriate balance among teaching, scholarship, and service—as well as many other elements. The risks that come under the purview of academic affairs include:

- Academic quality;
- Accreditation;
- Online Education;
- Faculty conflicts of interest;
- Faculty recruitment;
- International programs and global strategy;
- Medical centers;
- Program closures;
- New programs and entrepreneurial ventures;
- Research;
- Outcomes; and
- Tenure and promotion.

This is not a complete list; new risks will inevitably emerge, and some risks may not be relevant to all colleges, universities, and systems. The academic affairs committee is tasked with understanding the areas that pose the greatest risk to the institution, helping to identify potential gaps in risk identification and ensuring that mitigation plans are developed and followed. The committee should expect to see annual risk reports from senior administrators that designate the owner(s) of the top risks and document progress toward mitigation plans. (See page 23, Exhibit 8, for a sample report, and page 194, Appendix A, for a sample academic affairs risk register.)

The following discussions focus on some of the most common, challenging, and significant risks related to academic affairs, including:

- Academic quality;
- Tenure;
- Starting and closing programs;
- International programs;
- Research; and
- Medical centers.

The following pages are intended to offer insights to members of the board and the academic affairs committee so that they are better prepared to explore the risks and contribute to productive conversations with administrators.

ACADEMIC QUALITY

To open the dialogue the academic affairs committee should ask administrators:

1. How good is our academic product?
2. How good are we at producing our academic product?
3. Are our customers satisfied?
4. Do we have the right mix of programs to achieve mission and meet demand?
5. Do our academic products meet our quality standards?

The spotlight on academic quality is growing brighter as students, parents, legislators, and employers question the role of colleges and universities and the utility of skills graduates bring to the workplace.

The concept of a traditional undergraduate education is evolving, which brings increased scrutiny and new risks to leaders in higher education. Students, families, and increasingly legislators are questioning the value of an education and the return on their investment. This is reflected in public and political discourse on higher education: legislators looking to overhaul the Higher Education Act of 1965 (HEA) underscore the importance of "expand[ing] access, improv[ing] affordability, and promot[ing] completion for all students"[1] to ensure that higher education keeps up with changes in demographics and workplace demands.

While many board members are used to measuring financial health, tracking financial ratios, and reviewing balance sheets, overseeing the quality of the academic experience is new territory for most of them. The board needs to ask the administration if the perceived quality of the academic "product" and experience at the institution is sufficient to give the institution tuition pricing power. In light of the public's perception of the value of a college degree, can an institution market and sustain its traditional curriculum? If the institution is unable to align the academic program with student demand, and enrollment slips and tuition discounts increase, the institution may be on an unsustainable path. Instructional strategy is the responsibility of the faculty; ensuring that appropriate financial resources support that strategy is the responsibility of the president and board.[2]

> "Some colleges will choose to embrace a mission and accept the consequences to their revenue. Others will choose to pursue revenue and accept the consequences to their mission."
>
> —Nathan Mueller, principal, EAB

The board's oversight of academic quality can be a sensitive topic. The concept of shared governance keeps boards and administrators from developing or modifying curriculum, which is generally accepted as the sole province of the faculty. In ensuring academic quality—and mitigating risks that arise when the quality of the educational experience is less than students and parents can reasonably expect—the board's role is to remind faculty of their responsibility for developing curriculum and hold them accountable for its continuous improvement. In doing this, boards must walk a fine line.

Discussions within the academic affairs committee and with faculty leadership are a good starting place to ensure that instructional strategy and resource requirements are aligned. The academic affairs committee can help the board oversee educational quality by embracing the following five principles:

1. Curriculum is the faculty's responsibility; the board's role is to remind faculty of that and hold them accountable for that responsibility.
2. Stay focused on the academic experience as a strategic issue.
3. Expect and require a culture of evidence.
4. Recognize that evidence about academic quality raises issues but rarely provides final answers.
5. Make reviewing evidence of academic quality and improvement a regular and expected board-level activity.

ONLINE EDUCATION

Disruptive innovations in teaching and learning have further complicated oversight of educational quality. In the past, instructional strategy meant a faculty member decided whether a course would be better taught as a seminar or lecture. Now, instructional strategy might encompass not only lectures, seminars, labs, internships, externships, and service learning, but also online learning, online program managers (OPMs), massive open online courses (MOOCs), social media, and the like. And there are risks at both ends of the blended learning continuum. Some universities—sometimes driven by the board—are rushing to participate in OPMs without a full evaluation of how they fit within the institution's instructional strategy, broader strategic plans, brand, and overall financial picture. Other (often small, independent) colleges are choosing to downplay online learning opportunities rather

Insight: The Evolution of MOOCs, OPMs, and Their Impact on Education

Massive open online courses (MOOCs) rose in the early 2010s as a less expensive learning alternative that connects instructors with online learners from all over the world. The *New York Times* designated 2012 "The Year of the MOOC" as such institutions as Harvard University, the Massachusetts Institute of Technology, Stanford University, and Google developed platforms to offer courses online, typically at no cost.[3]

In 2019, however, a Google search for MOOCs invariably suggests the search query "the MOOC is dead."[4] Some MOOCs no longer exist, while some have had to cut costs drastically in order to survive.

As MOOCs have declined, OPMs (online program managers) have grown. Most online degree programs in 2019 were delivered through OPMs, which are companies that specialize in online course design, implementation, and delivery. While OPMs were ideal partners for universities as they sought to increase online enrollments—and tuition revenues—most partnerships failed to increase margins or reduce costs. OPMs often take a large percentage of revenues for marketing and administrative support. Some institutions are evaluating the merits of developing OPM capabilities in-house, weighing the significant investment with the potential long-term return.

The promise of education technologies has met the reality of higher education finance and the challenges of change. It has been a bumpy road for many institutions, and the outlook is just as trying with the release of promising new education technologies each year.

---

than getting ahead of the competition. In addition, all institutions must recognize that online learning and institutional websites have to meet accessibility standards of the Americans with Disabilities Act.

To some degree the greatest risk of technology-enabled education is an emerging risk: Will the institution be ready for whatever disruptions come next? Virtual reality courses, augmented reality assignments, artificial intelligence-aided instruction, and countless other education technologies are mostly still ideas, not reality. Will the institution be able to evaluate whether the next development in educational technology is a fad or a disruption? Will it be prepared to innovate on its instructional model to take advantage of new technologies? These are questions without easy answers, but they are crucial ones to ask as technologies promise to change how students learn.

> "It's not MOOCs that are going to close the gaps in the educational divide in the world—but they have stimulated the world's greatest institutions to start doing more digitally."
>
> —Simon Nelson, CEO, FutureLearn.[5]

Oversight of Educational Quality: If Not the Board, Then Who?

"There are reasons, of course, for keeping boards out of educational issues. Most college trustees are business executives or lawyers with no special knowledge of academic matters. Moreover education, like art and architecture, is a subject on which many inexperienced observers feel entitled to express views—views strongly held but often quite wrong. To faculty members, then, and even presidents, the prospect of having a board look at any part of the educational process may well seem threatening.

"Yet self-restraint also has its costs. Who else is capable of altering the current system of incentives and rewards to hold deans and presidents accountable for the quality of their educational leadership? No faculty ever forced its leaders out for failing to act vigorously enough to improve the prevailing methods of education. On the contrary, faculties are more likely to resist any determined effort to examine their work and question familiar ways of teaching and learning. Students cannot tell whether current practices are less effective than they might be, and alumni are too far removed to know what needs to be done. As a result, if trustees ignore the subject, no one may press academic leaders to attend to those aspects of the education program that are in greatest need of reform.

"Fortunately, the risks of unwise intervention are fairly low, so long as trustees do not try to dictate what courses should be taught and what instructional methods employed but merely ask for reports on the procedures used to evaluate academic programs and encourage innovation. It is surely within the prerogatives of the board to take an interest in these activities and to urge the president to work with the faculty to develop a process designed to ensure continuing improvement in the quality of education . . .

"Although . . . trustees can provide an important impetus for reform, and back it stoutly when it occurs, they cannot guarantee change by their own efforts. They can urge a process of self-scrutiny and innovation and give it greater legitimacy, but they cannot bring it about themselves. Real improvement requires the initiative and skills of academic leaders—presidents, provosts, and deans—who understand what needs to be done and appeal successfully to the sense of professional responsibility that most faculties share for the education of their students."

—Derek C. Bok, former president, Harvard University

Source: Derek Bok. *Our Underachieving Colleges: A Candid Look at How Much Students Learn and Why They Should be Learning More.* New Jersey: Princeton University Press, 2006. pp. 333–335.

TENURE

To open the dialogue the academic affairs committee can ask administrators the following questions about:

- **The role of tenure**. What goals does tenure meet and are the costs sustainable? What impact does tenure have on academic quality and student success?
- **Tenure policy**. Does the institution clearly articulate standards and procedures to guide tenure review and the award of tenure?
- **Legal review**. Have the faculty handbook and tenure policies been reviewed recently by legal counsel with expertise in higher education employment law?
- **Adherence to policies**. Are tenure review committees trained to ensure that current review practices consistently adhere to the institution's policies and faculty handbook?
- **Litigation**. If tenure litigation becomes inevitable, does the board have a process for testing its resolve?

Given their import, the full board can alternatively discuss these questions with the administration.

Academic tenure is an employment status unique to higher education, established to safeguard academic freedom by granting an indefinite appointment with the institution to deserving faculty members. Unlike other employment contracts that can be terminated at will, institutions may terminate a tenure appointment only by showing cause, such as incompetence or misconduct, or extraordinary circumstances, such as financial exigency and program discontinuation.[6] Otherwise, the faculty member can expect to remain employed by the institution until he or she retires.

Obtaining tenure is a time-intensive, rigorous process compared to other employment arrangements. Because lifetime employment is at stake, an institution's tenure policy and procedures must be clear and applied consistently.

PROGRAM CHANGES: STARTING NEW PROGRAMS AND CLOSING PROGRAMS

The academic affairs committee need not review business plans for each new program or entrepreneurial venture, but it does need to ensure that

Insight: Challenges to Tenure Review and Legal Implications

Tenure litigation is one of the most expensive, divisive, and time-consuming risks that educational institutions face. The stakes are extremely high. The core of a tenure denial lawsuit focuses on lifetime employment related to increasingly scarce positions, and all of the security and prestige associated with tenure status. Although much rarer than the denial of tenure for assistant professors, tenure revocation also occurs and often leads to litigation.

In a United Educators study published in 2017,[7] the average cost to defend a tenure denial lawsuit was $185,500, with the most expensive defense in the study costing $1.6 million. Settlements can also be costly given the loss of lifetime employment—the most expensive settlement in the study topped $600,000. Nearly all tenure claims alleged some type of discrimination. Gender discrimination was the most common allegation (34 percent of the claims in the study), followed by discrimination based on race (32 percent) and national origin (26 percent).

As a result, institutions must ensure that the promotion and tenure committee is trained regularly on an institution's tenure review procedures and that all faculty are trained on the institution's antidiscrimination and retaliation policies.

---

the administration has rigorous planning, management, and monitoring policies and procedures that are followed. To open the dialogue the academic affairs committee should ask administrators about:

- **New program planning.** Is there a detailed business plan including staffing needs, potential market, and costs to support each new program?
- **Annual reviews.** Are there annual reviews of ongoing programs to test the validity of assumptions, progress toward accreditation, financial results, and the strength and relationship of all partners?
- **Program closure.** When considering closing programs, are the key constituents involved? Are considerations related to faculty and students taken into account?

A significant shift occurring at colleges and universities is the pressure to become more entrepreneurial. Such initiatives may be domestic or international, online and through branch campuses, pursued alone or with partners. Their pace and scope are increasing. Institutions pursue new programs for a variety of reasons: to strengthen their core mission, to meet new and evolving constituent needs, and often to add revenue to replace declining state support and tuition.

For purposes of this discussion, programs are broadly defined to include academic, department, or school offerings within a larger institution. Especially for new programs, the rush to market poses heightened financial and reputational risks. Some of the most common problems relate to outsourcing (to online program managers, for example), accreditation, and academic quality. The academic affairs committee, in conjunction with other committees, should make sure that business planning exercises include the following:

- External market research validating demand for the new program;
- A pro forma financial plan with clear explanations of assumptions;
- Legal review of contracts, including employment, facilities, operations, and others;
- Documentation of accreditation required for successful program operation, with special attention to requirements needed to sit for external exams and licenses;
- Thorough review of marketing materials to ensure compliance with consumer protection laws, providing appropriate disclaimers for accreditation and potential future employment of program graduates; and

Insight: Conversations with Accreditors

Board members do not always have experience in higher education, finance, or law, which means that institutions may struggle to educate boards about important issues like accreditation. One accreditor noted cases in which administrators saw all the warning signs in advance, but failed to persuade the board when early signs were showing:

"We've had a number of closures in the recent past [when] the president has tried to get the board's attention and says, 'You know, we need to close.' And the board has been reluctant to do that [potentially because of] an emotional connection. A lot of them are alums. And in some cases in rural areas, they may be local board members who also know that if the college closes, it's an economic problem for the entire community."

In discussions with accreditors, it became clear that they want to help institutions succeed with accreditation and risk management initiatives. One leader at a regional accreditor stated, "I'm not quite a cheerleading squad, but kind of an advisory committee" or sounding board for institutions looking to navigate accreditation questions.

Ultimately, for boards to be most effective, one accreditor advised that boards can and should engage their accreditor before a financial crisis, and also seek out professional development opportunities to understand the accreditation process and interpret financial statements.

- Training for program administrators, including admissions staff, to ensure understanding of consumer protection laws.

As campuses evaluate new programs, ongoing reviews of current programs can result in a recommendation by the faculty and administration to close a program that no longer supports the mission, has shrinking enrollments, or can be better served through collaboration with another institution. Program closures can lead to lengthy and expensive lawsuits and reputational damage if not managed appropriately. Potential lawsuits can come from faculty and staff who may be terminated, students who may allege a breach of contract or consumer fraud, or partners who may allege a breach of contract. Boards should recognize that closing a program is not inexpensive, but, done well, the reputational damage will be minimized and the campus can focus on its ongoing mission.

When confronting a program closure, the academic affairs committee should ask administrators the following questions about:

- **Closure planning.** Were faculty involved in the review and decision to close a program? Were alternatives to closing the program considered?

Case in Point: Tales of Caution from the Claims Files

Accreditation status hits a snag: A comprehensive university contracted with an outside partner to offer a program for medical assistants. The program was run under the university's name but operated by the outside firm. Students were told that the program was fully accredited and that they would be able to sit for the three required licensing exams. However, the accreditation was secured only for two exams. Former students alleged that they were misled about the accreditation status. When the university applied to extend the accreditation to the third exam, it was denied. Then the outside partner experienced financial difficulties, leaving the university to settle the lawsuits.

Quality control is squeezed: A university offered financial incentives to departments and individual professors to teach short-term, off-site courses in several information technology disciplines. Recruiters promised a professional certification upon completion. In the rush to market, departmental oversight was not up to the same level demanded on the main campus. Course materials were late arriving at the off-site locations and, in some cases, were not current. The coursework did not lead students to the desired certifications. The university refunded tuition. Still, a group of students sued the institution, alleging it violated the state's deceptive trade practices act by luring them to quit steady jobs to take this certification course.

- **Personnel matters.** Is outside legal counsel with experience in reductions in force involved if faculty or employee layoffs are contemplated? Does the faculty handbook offer a definition and guidance for financial exigency if faculty positions are terminated? Are provisions established to help and support both terminated and remaining employees?
- **Student concerns.** Does the student handbook state that the institution reserves the right to terminate and reduce programs when deemed necessary by the institution? Is there a plan to "teach out" enrolled students or assist in transfers to other institutions?

INTERNATIONAL PROGRAMS

To open the dialogue the academic affairs committee can ask administrators about:

- **Due diligence.** Has appropriate due diligence been completed on all partners, suppliers, and agents involved in international programs?
- **Compliance.** Has a compliance checklist covering domestic and foreign regulations been developed and reviewed by counsel with expertise in international business and local counsel in the country of the foreign program?
- **Intellectual property.** Has the institution's name and intellectual property been registered and protected in foreign countries in which it will be doing business?
- **Exit strategy.** Does the institution have an exit strategy if the international program is terminated? Do agreements have clear guidance on dispute resolution?

While many colleges and universities are building a global curriculum and experience for their students and faculty in myriad ways, the most common international strategies and their attendant academic-related risks often fall into one of two areas: 1) overseas campuses and programs and 2) study abroad programs.

Overseas Campuses

Increasingly, large colleges and universities are building branch or independent campuses overseas, sometimes on their own and sometimes in partnership with a local entity. Institutions that lack the scale to launch overseas campuses are partnering with foreign universities to launch degree programs or collaborative academic experiences for students that expand beyond the confines of traditional study abroad.

The complexity of these ventures requires working with legal and academic experts who understand U.S. law and that of host countries. Initial areas to address in starting a formal program in another country include protecting the institution's name and intellectual property, adhering to U.S. laws safeguarding financial transactions, and establishing a clear understanding of faculty and administrator employment status.

While launching overseas campuses can spread the institution's global reputation, such initiatives can also damage that reputation. International campuses are high-profile efforts—when one fails it can drag down the institution's domestic brand as stakeholders question leadership's judgement and effectiveness. Specific stakeholder groups can also take issue with the institution's foreign operations, as well. For example, faculty in repressive countries may rebel against limited academic freedoms, or students and alumni may disapprove of the institution's affiliation with a government with a problematic human rights record. The U.S. government is increasingly questioning institutional practices related to the accounting of foreign assets and payments to foreign entities.

Before embarking on a new initiative, the academic affairs committee (in conjunction with other committees) should ensure that they receive regular reports on its academic offerings, in-country partnerships, and financial status, as well as a carefully designed exit strategy should circumstances suggest the need to end the program.

RESEARCH

To open the dialogue the academic affairs committee should ask administrators about:

- **Need**. Does the research agenda support the college or university's mission and priorities? Will the research fill an unmet need?
- **Total cost**. What is the total cost of new research initiatives, including the cost of constructing and maintaining facilities, infrastructure, and technology, supporting faculty and graduate students, and maintaining program operations?

- **Funding**. Does the university acknowledge the potential instability of outside support for research? Has senior leadership articulated the amount of internal funding that will be needed to support the research programs?
- **Compliance**. What funding exists for administrative oversight to ensure compliance with federal, state, and corporate mandates?
- **Conflicts of interest**. Does the university follow conflict-of-interest policies governing researchers' connections to funding sources and potential business ventures?
- **Technology transfer**. Do intellectual property policies clarify the roles of faculty researchers and the university to support technology transfer?
- **Reputation risks**. What is the potential reputational harm to the university for research misconduct?
- **Crisis planning**. Are there protocols in place to secure research (for example, materials in storage, animals, data) in the event of a power outage, a natural disaster, or human error? Is there a recovery plan in place in the event of a crisis?

Government Funding and Cost of Research

Basic research in the United States has been a partnership between federal and state governments and higher education institutions since the passing of the Morrill Acts in 1862. What began as a focus on the challenges to a young country as it addressed an agricultural and emerging industrial economy has evolved into a driving force in innovation and technological improvements, from DNA fingerprinting to weather forecasting to the Global Positioning System, the internet, and beyond. Boards, administrators, and faculty at research universities wonder how this centuries-old partnership may change and what risks and opportunities await.

Compliance and oversight covers a wide range of research activities, including animal and human subject protocols, export controls, intellectual property rights, scientific integrity, security, and safety. Research conducted in areas sensitive to national security carries added requirements, such as restrictions on access to labs and limitations on foreign student participation. While expenses related to compliance and oversight have increased, institutions typically negotiate a federal indirect cost recovery rate (the amount of administrative costs that can be recovered) that may or may not be enough to cover the expenses related to a particular grant. Unfunded mandates for compliance are now an integral part of any basic research program.

The total cost of university research is neither well understood nor completely accounted for, which can threaten an institution's ability to sustain facilities and research staff. Campuses have traditionally taken the upfront risk in building labs and investing in infrastructure with the hope that the cost of these capital investments will be covered in the future by indirect costs. That assumption is riskier now than it has ever been, and it warrants consideration by the academic affairs committee, as well as the finance committee.

Conflicts of Interest and Business Continuity

As part of its risk management assessment, the academic affairs committee should also consider the processes and policies related to research. It should make certain that policies and processes are in place to ensure the integrity of research findings and that honest and verifiable methods are used, that reports to funding agencies are timely and accurate, and that research practices reflect the institution's academic standards and professional norms. Appropriate training on the institution's standards—including ownership of intellectual property, publishing guidelines, effort reporting, and lab safety—should be in place and delivered to faculty members, researchers, and students.

Academic research is an integral part of many universities but is often left out of business continuity plans. Valuable research materials and data have been lost when natural catastrophes strike campus buildings. Institutions struggle to find insurance coverage for many academic

---

Case in Point: The Emerging Risk of Foreign Influence on Campus

One multicampus research institution pointed to foreign influence as a top emerging risk. In 2019, several research institutions dismissed researchers "over allegations they did not disclose foreign support for their work and ties to institutions in China."[8]

Institutions are not alone in their concern over foreign influence. Reports in the press include: "national security agencies, federal granting agencies, the White House and members of Congress have all signaled their increasing concern about international students or scholars who might seek to exploit the openness of the U.S. academic environment for their own—or their nations'—gain. . . ."[9] Given the federal government's increasing concern about the balance between scientific openness, national security, and economic competitiveness, boards and the academic affairs committee in particular should be attentive to any foreign interest or participation in institutional research.

> ### Federal Funding, Fraud, and Whistleblowers
>
> **Investigations under the federal False Claims Act (FCA) can be a significant risk** for institutions that receive federal support. The act imposes liability on individuals and institutions that defraud government programs. Although the FCA applies to misuse of any federal funds, research programs and the misuse of Medicare funds generate the greatest number of lawsuits. The FCA includes rewards (known as a "qui tam" provision) and protection for whistleblowers who report misconduct on federal grants. Many states and some cities also maintain FCA regulations.
>
> **Retaliation claims brought by whistleblowers are among the costliest and most disruptive lawsuits** for universities. They can reflect poorly on the research operation and ultimately damage an institution's reputation and ability to secure future research opportunities. In these types of suits, a whistleblower typically alleges that he or she suffered reprisal for reporting or complaining about wrongdoing, such as misuse of federal funds or violations of overtime laws. Most colleges and universities already recognize the need to prevent retaliation following an employee complaint about discrimination or harassment on the basis of race, sex, or another protected category. But they may not realize that they must be equally vigilant about preventing retaliation against employees who complain or simply raise questions about other types of illegal or improper conduct. Appropriate internal controls and audit functions, sound personnel practices (for example, grievance procedures and whistleblower policies), and training of supervisors can reduce the likelihood of FCA and retaliation claims.

research projects, increasing the importance of including research labs in disaster preparedness drills and providing protection of research animals, tissue, and data with generators and environmental controls.

ACADEMIC MEDICAL CENTERS

Academic medical centers (AMCs) are often the most complex and challenging part of any university. Addressing the risks associated with these centers is a monumental task. On behalf of the governing board, the academic affairs committee can start the dialogue by asking administrators about:

- **Strategy.** Does the AMC have a strategy in place to control costs and increase quality? Are merger and acquisition opportunities explored?
- **Innovation.** Does the AMC investigate innovative ways to attract and engage patients using new technology and delivery systems?
- **Data analytics.** Does the AMC harness data and analytics to improve delivery and patient care?
- **Mission alignment.** Are the research, clinical, and business strategies aligned to support the AMC's mission and focus on being a center of excellence?

AMCs support research, teaching, and clinical care are the backbone of the American medical system. They train future health care providers, produce basic research and medical breakthroughs, and care for the most challenging and risky patients. AMCs are decentralized and function with very slim operating financial margins. Since the 2010 Affordable Care Act, health care has navigated a state of transformation and uncertainty. Calls by politicians from all ideological perspectives ensure that change is here to stay. Regardless of policy changes, pressure will continue to build from consumers and health insurance providers to reduce costs, improve productivity, and increase technological investments. Meanwhile, shrinking federal support for basic research creates additional risks and opportunities for AMCs.

At the governing board level, and often through the academic affairs committee, issues that warrant careful consideration—above and beyond those particular to health care delivery—relate to financial and reputational assets. Some AMCs have separate, independent governing boards; others share board members or report to the university's governing board. The separation of reporting and fiduciary responsibilities, while important, does not address public perception of the link between the AMC and the university:[10]

- The public will not differentiate insurance fraud, patient abuse, or medical malpractice scandals at the university hospital from the university.
- Experts believe shrinking federal and state support for both reimbursement of services and basic research will lead to a further decline in net revenue for AMCs, which may strain the institution's financial health.

- The complexities of funding and cross-subsidization of clinical care, physician training, and research present distinct challenges for governing boards and administrators. Clinical trials, vital to academic research, present a major risk in terms of overall patient safety and for potential conflicts of interest related to the funding source (such as for drug research), which may be linked to commercial interests.

Student/Campus Life Committee

College and university boards are charged with governance responsibility to ensure that students receive a high-quality education from a well-managed institution. Although many of the areas involving students and campus life cross over to other board committees (for example, study abroad programs may be addressed by the academic affairs committee, student enrollment and retention is increasingly a finance committee focus), the student life committee is charged with:

1. Ensuring that the best interests of students are at the center of board considerations and decisions;
2. Educating itself and the board about students attending the institution and the services in place to support them;
3. Promoting and supporting institutional efforts to create a climate that is focused on student engagement both inside and outside the classroom; and
4. Ensuring that adequate resources for programs and services exist to support students in their learning and development.[11]

Risks that fall within the purview of the student or campus life committee may include:

- Alcohol and drug policies;
- Athletics;
- Campus security;
- Career services;
- Care teams/threat assessment;
- Commuting student programs;
- Experiential learning;

- Family Educational Rights and Privacy Act (FERPA) compliance;
- Financial aid/student debt;
- International students;
- Minors on campus;
- Residence halls;
- Services for nontraditional students (e.g., child care, tutoring, food pantries, or counseling);
- Service learning programs;
- Sexual assault/Title IX compliance;
- Student health and mental health centers; and
- Study abroad.

This is not a complete list; new risks will inevitably emerge, and some risks may not be relevant to all colleges, universities, and systems. The student life committee is tasked with understanding the areas that pose greatest risk to the institution, helping to identify potential gaps in risk identification, and ensuring that mitigation plans are developed and followed. The committee should work closely with senior members of the administration and receive annual reports that designate the owner of the risk and document progress on mitigation plans. (See Appendix A, page 197, for sample risk register.)

The following discussions focus on some of the most common, challenging, and significant risks related to the student experience outside the classroom. Unfortunately, some risks are, or have become, particularly high-profile issues for colleges and universities, including:

- Student health and safety;
- Campus security;
- Athletics; and
- Student activities, including study abroad programs and clubs.

The following pages are intended to offer insights to members of the board and the student life committee so that they are better prepared to explore the risks and contribute to productive conversations with administrators.

STUDENT HEALTH AND SAFETY

To open the dialogue student affairs committee members should ask about:

- **Common causes**. Does the administration regularly review reports of serious injury and death, looking for common causes and investigating appropriate responses to reduce recurring incidents?
- **Student mental health and substance abuse**. Does the student life committee regularly communicate the importance of student mental health and substance abuse prevention to the administration and community? Is a process in place for the administration to monitor and analyze student mental health and substance abuse reports and claims, as well as links to academic retention and student health and safety?
- **Student health services**. Does the administration clearly articulate and enforce policies on the types and levels of campus health services available to students and provide information on external sources of health care?
- **Student sexual assault**. Has the administration established institutional policies, procedures, and training aimed at preventing and responding to student sexual assault, and has it prioritized Title IX and VAWA-Campus SaVE Act compliance?

No higher education institution can promise a totally safe and risk-free experience to students and their parents. An important part of learning is being able to make mistakes, learn from them, and move on. But no family sends a child to college with the expectation that serious injury or death will result, and no president or dean ever wants to have to call a family about these circumstances. The climate of risk-taking and personal responsibility for taking risks has swung back and forth over the decades. Since the mid-1970s, the underpinnings of *in loco parentis* have eroded. Students over the age of 18 have been treated as adults, and institutions have not acted in a parental oversight role. Many courts recognized and supported this change, but today the pendulum is swinging back. Recent scholarly commentary, court decisions, and family expectations are again holding colleges and universities more responsible for the safekeeping of students. They do so under expanded notions of negligence or because of the "special relationship" that exists between institutions and students in

Insight: The Return of *In Loco Parentis*

High-risk student behavior may be considered to be part of moving into adulthood, but the shifting winds of *in loco parentis* and greater potential liability if serious injury or death occurs have placed a greater obligation on institutions of higher education to train student affairs staff, faculty, coaches, and other frontline staff on prevention and response strategies.

> "Mental illness is not sadness, insanity or rage (though it can involve these in some of its forms); it is not binary or exclusive, but complex and universal."
>
> —"Mental Illness: Is There Really A Global Epidemic?" *The Guardian*[12]

certain circumstances. Given this, it's critically important for the board's student life committee to focus on student health and safety issues, such as mental health, alcohol and substance abuse, and sexual violence which, unfortunately, are commonplace challenges for institutions today.

Student Mental Health

Student mental health is impacting all aspects of student life both inside and outside of the classroom, including academic success, extracurricular activities, relationships, and physical and mental well-being. Recent studies show that risks involving student mental health will remain severe and frequent over the next years.

Reports and Claims: Student Mental Health and Suicide

The 2018 National College Health Assessment by the American College Health Association (ACHA)[13] found that anxiety, depression, and stress are on the rise, and that students report that such mental health factors as anxiety, depression, insomnia, and stress have impacted their academic performance within the last 12 months. Reports find that feelings of loneliness and hopelessness are also up, and a greater number of students have seriously considered suicide, practiced self-harm, and attempted suicide within the last year. In 2015, students were 68 percent more likely to be diagnosed with anxiety and 34 percent more likely with depression than in 2009.[14] Over the same six-year period, students were 30 percent more likely to receive mental health services and 37 percent more likely to seek help in the future.

Student mental health risks also influence academic success and retention. Studies in England and Denmark found a link between student dropout rates in higher education and poor student mental health, including findings that the number of dropouts more than tripled as of 2015, and that men in higher education were five times more at risk of dropping out when they reported poor mental health.[15]

Students with mental health conditions are also making more legal claims against institutions alleging disability discrimination and improper counseling or medical malpractice. A 2018 United Educators claims study,[16] reviewing 223 claims reported from 2011 to 2016, confirmed some of the trends seen by the American College Health Assessment (ACHA). Nearly 70 percent of the claims involved deaths by suicide and suicide attempts, with the remaining 32 percent involving general mental health issues, such as anxiety, depression, or an eating disorder. Common reasons for students to pursue claims against their institutions included failure of a critical exam or expulsion from a program, dissatisfaction with the disability accommodation process or outcome, or discipline for inappropriate behavior. Relationship problems, illness, sexual assault, family problems, and changes in medication also appear to precipitate events to claims.[17]

Substance Use and Abuse

Alcohol remains the drug of choice for students, and according to the Higher Education Center for Alcohol and Drug Misuse Prevention and Recovery, "college students are more likely to be heavy drinkers than their noncollege peers."[18] In 2018, 62 percent of students reported consuming alcohol in the past 30 days. However, high-risk or "binge" drinking (defined as four or more drinks for women and five or more for men during one drinking session) is on the decline. According to statistics from the ACHA and the National Institute on Alcohol Abuse and Alcoholism (NIAAA),[19] high-risk drinking was on the rise until the early 2000s, but has decreased consistently since then, with only 27 percent of students reporting high-risk drinking in the last 30 days in 2018, down from 45 percent in 2005.

Nonetheless, institutions must remain vigilant. A 2017 publication by United Educators on the influence of alcohol in student claims revealed the following:

- **Student fights**: claims involving student fights cost 25 percent more on average than those not involving alcohol.
- **Sorority and fraternity activities**: more than half of the deaths involving sorority and fraternity activities involved alcohol.
- **Hazing**: more than half of claims involving student hazing involved excessive drinking.
- **Study abroad**: a third of study abroad claims involved alcohol.
- **Student sexual assault**: one or both parties consumed alcohol in more than half of student-perpetrated sexual assault claims.

Substance use impacts students in all aspects of their lives, from physical and mental health and safety, to classroom success, extracurricular activities, and life after graduation—all of which impairs the institution's ability to achieve its educational mission. According to a 2019 report by the American Council of Trustees and Alumni (ACTA), student GPAs drop in correlation to consumption of alcohol or drugs, and when students report using both, GPAs drop even lower. Alcohol use is among the strongest predictors of a student's academic success, even more than time spent in the classroom.[20] More research—including exit interviews for non-returning students and analysis of campus intervention efforts—is needed to better understand the correlation and causation of student behaviors and alcohol abuse, but initial studies reveal alarming trends.

While students have always turned to drugs as a result of stress, course loads, curiosity, and peer pressure,[21] drug availability and popularity continuously changes. Institutions must revise and adapt drug prevention programs as the landscape shifts.

Marijuana use among college students has markedly increased. A 2019 University of Michigan study reveals college students' use of marijuana is at the highest level over the past three and a half decades. Vaping of marijuana and nicotine doubled from 2017–2018. Studies show that there is a link between anxiety, student performance, and the use of marijuana on campus.[22] It will be worth noting how the dynamic of marijuana on campus develops as state and federal efforts continue to permit medicinal and recreational marijuana use.

Institutions must also consider the misuse of prescription drugs as part of drug prevention efforts. According to the Higher Education Center for Alcohol and Drug Misuse Prevention and Recovery, "there is a 'perfect storm' for the misuse of medications in the United States. The three fronts of this storm are: 1) the drug-taking culture in which we live, 2) easy access to prescription medications, and 3) misperceptions of safety and legality when misusing prescription drugs."[23] About one in ten students illicitly used prescription drugs and "study drugs" (used to treat attention deficit disorders) in the last 12 months.

Drugs like opioids, hallucinogens, and stimulants (cocaine, ecstasy, and molly) still have a presence on campus, despite ongoing prevention efforts. Student opioid (including OxyContin and Vicodin) use is down, and yet opioid misuse overall led to more than two-thirds of all overdose deaths in the U.S according to the National Institute on Drug Abuse. Ultimately, drugs remain a part of campus culture, and institutions must remain knowledgeable about all drugs and continue to provide students with substance abuse resources.

Cross-Functional Collaboration to Address Student Mental Health and Substance Abuse

The complexity of student mental health and substance abuse issues means that institutions cannot simply invest in more counseling resources. This risk requires a coordinated, cross-functional approach. The institution must engage all areas, including counseling and disability services, academics, student affairs, athletics, residential life, study abroad, faculty, staff, and public safety to develop meaningful programs to address student well-being and safety in and out of the classroom.

United Educators' mental health claims study revealed a high level of dissatisfaction with an institution's processes or outcomes following a student's request for a disability accommodation. It also is crucial for legal counsel to advise the institution in crafting policies and trainings to meet the privacy requirements of the ADA, Health Insurance Portability and Privacy Act (HIPAA), and Family Educational Rights and Privacy Act (FERPA), while ensuring student safety above all.

While counseling services, student affairs, and legal counsel should take the lead, evidence increasingly shows that students turn to their most trusted campus mentors—their closest faculty and staff members. Comprehensive training on reporting mental health concerns for all student-facing employees can elevate student mental health prevention and response beyond the counseling function.[24]

The board's student life committee can support reducing student mental health and substance abuse by:

- Elevating student mental health as a significant institutional risk;
- Asking the institution to work cross-functionally and proactively to develop a cohesive wellness program for all aspects of a student's time at the institution;[25]
- Supporting steady funding for training and awareness programs;
- Setting measurable goals for reducing student mental health issues and substance abuse, and tracking key indicators of success; and
- Holding administrators accountable for student health outcomes, including high-risk drinking and illegal drug use.

SEXUAL ABUSE AND MISCONDUCT

Recent sexual abuse and misconduct scandals have shown that institutions must develop a culture that encourages reporting and

> ## What is FERPA and When Does It Apply?
>
> Perhaps one of the most misinterpreted laws, the Family Educational Rights and Privacy Act (FERPA) creates confusion with academic and student affairs administrators and frustration with many families. In an effort to protect the privacy of academic records, this federal legislation was passed to limit the disclosure of student information with anyone other than the adult student. It contains, however, an important "student health and safety" exception that gives institutions significant latitude in what information can be shared and with whom.
>
> The board's student life committee should ensure that the institution has established policies and procedures that enable the appropriate sharing of information to protect the health of students and safety of the campus community. In particular, institutions must be clear on when they will disclose student health and safety concerns to parents and guardians. The administration should ensure that faculty and staff members are properly trained on FERPA obligations and understand the importance of sharing information as allowed by law.[26]

transparency, and includes clear policies, training, investigation and handling of complaints, and reporting. As a result, institutions may consider prevention of sexual misconduct and abuse across the entire community, including student sexual misconduct and Title IX, sexual misconduct by employees and other adults associated with the institution, and sexual abuse of minors. This section will discuss all three types of stakeholders, as well as details on how the board can encourage prevention and a culture of safety and transparency.

Student Sexual Misconduct

To open the dialogue student affairs/campus life committee members should ask administrators about:

- **Title IX**. Has your institution established training programs, policies, and procedures currently required by Title IX guidance? Does your institution have a Title IX coordinator to oversee (and monitor changes in) Title IX compliance?
- **VAWA-Campus SaVE Act**. Does your institution comply with the VAWA-Campus SaVE Act amendments to the Clery Act related to sexual violence and intimate partner violence?

Many trustees know Title IX as a 1972 amendment to the Civil Rights Act of 1964 and the groundbreaking legislation that opened doors for more women to participate in athletics. Since then, the legislation has expanded beyond the original scope of providing equal opportunities for women and men in all educational endeavors to addressing specific response and training in gender equality issues at educational institutions. What began as legislation to prevent discrimination based on gender has expanded (and contracted) to include specific requirements for training on and investigations and student adjudication of sexual harassment, sexual assault, and other forms of dating violence.

A United Educators study of student-on-student sexual assault claims on campuses showed that, today, institutions are nearly as likely to be sued by students alleged to have committed sexual assault as by those who suffered an assault. This demonstrates that an institution's policies and procedures seeking to curb student sexual violence almost invariably will result in the dissatisfaction of one party (and sometimes of both). The study also revealed other dynamics that add complexity to sexual assault matters, including:

- More than half of student-on-student sexual assault cases involved alcohol or drugs.
- In 21 percent of the attacks, the alleged victim had a history of prior mental health issues.
- In 22 percent of the attacks, the alleged victim and perpetrator had a romantic relationship or close friendship.
- In 16 percent of the attacks, the alleged perpetrator was an athlete, and athletes participated in 63 percent of attacks involving multiple perpetrators.

This claims study emphasizes the importance of developing and adhering to an institutional investigation policy that is thorough, prompt and, above all else, fair. It found that the allegations driving the student-on-student sexual harassment claims occurred when the institution did not follow its own policies and procedures, had confusing or unclear policies and procedures, did not respond promptly or reasonably to an assault report, and treated the victim or the perpetrator with bias. For example, no student population should be immune from investigation, including student athletes and fraternities and sororities. (See Insight: Sexual Abuse in Athletics in the Athletics section below.)

> "In recent years, multiple universities have faced sexual predator scandals involving scores of victims. Often the institutional leaders were uninformed about the allegations regarding incidents on their campuses. This failure of leadership oversight has many presidents and trustees wondering how to safeguard their communities from similar tragedies."
>
> —*Safeguarding Our Communities from Sexual Predators: What College Presidents and Trustees Should Ask*, United Educators[27]

Student sexual assault is subject to many of the same tides as other policy issues. Different U.S. Department of Education administrations place a different emphasis on a victim's and a perpetrator's rights, and courts are continuously interpreting institutions' obligations under Title IX and other sexual assault laws. To make matters more complicated, some states are passing laws that levy additional protections for victims and perpetrators. In those states, institutions may be caught between compliance with federal Title IX regulations and state-level victims' protections. As with other aspects of student health and safety, the student life committee should ensure that adequate policies and procedures are in place, that they are followed, and that they are periodically reviewed and adjusted to comply with legal expectations.

Student Sexual Assault by Employees

Some of the largest claims in higher education involve serial sexual abuse, including two widely reported settlements in 2018: a record-breaking $500-million settlement with more than 300 survivors of sexual abuse perpetrated by a former USA gymnastics team and university doctor/trainer, and a tentative settlement for $215 million for a potential class of thousands of female students claiming they were sexually abused during the course of treatment by a university gynecologist. The prevalence of claims in institutions of all sizes is a grim reminder that serial sexual abuse by an institution's employee can happen anywhere. Institutions must be proactive in managing this risk rather than assume that their campus is immune.

Leadership plays an important role in creating a safe environment for students and children participating in campus programs. United Educators published a resource for college presidents and trustees[28] about creating a culture of prevention and reporting in the context of sexual misconduct and abuse. Key questions that board members through the student life committee can ask include:

- **Be intentional with words and action**: Do board members speak out to foster a safe and inclusive environment on campus?
- **Understand the campus culture**: Does the institution have programs in place to address policies, trainings, reporting mechanisms, and investigation procedures?
- **Become informed about policies and procedures**: Do the institution's sexual abuse policies apply equally to employees at all levels, and are reporting mechanisms easily accessible and well publicized to the community?

Minors on Campus

To open the dialogue student life committee members should ask administrators about:

- **Inventory.** Does the administration maintain a current inventory of all programs and occasions when minors will be on campus or participating in campus programs?
- **Background checks.** Are background checks performed and training provided to all staff, faculty, volunteers, and students who have contact with minors?
- **Reporting.** Are the institution's sexual misconduct (molestation) policy and reporting requirements shared, at least annually, with the entire campus community?

The tragedy of the child sex abuse scandal at Penn State caused all of higher education to recognize that risks to minors are not exclusively a problem of K–12 schools and that colleges and universities must do more to protect minors on campus. Senior administrators, faculty, and board members are often surprised when they learn how many minors come into contact with the institution. Lab schools, childcare programs, summer camps, siblings' weekends, and high school student and student-athlete recruitment create opportunities for child molestation to occur.

Boundary training and background checks should be required for all faculty, staff, and students who come in contact with minors, including students who work with minors through volunteer programs, such as after-school recreational programs or tutoring. Clear policies on state and institutional reporting requirements should be disseminated throughout the campus. For example, a hotline to report suspected abuse can provide vulnerable staff members with a safe environment in which to report something they see.[29]

CAMPUS SECURITY

To open the dialogue student or campus life committee members should ask administrators about:

- **Security**. Are policies and procedures in place to ensure that security officers (whether armed or not armed) are thoroughly and regularly trained? Does campus security maintain effective relationships and agreements with local law enforcement?
- **Reporting**. Is regular training on Clery Act reporting provided to campus security and administrators? Does the institution submit an annual security report to the U.S. Department of Education, as required by the Clery Act?
- **Firearms and weapons**. Does the institution understand the extent to which it can regulate the presence of firearms under state law? Has it developed a policy that clearly communicates institutional expectations related to firearms?
- **Threat assessment and support**. Does the institution have a threat assessment and care team? Is regular training provided to faculty and staff, as well as specially designated gatekeepers and responders?

While a safe, crime-free campus is every board's goal, managing security and law enforcement creates significant risks for every campus. At the foundation of a sound security program are thoughtful decisions about a range of complex issues, such as: 1) creating policies and practices that comply with the Clery Act, 2) ensuring the campus security force is appropriately screened and trained, 3) managing the presence of firearms and weapons on campus, and 4) forging mutual aid agreements with local law enforcement.

Crime Reporting
The Jeanne Clery Disclosure of Campus Security Policy and Campus Crime Statistics Act (Clery Act), named for a Lehigh University student raped and murdered in her residence hall in 1986, requires colleges and universities

receiving federal funds to report campus crime data and detail efforts to improve campus safety. Each institution must maintain an up-to-date, publicly accessible crime log, (most institutions post the Clery report on the website), warn campus communities of immediate threats, and release an annual report (by October 1) detailing crime statistics for the prior three years. Institutions are also required to have written procedures on emergency response, evacuation, missing student notification (if they provide on-campus housing), and fire safety.

Security Forces

A threshold decision that many institutions consider to provide adequate security to their communities is whether or not to arm campus officers. There is no right answer; each campus must make this decision based on its particular context and needs. the International Association of Campus Law Enforcement Administrators, offers several considerations:

1. Internal department issues;
2. Local police/community considerations;
3. Budget considerations; and
4. Past incidents of weapons on or near campus.

Whether armed or unarmed, campus safety personnel should always be equipped and trained for the circumstances they face. For institutions choosing to arm public safety officers, the student life committee should look for the following best practices:

1. **Extensive background checks**. Once armed with guns, campus security officers most likely will be considered fully commissioned officers under state statute, with full powers of arrest that any state police officer would have.
2. **Use of force policy and training**. The college or university should establish protocols for the use of force and ensure that all officers are regularly trained on them.
3. **Awareness of state law**. Administrators should check with the state's law enforcement agency to determine whether armed guards have immunities that will limit legal responsibility for their actions.

Some campuses contract with outside security companies to provide campus security. Appropriate risk transfer language should be included

Insight: Excessive Force Claims

Institutions that decide to arm their police force must understand the risks associated with that decision. According to a 2017 United Educators study focused on claims resulting from a campus police officer's use of excessive force, many administrators ask how to avoid these claims, which often result in viral videos on social media, community protests, and news media attention[30] The study explored 45 claims from 2011 to 2015, resulting in more than $10.4 million in losses. An overwhelming majority of claims involved sworn police officers with full arrest powers as opposed to unarmed security guards. Incidents involving firearms, while used in only 18 percent of claims, resulted in 67 percent of costs incurred to defend the institution and reach resolution.

in the contract to ensure that the institution does not assume liability for the contractor's actions. Enforcing the institution's standards on background checks should also be included in the contract.

The student life committee should encourage the institution to carefully review any mutual aid agreements it has established with other police forces. Again, these agreements should include indemnification clauses to limit the liability that the college or university assumes for the other party's negligent acts. The institution at least should require a mutual indemnification agreement in which each party agrees to be responsible only for the losses it causes.

Firearms and Weapons on Campus

Gone are the days when administrators could simply ban firearms at their colleges and universities. Starting in 2013, state legislators began passing legislation to allow firearms, weapons, and concealed carry on campus. While adherence to state legislation is mandatory for public institutions in the state, some states allow them to opt out or use discretion, while others do not grant any discretion to opt out. In contrast, private institutions can opt-out of state legislation and have more discretion to make a campus-specific decision about whether to permit all or only certain firearms or weapons. Some private institutions permit firearms on campus, while others maintain strict policies banning firearms or weapons.[31]

The unsettled nature of federal and state law, and increased activism of groups both for and against gun control, present special challenges to boards and administrators. Today, more than ever, it is crucial that boards ask whether the institution:

- Has a clear policy on firearms and weapons on campus;
- Coordinates activities with campus security, local police, and the institution's interdisciplinary threat assessment team;
- Solicits input from campus law enforcement and/or public safety representatives, administration, legal counsel, student affairs,

counseling and psychological services, campus medicine, faculty, and students;[32]
- Educates the campus community and any campus visitors on the policy and offers or requires training on safe practices, where permissible by law.

Insight: School Shootings and Active Shooters

A 2019 report shows that within the last 10 years U.S. schools experienced 180 school shootings resulting in 356 victims as of the time of publication.[33] Unfortunately, it appears that these numbers are on the rise. These trends have changed campus culture, raising questions about campus safety, arming campus police, and active shooter training.

The U.S. Secret Service recently released the *Operational Guide for Preventing Targeted School Violence* as a tool for communities including schools and higher education institutions.[34] The report advises institutions to:

1. Establish a multidisciplinary threat assessment team;
2. Define behaviors;
3. Establish and provide training on a central reporting system;
4. Determine the threshold for law enforcement intervention, especially if there is a safety risk;
5. Establish threat assessment procedures that include practices for maintaining documentation, identifying sources of information, reviewing records, and conducting interviews;
6. Develop risk management options;
7. Create and promote a safe school climate built on a culture of safety, respect, trust, and emotional support; and
8. Provide training for all stakeholders, including school personnel, students, parents, and law enforcement.[35]

Similarly, a United Educators resource addressing active shooter preparedness[36] reminds boards to inquire whether the institution:

- Has developed and regularly updates its:
    - emergency management plans that address critical response practices (evacuations, lockdowns, student mental health services); and
    - crisis communications plan for honest and timely communications with all stakeholders;
- Trains staff on the institution's procedures;
- Conducts site assessments to identify security weaknesses;
- Has established community partnerships; and
- Conducts drills and tabletop exercises on a regular basis.

Care Teams and Threat Assessment

The tragedy at Virginia Tech in 2007 brought an increased awareness of the importance of training multidisciplinary teams to evaluate threats of violence in the educational setting based on troubling student behaviors observed in the classroom and on campus. Institutions call these teams by a variety of names: assessment and care team, behavioral evaluation team, student concern team, or alert team. Regardless of the name, the core functions are generally the same. These teams:

- Receive reports of troubling student behavior;
- Strive to understand a troubled student's circumstances by gathering information from team members and other available resources;
- Evaluate the facts to determine whether a student poses a risk of harm or needs additional assistance; and
- Recommend an intervention that connects the student to beneficial resources, de-escalates the threat posed, or both.

The student life committee should ask whether the institution has formed such a team, ensure that its scope and composition are appropriate, and support adequate recordkeeping and training of team members and potential reporters of concerns.[37]

STUDY ABROAD PROGRAMS

While overseas campuses and academic programs are a relatively new trend, study abroad programs predate the American higher education system. Programs have grown in complexity—and liability—for colleges and universities in recent years. To open the dialogue about study abroad risks student affairs committee members should ask administrators about:

- **Roster**. Does the administration maintain a list of all students, faculty, and staff traveling abroad?
- **Training**. Are processes in place for students, faculty, and staff to receive training on institutional policies, emergency preparedness, and other protocols prior to leaving the United States?

Three emerging trends related to study abroad programs create new risks: an increase in short-term study abroad programs, a shift from

European destinations to emerging nations, and an increase in accessibility needs as more students with disabilities study abroad.

While the term "study abroad" often creates visions of semester- or year-long trips to European cities, about 62 percent of students study abroad on short-term trips, often eight weeks or less, according to Institute of International Education.[38] Such short-term programs focus on service learning projects, research, and non-credit bearing work. Short-term programs are frequently organized shortly before departure by a faculty member who does not necessarily follow trip-planning procedures and typically occur during break periods when it may be difficult to contact the home campus for assistance. These programs can function under the radar of the study abroad office (for example, around a special research project by a well-intentioned professor), which can make tracking students, pre-trip training, and planning for appropriate infrastructure and support more haphazard.

The claims related to study abroad that United Educators sees are similar for short- and long-term trips. The vast majority—94 percent—relate to three types of injuries: sexual misconduct, physical injury or illness, and fatalities. The student affairs/campus life committee should encourage institutions to establish procedures to ensure that all students, their families, and trip leaders are: 1) briefed on the risks of traveling, 2) familiarized with emergency responses, and 3) trained on campus protocols for appropriate behavior and sexual harassment prevention, emergency response, and other safety issues.

Insight: Set Sail Safely

Even when risks to student safety seem similar at home and abroad, a United Educators claims study outlines key differences that the institution can help students anticipate and respond to:

- Unlike sexual assaults on American campuses, most study abroad victims do not know their attackers.
- Most claims occur during the student's "free time," or time outside of educational activities.
- One third of claims involve alcohol.
- Ten percent of claims involve a student as a driver or passenger of a vehicle.
- Ten percent of claims involve a student with a mental health condition and often a suicide or suicide attempt.

While the institution may face little to no liability for these injuries and accidents, it will almost always be asked to assist. Providing aid in a student's crisis, even when not obligated to do so, can support the mission and stem the risk of unfounded claims.

ATHLETICS

To open the dialogue the student life committee should ask about:

- **Mission.** Have the student or campus life committee and the board engaged in discussions on the role of athletics in the mission of the institution?
- **Costs/revenues.** Does the committee thoroughly understand the financial revenues and costs associated with intercollegiate athletics programs?
- **NCAA compliance.** Does the committee regularly receive reports on National Collegiate Athletic Association compliance for the institution?
- **Coach contracts.** Are there protocols in place to review contracts for highly compensated coaches?
- **Athlete academic success.** Does the committee receive reports on academic progress and majors of athletes?
- **Sexual abuse.** Are all athletics staff trained on the sexual abuse policies and reporting mechanisms? Does the policy establish boundaries for appropriate behavior?
- **Ethics.** What steps has the administration taken to ensure that coaches, athletics staff, and athletes meet the institution's ethical standards?

The most common and significant risks to an institution for athletics programs come in two forms: 1) the risk that athletics overwhelms the academic mission and values of the institution, and 2) the risk of physical harm to athletes. A distant third is crowd management challenges presented to all campuses that gather enthusiastic spectators, but it is particularly relevant for universities that draw huge crowds to athletic events.

> "Boards should consider and identify the appropriate board structure to help them meet their oversight responsibilities. For example, more than one standing committee may have oversight responsibilities for various aspects of the intercollegiate athletic program. These may include the finance or budget, student life committee, or compensation committee. Alternatively, some institutions might find a standing or advisory committee on athletics to be the most effective."
>
> —AGB Statement on Board Responsibilities for Intercollegiate Athletics (2009, revised 2018)

Countless high-profile examples shine light on governance gone astray when it comes to sports. Sex abuse scandals, coaches' contracts that turn into institutional liabilities, player recruitment violations, hazing, coaches bullying students, inappropriate booster club involvement, athlete mental health and substance abuse, academic fraud, and weak student athlete graduation rates demand board-level oversight and ownership at both large and small institutions.

In 2012, an AGB report, "Trust, Accountability, and Integrity: Board Responsibilities for Intercollegiate Athletics," asked, "Why do boards need to step up their oversight of intercollegiate sports?" The answer, the report emphasized, is that "as the fiduciary body charged with being the steward of their institution or system, they really have no other option." The report offered the following recommendations to guide board engagement in athletics:

- The governing board is ultimately accountable for athletics policy and oversight and should fulfill this fiduciary responsibility.
- The board should act decisively to uphold the integrity of the athletics program and its alignment with the academic mission of the institution.
- The board must educate itself about its policy role and oversight of intercollegiate athletics. (See Exhibit 17.)

Traumatic Brain Injuries (Concussions)

Medical injury is the more tangible risk related to athletics. At any given time, about 5 percent of student claims reported to United Educators involve athletic injuries. The largest number of claims have to do with club, intramural, and recreational sports, but the largest monetary losses come from injuries sustained in varsity sports. While everyone has long known that risk is inherent in sports, recent medical and scientific developments and high-profile lawsuits warrant new high-level attention.

Concussions or traumatic brain injuries (TBI) suffered while playing football, soccer, lacrosse, hockey, field hockey, and other contact sports are receiving heightened attention because of their long-term threats to mental and physical health.

The NCAA requires member institutions in all divisions to create and implement concussion management plans, which require athletics staff to identify and treat head injuries and work with athletes to ensure a safe return to play. In addition to NCAA requirements, all states have

> ### Insight: Sexual Abuse in Athletics
>
> Many scandals involving athletics center on sexual misconduct, including sexual abuse by coaches, trainers, and medical staff, as well as sexual violence perpetrated by student athletes. The imperative for boards and administrators to step up efforts to address sexual misconduct, ensuring the safety of the athletics and overall campus community, is clear.
>
> The student life committee can set the tone that Title IX complaints implicating student athlete perpetrators must be addressed like any other. That means these complaints are reported to the institution's Title IX office, properly investigated, and handled in a consistent manner under the institution's disciplinary procedures.

adopted concussion management laws, which mandate testing, waiting periods before returning to play, and other concussion management protocols.[39] An important inquiry for the student life committee is whether the institution has put protocols in place to comply with NCAA and state law mandates.

FRATERNITIES AND SORORITIES

Some of the most common—and most difficult—board and administration conversations about risk concern fraternities and sororities. On the one hand, fraternities and sororities are a quantifiable source of heightened risk. A four-year United Educators claims study accounted for $9 million of losses, with the average fraternity claim generating a $371,968 loss. The role of alcohol in many fraternities and sororities amplifies risk and often plays a contributing role in fraternity and sorority member fatalities. Incidents in recent years have shown that fraternities and sororities carry reputational risk for the institution. Occurrences of hazing, assault, racism, and sexual assault have placed institutions in a local and national spotlight that they prefer to avoid.

On the other hand, fraternities and sororities bring difficult-to-quantify benefits to a campus. As some prospective students explicitly seek fraternities and sororities when searching for a university, there's no doubt that these organizations help with recruitment of new students. Once on campus, these organizations can build a student's relationship with the institution, leading him or her to take advantage of academic resources and engage in philanthropy and community

Exhibit 17: The Board's Responsibility for Intercollegiate Athletics

Recommendation 1: **The governing board is ultimately accountable for athletics policy and oversight and should fulfill this fiduciary responsibility.**

- As the fiduciary body of the institution, the governing board bears responsibility for establishing a policy framework governing athletics.
- The board must act on this authority, establish high standards for transparency and ethics, and hold itself and the institution's chief executive accountable for the implementation of those policies.
- Athletic policy, as defined by the board, assists administrators with regulation.
- The board must inform itself about the risks and challenges of the athletics program and engage in policy questions that address those issues.
- While the board delegates management of intercollegiate athletics to the chief executive, it must recognize its ultimate responsibility.

Recommendation 2: **The board should act decisively to uphold the integrity of the athletics program and its alignment with the academic mission of the institution.**

- Policies that define the administration of athletics programs should be consistent with those for other academic and administrative units of the institution or system.
- The athletics program should be functionally integrated into the administrative structure and philosophically aligned with the mission of the institution.
- Boards should have a process in place to review contract agreements for highly compensated athletics personnel, financial information concerning athletics, and indicators of the academic progress and well-being of student athletes.
- The governing board should be informed of and consulted on issues related to conference membership, have final review of data ascertaining compliance with NCAA and conference regulations, and, on an annual basis, publicly certify that the institution is in compliance.

Recommendation 3: **The board must educate itself about its policy role and oversight of intercollegiate athletics.**

- The governing board of the institution must act intentionally to increase its collective span of knowledge concerning athletics, and each board member should be aware of the standards of behavior and regulations that apply to them individually.
- All board members should be informed about the business and challenges of intercollegiate sports, risk assessments, pertinent NCAA and conference rules, Title IX and other federal regulations, and the progress and well-being of student athletes.
- The board needs to be aware of the balance between appropriate oversight and involvement in institutional policy and intrusion into management prerogatives.

Source: John Casteen and Richard Legon. "Trust, Accountability, and Integrity: Board Responsibility for Intercollegiate Athletics" (Knight Commission on Intercollegiate Athletics), AGB, 2012.

service. After members graduate, they may feel more inclined to donate to the institution as alumni.

These competing opportunities and risks, as well as many board members' experience as a fraternity or sorority member, make risk management in this arena challenging. Boards should consider their risk tolerance for fraternities and sororities, carefully weighing the benefits against the potential costs of supporting these organizations. If boards are willing to accept the risks associated with them, they should advise administrators to mitigate risk by considering the following questions:

- Who owns and is responsible for maintenance of fraternity and sorority housing? How is risk allocated between the institution and fraternities and sororities?
- Are fraternities and sororities required to carry adequate insurance that indemnifies the institution for risks within its control and responsibility? Does the institution carry adequate insurance for potential fraternity or sorority exposures?
- Does campus security supervise events and parties?
- What efforts does the institution make to protect students from hazing?
- How are fraternity and sorority members trained in risk management and how to report unsafe incidents to campus administration?

Insight: Clubs

Risks associated with fraternities and sororities are not exclusive to the fraternity/sorority house. The student life committee should understand that student clubs can create the same social pressures that lead to similar incidents of hazing, sexual assault, alcohol abuse, and discrimination. While claims are less likely from any single student club than a fraternity or sorority, clubs present distinct risks because of the large numbers of student participants, the wide range of activities, and the light or minimal institutional oversight. For example, United Educators has been asked to underwrite high-risk clubs such as drone, robotics, lumberjack, rocketry, and blacksmithing clubs, among others.

The student life committee should encourage the student life staff to vigilantly monitor club activities for potential risks.

Student Experience Warning Signs and Board Actions

The board can get a sense of whether additional coordination or internal oversight around operational issues are needed by considering the following warning signs:

Board Inquiry	Student Experience Warning Sign	Possible Board Actions
Is the institution adapting academic affairs strategies to meet market demand, learning trends, immigration policies, and global changes?	The institution's peers are increasing their new student enrollments faster than the institution.	Ask administrators to conduct regular market research to compare academic programs and practices with peers.
Does the institution have consistent policies to manage admissions, enrollment, student health and safety, campus security, and athletics administration?	The institution reacts to crises involving admissions, enrollment, student health and safety, campus security, and athletics rather than planning proactively.	Consider requiring the institution to develop proactive strategies, including updating written plans, training, and tabletop exercises for each area of operational risk.
Does the institution have a single wellness plan to address student mental health, physical well-being, and/or sexual misconduct?	The institution is seeing increased student mental health, physical health, and sexual misconduct reports or claims.	Require the institution to develop a cross-functional student well-being committee to address the student mental and physical health risk proactively across the entire institution and regularly report to the student life committee.

Chapter 9
Advancing Reputation

"It takes 20 years to build a reputation and five minutes to ruin it. If you think about that, you'll do things differently."
—Warren Buffett

INSTITUTIONS SPEND GENERATIONS BUILDING A REPUTATION THAT can be tarnished in a very short time. In today's environment of prolific internet commentary and always-on social media, combined with the persistence of 24-hour cable news and traditional news media, events that used to occur entirely on campus now spill into public view almost instantly. With little or no warning:

- Innocuous student activities can become national news;
- Differences in opinion between institutional leaders and board members can become public disputes;
- Allegations of serious misconduct, both founded and unfounded, are contested publicly; and
- Minor institutional shortcomings become glaring defects.

As fiduciaries of an institution of higher education, board members protect its financial, physical, human, and cyber assets, which cumulatively form the institution's reputation. This is a shared responsibility of the full board. An institution's reputation is essential to recruiting and retaining students, faculty, and major donors. Intentionally or not, most of the risk management actions at the board level are focused on preserving that treasured reputation.

Reputational Risk and ERM

Reputational risk is the risk that an institution will fail to meet the expectations of its stakeholders, resulting in tangible harm to the institution. Reputational risk is a second-order risk; reputational harm results from other major categories of risk, such as strategic, financial, operational, and compliance. For example, an institution that mishandles allegations of sexual misconduct or responding to a dormitory fire faces not only the direct consequences of those events, but also possible reputational harm as a result of its failure to do what its stakeholders expect. For this reason, institutions can use their enterprise risk management (ERM) program to manage reputational risk.

Indeed, it is increasingly vital that institutions do so. The costs or consequences of a reputational event can be significant, including for example:

- The capital campaign does not reach its goal in the stated time period;
- The institution's bond rating is downgraded, increasing the cost of borrowing;
- Faculty decide to accept competing job offers;
- Key institutional leaders, including the president, are forced to resign; and
- Students decide to study elsewhere, taking their talents and tuition to a competing institution.

We live in a world in which institutions continually face reputational events, including major scandals, operational failures, and strategic setbacks. Social media and news do not cause reputational risk, but they do make it worse by adding fuel to the fire. Reputational events consume institutional focus and resources. Time spent responding to reputational events is time not spent attending to the institution's strategy or mission.

Why do some institutions and their leaders survive these reputational firestorms unscathed, while others suffer tremendous harm? Institutions that manage reputational risk well approach it proactively. In a 2017 UE-AGB survey of board members and administrative leaders, institutions that believed they were performing "substantially higher" or "higher" than their peer groups in managing reputational risk were more likely to be proactive in their approach.[1]

Specifically, institutions that take a proactive approach:

- Recognize that board members have a vital role in preserving reputation;
- View reputation as a shared responsibility, with everyone from students and faculty to senior administrators and board members having a role to play; and
- Have a strong foundation for managing reputational risk, as well as dedicated processes that ensure follow-through.

Being proactive about reputation is more easily said than done; in the same UE-AGB survey, only 26 percent of survey respondents believed that their institution's response to reputational risk was consistently proactive.

But institutions that want to survive in the coming years must aggressively manage their reputations. Reputational risk is unavoidable, and while institutions can buy adequate insurance to cover some specific risks, insurance does not cover reputational losses, which can greatly overwhelm insured losses. The only effective way to treat reputational risk is to manage it. ERM can be uniquely helpful in doing so.

Start at the Top

Effective reputational risk management starts at the top, with a commitment from the board and senior leadership. The first step is to recognize that the institution's reputation is a valuable asset that the board and administration must protect.

To open the dialogue the full board should discuss with administrators:

- **Shared understanding of the institution's reputation**. Does the institution know what components of its reputation are the most valuable?
- **Consequences of reputational harm**. Do board members and administrators agree on the potential consequences of a diminished reputation?
- **Commitment to protecting the institution's reputation**. Has senior leadership made managing reputational risk a priority for the institution?

Boards and senior leaders should develop a common understanding of the institution's reputation. What is the value the institution derives from its reputation among its stakeholders? Reputation is often seen as an abstract concept, so it is important to understand what's at stake with an institution's reputation.

Consider the results of in-person interviews or surveys of stakeholders, including students, alumni, faculty, staff, and community members. Analyze social media mentions of the institution. Review such college and university guides as the *Fiske Guide to Colleges*, *The Princeton Review*, and *U.S. News & World Report*. Using these inputs, board members and senior administrators should come to agreement on the potential consequences of a diminished reputation. Given the foreseeable costs of reputational risks, what resources should the institution commit to managing them? Boards and senior leaders need to understand the business case for protecting the institution's reputation and developing (and implementing) recovery plans, and then commit to using them.

Identify Reputational Risks

To manage reputational risks, you must identify those that matter most. To open the dialogue the board and senior leadership should discuss the following:

- **Reputational Risk Register.** Does the institution have a risk register identifying top reputational risks, or alternatively does it score the top risks on its register for reputational impact?
- **Reputational Risk Ownership.** Does every reputational risk have an owner?

As discussed in chapter 2, a risk register is an important tool for identifying and managing risks. Indeed, every risk on an institution's

---

Insight: Seek Alignment on Reputational Risks

One surefire way for an institution to suffer reputational harm is for the board and senior leadership to publicly air differences during a crisis. "Where we tend to see things really go pear-shaped is when there is space between the board and the president and everybody is trying to make their case in the media," said Erin Hennessy, vice president of TVP Communications.

To avoid public disputes, it is important for senior administrators and boards to agree on how they will address a reputational event before the crisis hits. The board should be comfortable with the senior administrators' plan for protecting the institution's reputation so that during times of crisis, they can follow through on that plan, avoiding any surprises or conflicts with trustees.

risk register has reputational implications. Each of the known risks involving sexual misconduct, athletics, admissions, academics, finances or operations can have a major reputational impact.

For additional reputational risks, consider the table below, which is a list of risks that commonly have major reputation impacts.

Area	Examples of Areas to Assess for Reputational Impact
Academic Programs	• Quality and integrity of academic programs • Quality of students and faculty • Faculty conduct • Integrity of researchers and federal grant administration
Accreditation	• Actions taken by accreditors relating to accreditation status • Failure or poor scores on licensing exams
Athletics	• NCAA compliance • Athlete conduct • Coach behavior • Athletic conference
Business Model	• Enrollment trends • Fiscal management • Staffing levels • Tuition management
Campus Climate	• Diversity and inclusion of student body • Diversity and inclusion of senior administration • Controversial speakers
Cybersecurity	• Loss of data due to technology breaches • Phishing, ransomware, and other cyber events
Leadership Behavior and Talent Retention	• Quality of leadership • Leadership changes • Talent acquisition and retention • Fiscal responsibility
Sexual Assault/Title IX	• Prevention and response to student-on-student sexual assault • Title IX compliance
Student Behaviors	• Greek organizations • Campus safety • Student mental health • Inclusion of international students

Source: Abraham, Janice M. and Paul L. Walker, "ERM and Reputational Risk: More Talk Than Action?," 2017; available at https://www.ue.org/uploadedFiles/ERM%20and%20Reputational%20Risk%20White%20Paper.pdf

When identifying potential sources of reputational risk, be sure to consider any iconic programs, people, and traditions that exist at every institution and seem to be above reproach. These institutional areas require reputational risk management as much as any other—if not more so, given the often-conflicting expectations of stakeholders such as alumni, donors, and even the broader public.

Similarly, satellite programs that are not front and center to the administration may be a source of reputational risk. Misconduct at summer camps and field research sites can lead to harmful headlines, so it's important to consider areas that might ordinarily avoid scrutiny. One risk manager explained that he is especially concerned about areas at his institution that he doesn't hear about. He assumes that's where most of the bad things are likely to arise.

Insight: Different Approaches to Including Reputation in ERM

There are many ways to manage reputational risk in relation to ERM. Some institutions consider reputational risk as part of other ERM activities, while others have a dedicated program focused just on reputation. The right model depends on the institution's resources and appetite.

For example, one major research university maintains a reputational risk dashboard that tracks major reputational events involving other educational institutions, the impact a similar event would have on its own reputation, and how it mitigates that risk through its ERM program. This dashboard serves as a central discussion piece during ERM sessions at board meetings.

Another research university uses reputational impact as the only risk impact score it assigns when assessing risks. For that institution, reputational impact is paramount, and prioritizing risks based on reputational impact rather than financial impact enables it to focus on the risks that matter most to it.

Perhaps the simplest approach is to add a reputational dimension when assessing the likelihood and impact of the risks on the risk register. On a scale of from 1 to 5, rate how significant the reputational impact of each risk would be and then multiply this score, along with impact and likelihood of the risk, to arrive at a total risk score weighted for reputation.

Manage Reputational Risk

An institution's ERM program should manage reputational risks using the same process as other risks. To open the dialogue the board should ask senior leaders:

- **Monitoring**. Does the institution have systems in place to know when a reputational event occurs?
- **Response**. Does the institution have processes in place to manage all major reputational events? How would the institution respond to a peer institution's reputational event?
- **Recovery strategy**. Does the institution have a reputation recovery strategy that moves beyond a crisis response or business continuity plan?
- **Priority stakeholders**. Who are the stakeholders who matter to the institution's reputation? During a reputational event, which stakeholders will leadership reach out to first? Which are secondary priorities?
- **Goodwill**. Where does the institution stand with each stakeholder group? Does the institution have sufficient goodwill to survive a reputational event?

PROCESSES FOR REPUTATIONAL RISK

The time to manage risk is before the reputational event occurs. In the middle of a crisis, there isn't time to plan a response and understand who the impacted stakeholders are. Campus leaders should create a mitigation plan for each reputational risk on its register, and the board should review the register and those plans regularly. The board should have confidence in the institution's ability to deploy appropriate resources to prepare for reputational events. It needs to understand how the institution will respond, as well as its ability to be resilient and withstand and recover from such an event.

The institution also needs some way of knowing when a reputational event has occurred. It should establish a monitoring system that will provide early notification of emerging reputational damage. Most institutions have established social media monitoring capabilities. The system for monitoring should be flexible enough to detect unforeseen events and minimize surprises.

Also, while it is increasingly difficult to keep secrets in the age of mobile devices and social media, consider whether there is some way to conceal a potential reputational event from outsiders. According to the 2017 AGB–UE survey mentioned earlier, high performing institutions reported being better at keeping events inside the system: 50 percent of high performers reported the occurrence of "significant reputational risk events . . . that never became known."

Finally, recognize that an institution may suffer reputational harm through no fault of its own. Major scandals involving a large donor (living or deceased) can tarnish an institution's reputation through negative news coverage or simply a photo of a suddenly reviled benefactor wearing the college's T-shirt. Campus statues and names of buildings can quickly become controversial, along with honorary degrees (and even earned ones). Sometimes, a major scandal at one institution will impact another's reputation—and indeed the reputation of all higher education. Consider the potential impact of these external risks to the institution's reputation. To manage them, goodwill is essential. (See "Insight: Build Goodwill Before You Need It" on page 183.)

STAKEHOLDERS AND REPUTATIONAL RISK

As noted earlier, stakeholders and their expectations are key to reputational risk. The institution's priority stakeholders can be different for different risks, but to manage reputational risk effectively, institutions have to prioritize their stakeholders and develop a plan for responding to major reputational risks. Everyone, including the board and senior leadership, must agree on which stakeholders come first during a reputational event.

A challenge facing higher education is that each institution has many stakeholders, which range from internal to external:

- Internal—Students/faculty members/administrators/board members
- Involved—Parents/alumni/donors
- Adjacent—Community members/accreditors/key partners (including insurers)
- External—Legislators/regulators/media representatives

This list is meant to be representative, and no doubt any given institution may have dozens of additional stakeholders.

Advancing Reputation

Internal
- Students
- Faculty
- Staff
- Administrators
- Board members

Adjacent
- Local community
- Accreditors
- Business partners

Involved
- Parents
- Alumni
- Donors

External
- Legislators
- Regulators
- Media representatives

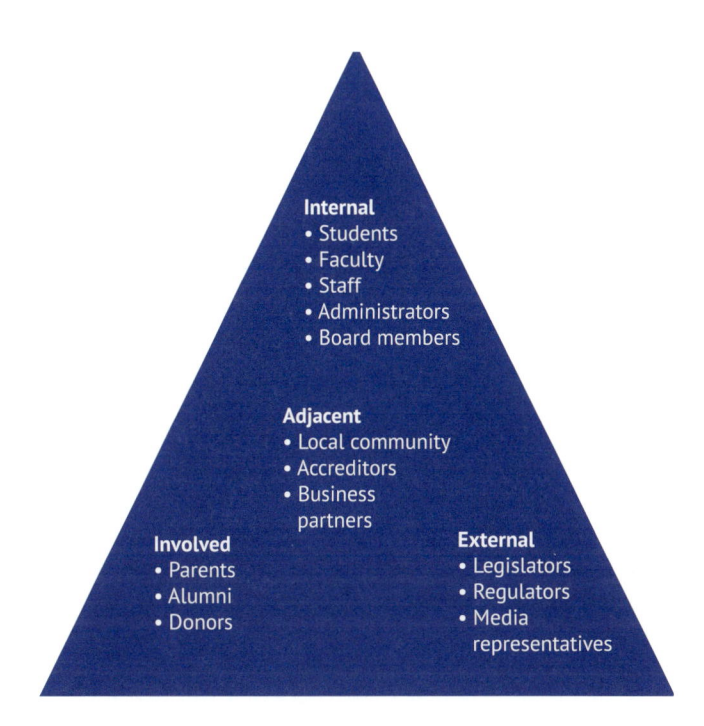

When managing reputational risks, it is important to consider the expectations of these stakeholders. With so many stakeholders, it is impossible to consistently meet all of their expectations, so leadership will need to decide which stakeholders matter most during a reputational event and act accordingly. For each reputational risk on the register, identify the priority stakeholders implicated by the risk and make a plan for responding to each one.

Insight: Build Goodwill Before You Need It

The most effective way to manage reputational risk is to accrue the goodwill needed to weather reputational events well in advance of needing it. An institution that cares about its reputation is one that is continually garnering such goodwill.

Everything an institution and its constituents do can have a reputational impact, and that is especially true for senior leadership. For example, new presidents and other senior leaders must start building goodwill on day one. Explains another communications expert: "We do some work with institutions on presidential rollouts. We try and set them up right from the start so that they are earning that goodwill and banking it so that when they do have to make the tough decision, they have some capital, they have some trust." It's never too soon to begin building goodwill. Leadership's ability to protect the institution's reputation (along with their own) depends upon it.

RISK MANAGEMENT

Insight: What About the Media?

It can be particularly difficult to respond effectively to the news media during a reputational event. In this era of increasingly polarized coverage, as the news cycle picks up stories about higher education, institutions may be tempted to address every news story directly. This is an ill-considered approach, counsels a leader at a communications firm: "I would not advise any client to go on [a cable news program] because you are just helping [the media outlet] sell advertising at that point." That communications expert discourages institutional leaders from going on news programs because their viewership "is not on that list of people whom institutions care about."

As the leader at the communications firm points out, the media is not as important to the institution as the stakeholders who rely on it, including alumni, parents, and major donors. For this reason, those stakeholders should come first during a reputational event: "What [institutions] will deal with, though, is the alum or the board member who is part of that readership or viewership coming to you and saying, 'I saw this and I'm worried about it.' We really encourage [institutions] to [have] that one-on-one conversation."

Given that social media and the web have made it easy for anyone to share opinions about any topic, communications firms advise the same in responding to social media stories by individuals who are not institutional stakeholders, such as students, parents, alumni or donors. Institutions should consider whether their key stakeholders are consuming negative or inaccurate content and tailor their response based on their needs.

Reputation Warning Signs and Board Actions

The board can get a sense of whether additional coordination or internal oversight around reputational questions are needed by considering the following warning signs:

Board Inquiry	Reputational Risk Warning Sign	Possible Board Actions
Is the institution's chief communications officer involved in ERM and risk management?	The communications officer is not involved in risk management and planning prior to crises.	Mandate that the communication's officer actively participate in the institution's ERM processes.
Has the institution identified key reputational risks and their major stakeholders? Has the institution prioritized which stakeholders it will respond to first in a reputational event?	The institution responds to all media comments about the institution, including external parties that have no relationship with or stake in the institution's mission or objectives.	Ask the institution to partner with communications to identify key stakeholders, as well as external parties that are not considered part of the institution's stakeholders.
Does the institution have a response plan and an overall approach for responding to a reputational event?	The institution does not have a proactive and collaborative process for considering and managing its reputation.	Ensure that the institution develops a response plan in collaboration with the communications officer.
Does the institution have a monitoring system to detect reputational events?	The institution lacks a monitoring system.	Suggest the institution implement a monitoring system for reputational events, including social media as well as transitional media.
Does the institution train its leaders about reputation, goodwill, and response prior to reputational events?	The institution does not implement regular tabletop exercises or train its leaders on reputational risk.	Consider instituting regular tabletop exercises and training related to reputational risk and event response.

CONCLUSION
Lessons for Boards

Chapter 10
A Call to Action

In 1998, AGB published a 15-page booklet, *Board Basics: Essentials of Risk Management*. In 2009, AGB and United Educators published a 28-page guide, *The State of Enterprise Risk Management at Colleges and Universities*. In 2013, AGB and United Educators published the first edition of this book, *Risk Management: An Accountability Guide for University and College Boards*. And most recently in 2017, AGB assisted United Educators in a survey forming the basis of a nine-page study focused on a single risk and titled "ERM and Reputational Risk: More Talk Than Action."

Now, in recognition of the complexity of risk management, this book challenges boards and senior administrators to embrace enterprise risk management (ERM) as a way to proactively address institutional risks that higher education faces. This book aims to help campus leaders answer not only "What keeps you up at night?" but also the more important question: "What gets you up in the morning?"

Understanding both the opportunities and downside of risk is essential. To that end, this book concludes with 10 important lessons gleaned from the experience and wisdom of a multitude of professionals who have devoted their careers to understanding the risks and rewards of institutions of higher education. To build a robust risk management program, start small and revisit this list and the book's chapters over time.

10 Important Lessons in Risk Management

1. **Prioritize**. Emphasize treating prioritized risks. Risk identification is merely a springboard for risk prioritization, not merely an effort to catalogue every risk on campus.
2. **Focus**. Senior administrators should focus their energy on high-priority risks rather than those that will have only a modest impact on the institution.
3. **Plan**. Follow through by developing mitigation plans and improving those plans.
4. **Borrow**. As a start, use risk registers and lists developed by peer institutions (and included in this book) and interview senior leaders to verify applicability to your campus. Move deeper into the specific concerns of your own institution in future years.
5. **Talk**. Be ready, willing, and able—on campus, in committees, and at board meetings—to talk about the tough issues. Avoid following the timeworn code of silence on the most critical risks.
6. **Practice**. Use crises at other institutions as a drill or practice to ask, "How would we respond if that happened here?"
7. **Engage board oversight**. The board does not own the ERM process, the administration does. The board's role is to remind the administration of that and hold them accountable.
8. **Hold the president accountable**. The president should lead the ERM effort (if not throughout the entire process, at a minimum to get it started) and stay engaged throughout the deliberations. Managing ongoing ERM activities should belong to a member of the president's cabinet.
9. **Involve administrators**. Each risk brought to the board must have an administration owner, someone who is accountable.
10. **Call on subject-matter experts**. Call upon subject-matter experts from time to time to ensure that the administration is not missing important trends and developments in the risk identification process.

Appendix A
AGB/UE Enterprise Risk Management Risk Registers

THE RISK REGISTER LISTS OFFER BROAD CATEGORIES of potential risk areas for senior administration to evaluate for urgency for and relevance to their institutions. Some of these risks will not rise to the level reported to the board but can serve as a road map for campus administrators.

Strategic and Shared Risks

	Urgency Rating				Person to Address
	1	2	3	NA	(If rated "1")
Business continuity					
Campus unrest and controversial events					
Community relations					
Crisis response					
Cybersecurity					
Faculty recruitment and retention					
Market position					
Mission alignment					
Succession planning					
Technology strategy					
Additional Strategic and Shared Risk Areas:					

Appendix

Risks to Board Governance

	Urgency Rating				Person to Address
	1	2	3	NA	(If rated "1")
Board member independence					
Board performance assessment					
CEO compensation and assessment					
Conflicts of interest					
Governance policies					
IRS Form 990					
Board member participation					
Additional Board Governance Risk Areas:					

Risks to Finances

	Urgency Rating				Person to Address
	1	2	3	NA	(If rated "1")
Auditor independence					
Budget					
Cash management					
Conflicts of interest					
Contracting and purchasing					
Cost management					
Depletion of endowment principal					
Enrollment					
Financial aid					
Financial exigency plan					
Fundraising					
High-risk investments					
Insurance					

	Urgency Rating				Person to Address
	1	2	3	NA	(If rated "1")
Investment oversight					
Long-term debt					
Reserve fund					
Tuition dependency					
Additional Financial Risk Areas:					

Risks to Operations

Facilities

	Urgency Rating				Person to Address
	1	2	3	NA	(If rated "1")
Accessibility					
Auto/fleet					
Disaster preparedness					
Deferred maintenance and physical plant condition					
Employee safety					
Outsourcing					
Pollution					
Security					
Student and community safety					
Transportation					
Additional Facilities Risk Areas:					

Appendix

Academic Affairs

	Urgency Rating				Person to Address (If rated "1")
	1	*2*	*3*	*NA*	
Academic freedom					
Academic quality					
Accreditation					
Education technologies					
Faculty conflicts of interest					
Graduation rates/student learning outcomes					
Grievance procedures					
Joint programs					
Online education					
Academic program portfolio					
Promotion and tenure					
Recruitment/competition					
Additional Academic Affairs Risk Areas:					

Human Resources

	Urgency Rating				Person to Address (If rated "1")
	1	2	3	NA	
Affirmative action					
Background checks					
Benefits					
Code of conduct					
Employee handbook					
Executive succession					
Grievance procedure					
Harassment prevention					
Labor relations					
Nondiscrimination					
Performance evaluation					
Recruitment and retention					
Sexual molestation prevention					
Termination procedures					
Workplace safety					
Additional Human Resources Risk Areas:					

Appendix

Information Technology

	Urgency Rating				Person to Address
	1	2	3	NA	(If rated "1")
Back-up procedures					
Communications systems					
Cyber liability					
Data governance					
Data protection					
Incident response					
Network integrity					
Privacy					
Security					
Staffing and support					
System capacity					
Third-party vendors					
Unauthorized data disclosure					
Additional Information Technology Risk Areas:					

Research

	Urgency Rating				Person to Address
	1	2	3	NA	(If rated "1")
Accounting					
Animal research					
Clinical research					
Environmental and lab safety					
Hazardous materials					
Human subjects					
Lab safety					
Patenting					

AGB/UE Enterprise Risk Management Risk Registers

	Urgency Rating				Person to Address
	1	2	3	NA	(If rated "1")
Security					
Technology transfer					
Additional Research Risk Areas:					

Student Affairs

	Urgency Rating				Person to Address
	1	2	3	NA	(If rated "1")
Academic standards					
Admissions/retention					
Alcohol and drug policies					
Athletics					
Code of conduct					
Crime on campus					
Diversity					
Experiential programs					
Financial aid					
Fraternities and sororities					
Free speech					
International students					
Privacy					
Sexual abuse					
Student debt					
Study abroad					
Additional Student Affairs Risk Areas:					

Appendix

Compliance

	Urgency Rating				Person to Address (If rated "1")
	1	*2*	*3*	*NA*	
Animal research					
Athletics					
Clinical research					
Copyright and "fair use"					
Environmental					
Government grants					
Higher Education Act					
HR/Employment					
Intellectual property rights					
Privacy					
Protection of minors					
Record retention and destruction					
Taxes					
Title IX					
Whistleblower policy					
Additional Compliance Risk Areas:					

Appendix B
Sample Universitywide Risk Management Committee Charter

THE FOLLOWING IS A SAMPLE CHARTER OF an institutionwide risk management committee. This standing committee—in this illustrative example, it is called a council—is composed of senior administrators and supports the administration and the governing board. This charter is reprinted with permission from Cornell University.

Cornell University Risk Management Council Charter

CHARGE

As delegated by the Board of Trustees and charged by the President, the University Risk Management Council is responsible for providing oversight, guidance, and coordination of university-wide efforts aimed at identifying, assessing, and reducing risks that may jeopardize life and safety of individuals, and the assets, operations, reputation, and legal interests of the institution. In fulfilling its oversight responsibility, the Risk Council will assist the administrators who have lead or shared responsibility in managing risks within their assigned areas, in terms of monitoring risk mitigation strategies and marshaling sufficient organizational support. Further, the Risk Council will advise university senior leadership concerning strategic risks to the institution, as well as risks that fall between or above assigned risk areas. The Risk Council will also coordinate the presentation of periodic status reports to the Board of Trustees and subordinate committees which are relegated risk review responsibility.

Appendix

COMPOSITION

The University Risk Management Council is a university-wide standing committee; it is vested with oversight and advisory authority, but has no executive or supervisory powers. The President designates the chair and vice chair, who in turn are authorized (by the President) to appoint the members. Individuals are appointed because of their leadership roles within the University and their informed insights concerning the control of risks both within and across their areas of risk responsibilities.

- University Counsel and Secretary of the Corporation (Chair)
- Executive Vice Provost for Administration and Finance, Weill Cornell Medical College (WCMC) (Vice-Chair)
- Vice President for Human Resources and Safety Services (Vice-Chair)
- Vice President for University Communications
- Senior Vice Provost for Research
- Associate Vice President for Campus Health
- Vice President for Finance and CFO
- University Auditor
- Vice President for Cornell NYC Tech
- Chief Administrative Officer, WCMC-Qatar
- Senior Director of Risk Management and Insurance, WCMC
- Director of Risk Management and Insurance
- Vice President for Student and Academic Services
- Vice Provost for International Relations
- Associate Chief Information Officer for Information Technologies
- Assistant Dean for Research Integrity, WCMC
- Associate Vice President for Environmental Health and Safety
- Director of Environmental Health and Safety, WCMC
- Senior Director, WCMC IT Security Officer
- Vice President for Facilities Services
- Chief of Police

GUIDING PRINCIPLES

In performing its oversight and advisory responsibilities the Risk Council will be guided by the following principles:

- Emphasize to Cornell leadership and governance that for "plans" writ large (strategic plans, master plans) or small (discrete projects, initiatives), proper attention must be paid to potential risks to the University's people, property, and reputation in the planning and decision-making stage.
- Instill university-wide awareness among everyone engaged to act on Cornell's behalf that the recognition and reduction of risk are both a continuing concern and a collaborative responsibility.
- Provide a comprehensive approach to manage risks across the entire institution
- Take stock of external and internal forces and factors that influence the university risk landscape.
- Identify the main and specific risks to the university and ensure that specific risks have responsible managers.
- Enable an efficient system of guidance and support to individuals "in charge," through development of appropriate policies and assistance of risk advisory committees (ad hoc and standing), and elimination of silos which may inhibit institutional risk management efforts.
- Gauge the most "serious risks" in terms of perceived impact and likelihood and assess whether organizational and operational structures and dedicated resources are adequate to the task of managing such serious risks.
- Make recommendations to the president and provost for areas requiring additional resources to minimize high impact risks.
- Recognize that perceived risks must be balanced against risk control costs, and that some level of risk may have to be tolerated.
- Review from time to time risk management strategies to assure they remain current with regulatory, operational, and legal changes, as well as business and financial objectives.

MEETINGS

The Council will meet at least once a quarter and more frequently if deemed necessary. There may be email communication to arrive at a consensus on an issue. Non-council members may be invited to attend meetings as needed.

Appendix C
Sample List of Insurance Policies for Colleges and Universities

Sample List of Insurance Policies for Small and Medium-Size Colleges

1. **Property**: Replacement of campus buildings, equipment, fine arts, and valuable collections due to fire, earthquakes, vandalism, and weather-related events Including floods, and wind or ice storms. May include extra expenses for business interruption
2. **Automobile/fleet**: such as auto physical damage, auto liability
3. **Educators' Legal liability**: Coverage for the institution, board, directors and officers, employees and volunteers
    - Educational malpractice
    - Employment practices
    - Sexual harassment
    - Tenure denial
    - Violation of fiduciary duties
    - Violation of intellectual property
    - Discrimination rights
4. **Fiduciary liability**: Employee benefit plan administration
5. **General liability**:
    - Primary: defense and indemnification from liability claims alleged by third parties, including students, visitors, and guests
    - Excess/Umbrella: catastrophic coverage above the primary general liability

Appendix

- Crime: Employee fraud and dishonesty
- Professional Liability/Medical Malpractice: Covering health care providers employed by institutions
- Business Travel Accident: Employee benefit for faculty and staff
- Accidental Death and Dismemberment: Employee benefit for faculty and staff
- International Travel: Foreign travel accident and sickness, medical evacuation, and repatriation

6. **Workers' Compensation**: Mandated by states providing wage replacement and medical coverage for injuries of faculty and staff performing job responsibilities

Sample List of Insurance Policies for Large Research Universities

General Liability—Primary
General Liability—Excess or Umbrella
Educators' Legal Liability—including directors and officers, employment practices liability and errors and omissions
Fiduciary Liability
Special Crime Kidnap and Ransom Business Travel Accident
Student Travel Accident Field trip
Medical Evacuation and Repatriation
Intercollegiate Athletics Travel Accident
Intercollegiate Athletic Accident Injury
Intercollegiate Athletic Catastrophic Injury
Student Club Insurance
Experiential Learning/Student Internship
Student Club Catastrophic Injury
Tenant User Liability Insurance Policy (TULIP)
Concert Promoters Liability Policy
Student EMS Voluntary Workers Compensation
Student EMS Professional Liability International Liability
Professional Liability Medical Malpractice Veterinary Malpractice
Workers Compensation—Primary state
Workers Compensation—other states
Workers Compensation—Defense Base Act

Sample List of Insurance Policies for Colleges and Universities

Workers Compensation—Long shore and Harbor Workers
Workers Compensation—International
Owner Controlled Insurance Policy (OCIP)—Construction Wrap-up
Auto—Primary State
Auto—Other states
Auto—International
Environmental—1st and 3rd Party Pollution
Property—Multiple layers
Inland Marine
Ocean Marine
Aircraft—Liability
Aircraft—Hull
Fine Arts
Crime
Protection and Indemnity
Water Craft-Hull
Cyber Liability—1st and 3rd party
Aerospace and Satellite Launch
Student Personal Property
Student Personal Liability
Student Health Insurance
Business Interruption
Foreign Terrorism Liability
Clinical Trials Liability
Nuclear Liability

Appendix D
Models for Managing Compliance

To understand compliance better, board members should know that compliance models can differ given that organizational structure often depends on institutional history. Some institutions have the culture and leadership buy-in in place to centralize compliance, while others may prefer a more decentralized approach.

Four predominant models for managing compliance include:

- **Centralized compliance management**: a coordinated approach where a single department oversees and manages compliance across the institution, coordinating the efforts of many different stakeholders in a centralized fashion;
- **Topical compliance management**: a hybrid model where departments sharing a compliance risk coordinate their approach based on the topic to ensure a unified, comprehensive, and efficient process;
- **Departmental compliance management**: a hybrid approach where departments consider all departmental compliance requirements as a whole but do not coordinate with others across the institution; and
- **Decentralized compliance management**: neither the institution nor the department consider compliance as a whole, and individual stakeholders manage pieces of compliance without coordinated reporting to any department or the institution.

These models are not mutually exclusive, and some institutions may combine them when managing different compliance risks.

Appendix

Centralized Compliance Management	Topical Compliance Management
Compliance Office(r) → Risk 1, Risk 2, Risk 3 → Risk 1 Depts, Risk 2 Depts, Risk 3 Depts → Outcome: *Compliance Program for Risk 1*, *Compliance Program for Risk 2*, *Compliance Program for Risk 3*	Compliance Risk 1: Dept A, Dept B, Dept C → Outcome: *Compliance Program for Risk 1* Compliance Risk 2: Dept D, Dept E, Dept F → Outcome: *Compliance Program for Risk 2*
Departmental Compliance Management	**Decentralized Compliance Management**
Department A → Risk 1, Risk 2, Risk 3 → Outcome: *Dept. Compliance Program for Risk 1*, *Dept. Compliance Program for Risk 2*, *Dept. Compliance Program for Risk 3* Department B → Risk 1, Risk 2, Risk 3	Compliance Risk 1, Compliance Risk 2, Compliance Risk 3, Compliance Risk 4, Compliance Risk 5 Outcome: *Scattered Compliance Efforts*

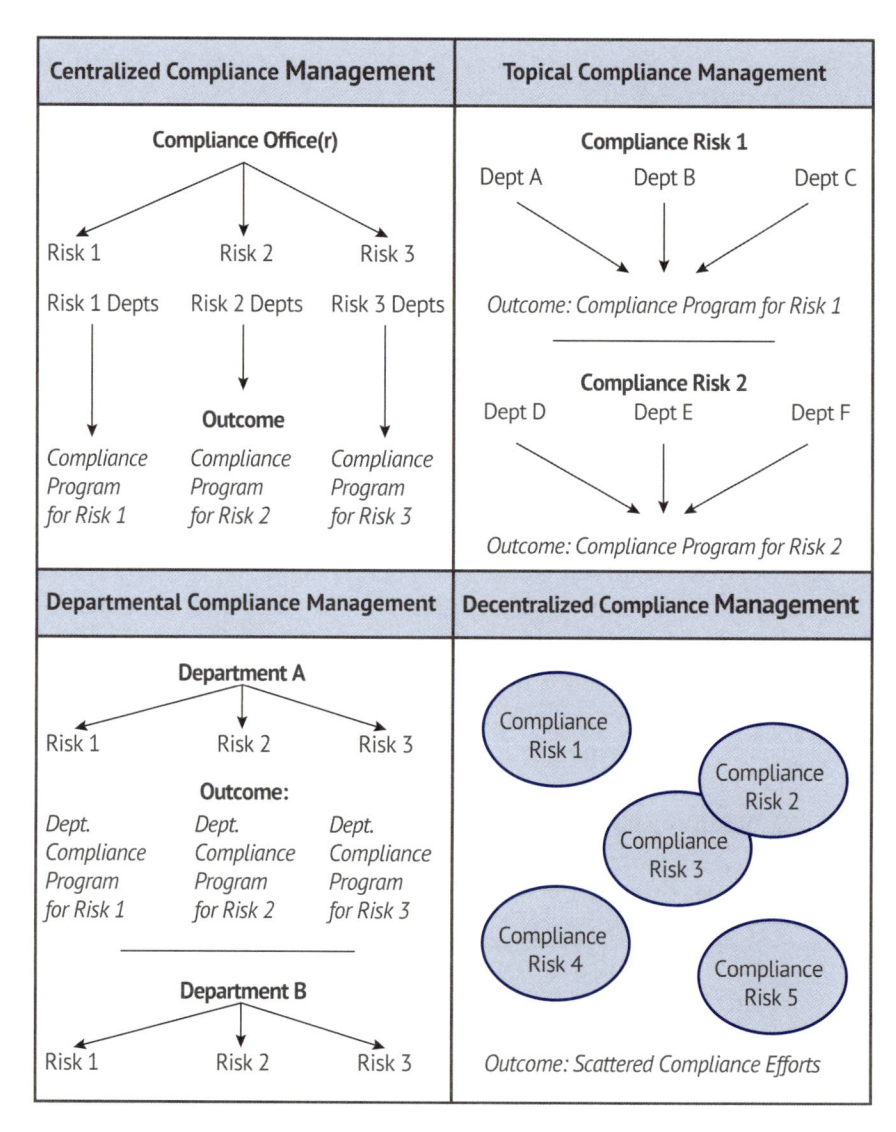

Figure 2—Compliance Management Models

Centralized Compliance

The most cohesive approach towards compliance is a centralized compliance model. As higher education becomes more regulated, the financial and reputational stakes for noncompliance continue to increase. As a result, more institutions are centralizing compliance, much like the ERM model for risk management.

A central compliance office is responsible for managing all compliance risks, assigning and overseeing risk owners, and ensuring a cohesive compliance strategy is in place. Given that centralizing compliance practices across an institution can take significant effort, larger institutions have been at the forefront of managing compliance in a centralized fashion, with an institutionwide compliance office that oversees the compliance operations of all areas of the college or university.

For example, one large research institution with centralized compliance management has a compliance office responsible for overseeing compliance efforts across all areas. The office develops and publishes all compliance policies and is responsible auditing practices and regularly updating policies. This ensures timely updates to policies that reflect changes to compliance requirements or institutional practices, rather than a scattered approach where it is unclear who owns updates. From the legal perspective, nothing is worse than a policy that is outdated, impossible to follow in the practical sense, or applied inconsistently, as these gaps allow outsiders to point to institutional wrongdoing.

In this case, the compliance office also serves as a central resource on all things compliance—the office's website lists all policies, trainings, and reporting requirements. This process eliminates the potential for multiple conflicting policies about the same risk and ensures a clear process that everyone is expected to follow. What's more, because it is so simple to locate policies, stakeholders no longer have the familiar excuse for failing to follow institutional policies: "I could not find the policy." A central location for policies allows stakeholders to identify and contact compliance risk owners as questions arise or to request training, addressing the challenge of unclear responsibilities at decentralized organizations.

While every institution operates differently, centralized compliance appears to be the predominant model at larger institutions, including public and research institutions.

TOPICAL COMPLIANCE

Institutions may manage compliance based on a risk or topic. In some cases, a central office might coordinate compliance efforts around a single risk to ensure cohesive policies and practices are in place. Even institutions that do not centralize compliance across the institution often ask departments to collaborate on managing risks with significant compliance requirements.

Appendix

Insight: Achieving Centralized Compliance on a Budget

In some cases, leadership may allocate resources to create a single role or an entire office to oversee compliance. In this case, individual departments may still manage the day-to-day operations of compliance like Title IX, accessibility, or health and safety, while a central officer is responsible for centralizing written procedures, trainings, and reporting to leadership on all compliance efforts.

Some institutions face budgetary constraints or may not have sufficient compliance management responsibilities to justify a full-time position dedicated to compliance. For instance, one institution could not authorize resources to create a single compliance officer role, but it updated a regulatory position so that managing institutional compliance was half of that role's responsibilities. For smaller institutions in particular, this approach can ensure centralized compliance oversight without dedicating a full position or office.

For example, institutions frequently manage the risk of student misconduct as a cross-functional task force because the risk has so many moving pieces including student academics, conduct, housing, and sexual misconduct. In addition to managing the safety and well-being of the campus community, the institution must follow stringent compliance requirements including:

- Title IX of the Education Amendments Act (Title IX)
- Jeanne Clery Disclosure of Campus Security Policy and Campus Crime Statistics Act (Clery Act)
- Americans with Disabilities Act (ADA)
- Fair Housing Act (FHA)
- Family Educational Rights and Privacy Act (FERPA)
- Health Insurance Portability and Accountability Act (HIPAA)
- Additional applicable local and state requirements.

Operational areas that frequently collaborate to manage this risk and ensure compliance may include the student affairs, academics, athletics, housing and residence life, Title IX, counseling services, disability services, public safety, and legal counsel.

Beyond the obvious risk to the well-being of students and others in the community, failing to coordinate on response can include expensive fines and legal expenses. For the Clery Act alone, the U.S. Education Department imposed 40 fines involving Clery Act regulations between 2010 and 2017 for a total of $5 million in fines. While the median fine during that period was $47,250, the largest fines for institutions failing to report forcible sexual offenses ranged from $1 million to $2.4 million.

Departmental Compliance

Institutions move towards centralized compliance when departments consider compliance proactively by planning around what risks fall under their purview and tracking compliance obligations at regular increments. The institution may not have a centralized compliance model or even consider risks topically across multiple departments, but individual departments are able to get ahead of managing compliance by thinking proactively and collaboratively within the department.

One common example is laboratory safety, which addresses the need to ensure student safety first, followed by external compliance and reporting requirements. Institutions often have a single lab safety manager or faculty member tasked with compliance across all areas. Eventually, this department may consider partnering with all areas that manage safety to develop a topical compliance program.

While this approach may not allow coordination with other departments, it helps departments to get ahead of compliance risks on an internal level rather than thinking reactively. Managing compliance risks at a departmental level can also be a starting point towards centralizing compliance efforts when there is no leadership buy-in for institutional compliance.

Decentralized Compliance

In the absence of a structured approach to managing compliance, institutions operate in a decentralized fashion. Individual positions manage compliance topics without coordinating within a department or across them.

While boards will not be involved at this level of compliance, it is important to remember that stakeholders managing compliance on a daily basis typically do not have an auditing, legal, finance, or risk management background. They are experts in their roles and may understand related regulations, but may not know how to respond to complex issues or be able to balance conflicting compliance priorities.

Examples of areas that manage compliance programs include:

- Leaders in student life and public safety oversee components of Title IX and Clery Act reporting related to sexual misconduct and crimes on campus.
- Human Resources oversees EEO, hiring, and reporting requirements involving employees.
- Financial aid oversees Title IV and other finance and financial aid requirements.
- Faculty and researchers working on complicated research must understand grant requirements and research funding.

For example, at institutions with decentralized compliance management, each research department creates its own laboratory safety standards and policies rather than one institutional contact overseeing laboratory safety for all departments.

The challenge with this model is that oversight might not be sufficient to ensure that the institution is meeting all of its compliance requirements, even within a single department or compliance topic. Stakeholders may not be properly trained to manage compliance and reporting efforts. Some sub-risks may fall through the gaps when no clear owner or expert on that topic guides all areas.

Resources

Resources

"10 years. 180 school shootings. 356 victims," CNN, August 2019.

Arria, Amelia and Greta Wagley, "Addressing College Drinking and Drug Use, A Primer for Trustees, Administrators, and Alumni," ACTA, June 2019.

"Assessing Marijuana Use, Anxiety, and Academic Performance Among College Students," Higher Education Center for Alcohol and Drug Misuse Prevention and Recovery, July 22, 2019.

Abraham, Janice M. and Paul L. Walker, "ERM and Reputational Risk: More Talk Than Action?" United Educators, 2017.

"Beating Turnover in Higher Ed: New Findings from Academic Impressions," Academic Impressions, 2019.

Bell, David A. and Judith H. Van Gorden, "Piloting the Portfolio," *Business Officer*, December 2012.

Bernstein, Peter L., *Against the Odds: The Remarkable Story of Risk*, Hoboken, N.J.: John Wiley & Sons, Inc., 1996.

Choudaha, Rahul, PhD, assisted by Li Cjang and Kata Orosz, "Not All International Students Are the Same: Understanding Segments, Mapping Behavior," *World Education News & Reviews*, August 2012.

Crist, Carolyn, "Mental Health Diagnoses Rising among U.S. College Students," *Reuters*, November 1, 2018.

DeCrappeo, Anthony, *Managing Externally Funded Research Programs: A Guide to Effective Management Practices*, Council on Governmental Relations, 2009.

Denneen, Jeff and Tom Dretler in collaboration with Sterling Partners, *The Financially Sustainable University*, Bain & Company, July 2012.

"Diversity and Inclusion Defined," George Washington University, Office of Diversity, Equity and Community Engagement, 2019.

"Don't Stop Believin' (in the value of a college degree): Committee on Education and Labor Report," U.S. House of Representatives, March 2019.

"Excessive Force by Campus Security," United Educators, February 2017.

"Faculty Governance in Higher Education," National Education Association, 2019.

"Firearms and Weapons Policies," United Educators, July 2019.

"A Framework for Integrating Young Peers in Recovery into Adolescent Substance Use Prevention and Early Intervention," Higher Education Center for Alcohol and Drug Misuse Prevention and Recovery, August 29, 2019.

"Get the Facts," Higher Education Center for Alcohol and Drug Misuse Prevention and Recovery, September 2019.

Grawe, Nathan, *Demographics and the Demand for Higher Education*, Johns Hopkins University Press, 2018.

"Good Practice in Tenure Evaluation," A joint project of the American Council on Education, the American Association of University Professors, and United Educators, American Council on Education, 2000.

Governance for a New Era: A Blueprint for Higher Education Trustees, American Council of Trustees and Alumni, 2014.

Greene, Randy, Chuck Shaw, and Ron Salluzzo, "Made to Measure," *Business Officer*, March 2012, pp: 28–29.

Gunza, Nancy, "High Tech, High Stakes," *Business Officer*, September 2012, p. 31.

Hampton, John J., *Fundamentals of Enterprise Risk Management*, American Management Association, 2009.

The Health Research Institute, "The Future of Academic Medical Centers: Strategies to Avoid a Margin Meltdown," PricewaterhouseCoopers, February 2012.

Jaschik, Scott and Doug Lederman, "2019 Survey of College and University Business Officers," *Inside Higher Ed* and Gallup.

Kelchin, Robert, *Higher Education Accountability*, Johns Hopkins Press, 2018.

Kloman, H. Felix, *The Fantods of Risk: Essays on Risk Management*, Lyme, Conn.: Seawrack Press Inc., 2008.

Kloman, H. Felix, "Enterprise Risk Management: Past, Present and Future," *Risk Management Reports*, May 2003.

Lederman, Doug, "MOOC Platforms' New Model Draws Big Bet From Investors," *Inside Higher Ed*, May 22, 2019.

"Liability and Lessons from General Mental Health Claims," United Educators, October 2018.

McChesney, Jasper, "Representation and Pay of Women of Color in the Higher Education Workforce," CUPA-HR, 2018.

"Mental Health and School Dropout across Educational Levels and Genders: a 4.8-Year Follow-up Study," U.S. National Library of Medicine, National Institutes of Health, September 2016.

"MOOCs Are Dead—Long Live the MOOC," *Wired*, August 2014.

Mondou, Sherry B., "A Beneficial Bet," *Business Officer*, September 2012, p. 33.

"National College Health Assessment," American College Health Association, Fall 2018.

National Research Council of the National Academies, *Research Universities and the Future of America: Ten Breakthrough Actions Vital to Our Nation's Prosperity and Security*, Washington, D.C., The National Academies Press, 2012.

"NIH has referred 16 allegations of foreign influence on U.S. research to investigators," *Stat News*, June 2019.

Pappano, Laura, "The Year of the MOOC," *New York Times*, November 2, 2012.

Pearlman, Jay, "Decent Exposure: Reducing Facilities Risk in the Post-Downturn Environment," *Net Assets*, July/August 2012, pp. 25–27.

"Problems Arising From Tenure Denials: A Review of Recent Claims," United Educators, June 2017.

Redden, Elizabeth, "Science vs. Security," *Inside Higher Ed*, April 2019.

"Report to the Nation on Occupational Fraud and Abuse," Association of Certified Fraud Examiners, 2012.

"Report of the Special Investigative Counsel Regarding the Actions of The Pennsylvania State University Related to the Child Sexual Abuse Committed by Gerald A. Sandusky," Freeh, Sporkin & Sullivan, LLP, July 12, 2012.

Rice-Oxley, Mark, "Mental illness: is there really a global epidemic?" *The Guardian*, June 3, 2019.

"Safeguarding Our Communities from Sexual Predators: What College Presidents and Trustees Should Ask," United Educators, January 2019.

"Taking Inventory of Your Off-Campus Real Estate," United Educators, June 2017.

Tahey, Phil, Ron Salluzzo, Fred Prager, Lou Mezzina, and Chris Cowen, *Strategic Financial Analysis for Higher Education: Identifying, Measuring & Reporting Financial Risks*, Seventh Edition, KPMG, Prager, Sealy & Co., and ATTAIN, 2010.

"Tenure," American Association of University Professors, 2019.

Thomason, Andy, "Is College President 'the Toughest Job in the Nation'?," *Chronicle of Higher Education*, 2018.

"U.S. Secret Service Releases Operational Guide for Preventing Targeted School Violence," U.S. Department of Homeland Security, July 13, 2018.

Walker, Paul L., William G. Shenkir, and Thomas L. Barton, "Improving Board Risk Oversight Through Best Practices," Institute of Internal Auditors Research Foundation, 2011.

Warner, John, "One Small Step to Address the Student Mental Health Crisis," *Inside Higher Ed*, February 24, 2019.

Key Resources from AGB

AGB REPORTS AND SURVEYS

- *State of Enterprise Risk Management (ERM) in Colleges and Universities Today*, AGB and UE, 2009.
- *AGB Survey of Higher Education Governance*, 2011 and 2012.
- *Trust, Accountability, and Integrity: Board Responsibilities for Intercollegiate Athletics*, AGB with support from The Knight Commission on Intercollegiate Athletics, 2012.
- *Tuition and Financial Aid: Nine Points for Boards to Consider In Keeping College Affordable*, 2011.
- *Front and Center: Critical Choices for Higher Education*, 2011.

AGB PUBLICATIONS

- *Institutionally Related Foundation Boards: An Introductory Guide for Board Members*, 2019.
- Baum, Sandy, *Financial Aid and Enrollment: Questions for Boards to Consider*, 2015.
- Bobowick, Marla J., and Merrill P. Schwartz, *Assessing Board Performance: A Practical Guide for College, University, System, and Foundation Boards*, 2018.
- Chabotar, Kent John, *Strategic Finance: Planning and Budgeting for Boards, Chief Executives, and Finance Officers*, 2006.
- Dreier, Alexander E. and Martin Michaelson, *A Guide to Updating the Board's Conflict of Interest Policy*, 2006.
- Ewell, Peter T., *Making the Grade: How Boards Can Ensure Academic Quality*, 2012.
- Hites, Michael, George Finney, and Joseph D. Barnes, *What Board Members Need to Know About Cybersecurity*, 2018.
- Jackson, Patricia P., *The Board's Role in Fundraising*, 2013.
- Kraus, Nicole Wellmann, Hilda Ochoa- Brillembourg, and Jay A. Yoder, *Endowment Management for Higher Education*, 2017.
- Legon, Richard G., *Margin of Excellence: The New Work of Higher Education Foundations*, 2005.
- MacTaggart, Terrence, *Leading Change: How Boards and Presidents Build Exceptional Academic Institutions*, 2011.
- Schrum, Jake B., *A Board's Guide to Comprehensive Campaigns*, 2000.
- Shinn, Larry D., *Strategic Thinking and Planning in Higher Education: A Focus on the Future*, 2017.
- Worth, Michael J., *Foundations for the Future: The Fundraising Role of Foundation Boards at Public Colleges and Universities*, 2012.
- Worth, Michael J., *Securing the Future: A Fund-Raising Guide for Boards of Independent Colleges and Universities*, 2005.

AGB EFFECTIVE COMMITTEE SERIES

- *The Audit Committee* by Richard L. Staisloff, 2011.
- *The Academic Affairs Committee* by Susan Whealler Johnston, 2014.
- *The Compensation Committee* by Thomas K. Hyatt, 2012.
- *The Development Committee* by Peyton R. Helm, 2012.
- *The Executive Committee* by Richard D. Legon, 2012.
- *The Facilities Committee* by Harvey H. Kaiser, 2012.

Resources

- *The Finance Committee* by Ingrid Stafford, 2013.
- *The Governance Committee (Foundation Boards)* by James L. Lanier and E.B. Wilson, 2014.
- *The Governance Committee (Public Institutions)* by Carol Cartwright, 2019.
- *The Governance Committee (Independent Institutions)* by E.B. Wilson and James L. Lanier, 2013.
- *The Investment Committee* by Jay A. Yoder, 2011.
- *The Student Affairs Committee* by Shannon Ellis, 2011.

AGB REPORTS AND STATEMENTS (ISSUED TO HELP DEFINE AND CLARIFY THE RESPONSIBILITIES OF GOVERNING BOARDS):

- *AGB Statement on External Influences on Universities and Colleges*, 2012.
- *AGB Statement on Board Responsibility for the Oversight of Educational Quality*, 2011.
- *AGB Statement on Board Responsibility for Institutional Governance*, 2010.
- *AGB Board of Directors' Statement on Conflict of Interest with Guidelines on Compelling Benefit*, 2013.
- *AGB-CHEA Joint Advisory Statement on Accreditation & Governing Boards*, 2009.
- *AGB Board of Directors' Statement on Governing Boards' Responsibilities for Intercollegiate Athletics*, 2018.
- *AGB Statement on Board Accountability*, 2007.
- *A Wake-up Call: Enterprise Risk Management at Colleges and Universities Today*, 2014.
- Bass, David, "Spending and Management of Endowments Under UPMIFA," 2010.
- *How Boards Oversee Educational Quality: A Report on a Survey of the Assessment of Student Learning*, 2010.

AGB *TRUSTEESHIP* ARTICLES:

- Abraham, Janice, "Are You Sacrificing Your Reputation to Protect Sacred Cows?" *Trusteeship*, September/October 2014.
- Abraham, Janice, "Heat Map: Is Your Institution at Risk? Protecting Minors on Your Campus," *Trusteeship*, March/April 2012.

- Abraham, Janice, "Vitiating Vulnerability," *Trusteeship*, September/October 2007.
- Alexander, Lamar, "What Do American Auto Manufacturers and Higher Ed Have in Common?," *Trusteeship*, January/February 2012.
- Bacow, Lawrence and Laura Skandera Trombley, "Making Metrics Matter: How to Use Indicators to Govern Effectively," *Trusteeship*, January/February 2011.
- Bahlman, David, John Walda, and Verne Sedlacek, "Higher Education Endowments Return," *Trusteeship*, March/April 2012.
- Bahls, Steven C., "Board Complacency and the Experienced President," *Trusteeship*, January/ February 2011.
- Bass, David and Jim Lanier, "What Lies Ahead for University-Foundation Relations?," *Trusteeship*, November/December 2008.
- Bass, David, "College Fundraising: Is There a 'New Normal'?" *Trusteeship*, November/December 2009.
- Bass, David, "What's a Prudent Payout from an 'Underwater' Endowment," *Trusteeship*, May/June 2009.
- Baum, Sandy, "The Link between Financial Aid and Enrollment," *Trusteeship*, May/June 2015.
- Baum, Sandy, "Taxing the Endowment," *Trusteeship*, May/June 2019.
- Beyer, Rick, "Mergers and Affiliations," *Trusteeship*, May/June 2019.
- Bernard, Pamela J., "Does Your Institution Need a Social-Media Policy?" *Trusteeship*, September/ October 2010.
- Bernard, Pamela J., "New Federal Rules Elevate E-mail as a Risk for Boards and Presidents," *Trusteeship*, March/April 2008.
- Bernard, Pamela J., "Do Emergency Planners Know When and How to Share Confidential Student Records?," *Trusteeship*, May/June 2008.
- Bossle, Frank, Betty McPhilimy, and Michael Somich, "Who Audits the Auditor? Assessing the Quality of the Internal Audit Function," *Trusteeship*, May/June 2015.
- Bourbon, Julie, "University of Iowa Flooding: The Expected and the Unexpected," *Trusteeship*, September/October 2008.
- Brennan, Joseph A., "Object Lesson: The Crucial Role of Trustees in Facing Crisis," *Trusteeship*, July/August 2017.
- Chynoweth, Lyn Trodahl, "Creating Solutions in Times of Crisis," *Trusteeship*, November/December 2011.

- Connell, Christopher, "Stronger Together: Building Better Relationships Between Foundations and Universities," *Trusteeship*, January/February 2020.
- Curry, John R. and Lyn Hutton, "Why Cash Flow Is No Longer for Wimps," *Trusteeship*, September/October 2012.
- Denna, Eric, "Higher Education's Return on Information Technology," *Trusteeship*, special issue 2015.
- Dobkin, Bethami A., "Creating Inclusive Board Culture," *Trusteeship*, March/April 2019.
- Dunham, Steven, "Compliance Policies and the Law," *Trusteeship*, March/April 2019.
- Dunham, Steven, "Risk Management and the Law," *Trusteeship*, May/June 2019.
- Dunham, Steven, "Crisis Management and the Law," *Trusteeship*, November/December 2019.
- Eells, Gregory T., "Rx for Students' Mental Health: What Boards Can Do," *Trusteeship*, September/October 2011.
- Ewell, Peter T., "The Growing Interest in Academic Quality," *Trusteeship*, January/February 2014.
- Gellman-Danley, Barbara, "Accreditation and Quality Assurance," *Trusteeship*, November/December 2017.
- Green, Kenneth C., "Mission, MOOCs, and Money," *Trusteeship*, January/February 2013.
- Griswold, John, "What Should We Know About Investments and Endowments?" *Trusteeship*, January/February 2013.
- Hinton, Mary Dana, "The Importance of Academic Oversight," *Trusteeship*, September/October 2019.
- Hodge-Clark, Kristen, "Losing Ground on Risk Assessment," *Trusteeship*, May/June 2014.
- Hrabowski III, Freeman A., "Diversity, Access, and the American Dream," *Trusteeship*, May/June 2014.
- Humber, Jeffrey, Jonathan Alger, Loretta Martinez, Jeffrey B. Trammell, Marc A. Nivet, Anne C. Berlin, "Why Boards Must Become Diversity Stewards," *Trusteeship*, May/June 2014.
- Hyatt, Thomas K., "Show Me What I'm Looking For: A Trustee's Guide to Reviewing the New IRS Form 990," *Trusteeship*, January/February 2008.
- Ikenberry, Stanley, Peter Ewell, and George Kuh, "Governing Boards and Student Learning Outcomes Assessment," *Trusteeship*, January/February 2016.

- Johnston, Susan Whealler, "Risking Your Reputation," *Trusteeship*, November/December 2017.
- Kaiser, Harvey H., "Protecting and Enhancing Campus Facilities: 6 Principles for Boards," *Trusteeship*, March/April 2012.
- Kirch, Darrell G., "Higher Education in the Age of Obamacare," *Trusteeship*, July/August 2013.
- Kirch, Darrell G., "Higher Education and Health Care at a Crossroads," *Trusteeship*, March/April 2011.
- Kinzie, Jullian, Alexander C. McCormick, and Robert M. Gonyea, "Using Student Engagement Results to Oversee Educational Quality," *Trusteeship*, January/February 2016.
- Krisberg, Kim, "Campus Carry Laws and the Challenges for Leadership," *Trusteeship*, September/October 2017.
- Krisberg, Kim, "Can Institutions Learn to Live with Campus Carry?" *Trusteeship*, September/October 2018.
- Loughry, Andrea J., "Stay Alert to Financial Oversight and Risk Assessment on the Audit Trail," *Trusteeship*, November/December 2007.
- Mactaggart, Terrence, "Leadership in a Time of Crisis," *Trusteeship*, July/August 2019.
- MacTaggart, Terrence, "The Risks of Trustee 'Managerialism,'" *Trusteeship*, January/February 2007.
- McLaughlin, Gerald W. and Josetta McLaughlin, *The Information Mosaic: Strategic Decision Making for Universities and Colleges*, 2008.
- Mendez, Angel L., "Need IT With That? How one Board Effectively Oversees Technology," *Trusteeship*, special issue 2015.
- Michaelson, Martin, "How is Your Institution Doing on Conflicts of Interest?" *Trusteeship*, November/December 2007.
- Novak, Richard, "State Policies and Practices to Improve Board Governance," *Trusteeship*, September/October 2012.
- O'Brien, John, "IT: The New Strategic Imperative," *Trusteeship*, March/April 2018.
- O'Neil, Robert, "Updated Board Bylaws—and Beyond," *Trusteeship*, March/April 2013.
- Pelletier, Stephen G., "Taming 'Big Data': Using Data Analytics for Student Success and Institutional Intelligence," *Trusteeship*, special issue 2015.
- Pelletier, Stephen G, "High-Performing Committees: What Makes Them Work?," *Trusteeship*, May/June 2012.

- Pelletier, Stephen G., "Campus Security Under the Microscope," *Trusteeship*, January/February 2008.
- Pelletier, Stephen G, "New Strategies for Managing Risks: A Balancing Act for Boards," *Trusteeship*, January/February 2012.
- Schwartz, Merrill, "The Big Risk in Not Assessing Risk," *Trusteeship*, January/February 2012.
- Schwartz, Merrill, "Making Sense of Tuition Prices and College Costs," *Trusteeship*, July/August 2011.
- Sedlacek, Verne, "The Importance of Stress Testing in Higher Education," *Trusteeship*, September/October 2019.
- Sedlacek, Verne, "How Can Institutions Use Financial Stress Testing to Ensure Their Fiscal Health?" *Trusteeship*, January/February 2019.
- Twigg, Carol A., "Transforming Learning Through Technology: Educating More, Costing Less," *Trusteeship*, September/October 2011.
- Vekich, Michael and Daniel Cobom, "Accountability is a Calculated Effort," *Trusteeship*, September/October 2004.
- Weiss, Jeff A., "Growth and Transformation: A New Era of Mergers," *Trusteeship*, January/February 2018.
- White, Lawrence, "The Principle of Indemnification and Why Trustees Should Care About It," *Trusteeship*, March/April 2012.
- White, Lawrence, "Governing During an Institutional Crisis: 10 Fundamental Principles," *Trusteeship*, January/February 2012.
- White, Lawrence, "The Whys and Wherefores of Whistleblowing." *Trusteeship*, January/February 2012.
- White, Lawrence, "What the New and Invigorated Americans with Disabilities Act Means for Boards," *Trusteeship*, May/June 2011.
- White, Lawrence, "Why Do So Many Lawsuits End in Settlement? Check Your E-Mail," *Trusteeship*, September/October 2011.
- Williams, Lee Burdette, "Under Pressure: The Growing Demand for Student Mental Health Services," *Trusteeship*, May/June 2017.

Notes

Chapter 1: Good Risk Management is Good Governance

1. For additional resources from AGB, see
   - Merrill Schwartz, "The Big Risk in Not Assessing Risk," *Trusteeship*, January/February 2012.
   - Kristen Hodge-Clark, "Losing Ground on Risk Assessment," *Trusteeship*, May/June 2014.

2. For additional resources from AGB, see Lamar Alexander, "What Do American Auto Manufacturers and Higher Ed Have in Common?" *Trusteeship*, January/February 2012.

Chapter 2: Enterprise Risk Management: A Guide for Administrators

1. For additional resources from AGB, see Janice M. Abraham, "Vitiating Vulnerability," *Trusteeship*, September/October 2007.

2. For additional resources from AGB, see:
   - Stephen G. Pelletier, "New Strategies for Managing Risks: A Balancing Act for Boards," *Trusteeship*, January/February 2012.
   - *A Wake-up Call: Enterprise Risk Management at Colleges and Universities Today*, 2014.

Chapter 3: External and Internal Stakeholders in Risk Management

1. To see the range of compliance standards institutions must meet, see the Higher Education Compliance Alliance's Compliance Matrix at https://www.higheredcompliance.org/compliance-matrix/

2. Robert Kelchin, *Higher Education Accountability*, Baltimore: Johns Hopkins Press, 2018, pg. 96.

3. For additional resources from AGB, see:
   - Stephen G. Pelletier, "High-Performing Committees: What Makes Them Work?," *Trusteeship*, May/June 2012.

- Steven Dunham, "Compliance Policies and the Law," *Trusteeship*, March/April 2019.
- Steven Dunham, "Risk Management and the Law," *Trusteeship*, May/June 2019.
- Theodore E. Long, *Restructuring Committees*, 2018.

4. For additional resources from AGB, see:
- Michael Vekich and Daniel Cobom, "Accountability is a Calculated Effort," *Trusteeship*, September/October 2004.
- Barbara Gellman-Danley, "Accreditation and Quality Assurance," *Trusteeship*, November/December 2017.

Part II: Risk from the Board's Perspective

1. "Board Structure of a Higher Education Institution," BoardEffect, August 2018, https://www.boardeffect.com/blog/board-structure-higher-education-institution/

Chapter 5: Risks to Effective Governance

1. For additional resources from AGB, see Richard D. Legon, *The Executive Committee* (Effective Committee Series), 2012.

2. For additional resources from AGB, see:
- Steven C. Bahls, "Board Complacency and the Experienced President," *Trusteeship*, January/February 2011.
- Terrence J. MacTaggart, "The Risks of Trustee 'Managerialism,'" *Trusteeship*, January/February 2007.
- Richard Novak, "State Policies and Practices to Improve Board Governance," *Trusteeship*, September/October 2012.
- E.B. Wilson and James Lanier, *Governance Committee (Foundation Boards)*, 2014.
- Carol Cartwright, *The Governance Committee (Public Institutions)*, 2019.

3. For additional resources from AGB, see Stephen G. Pelletier, "High-Performing Committees: What Makes Them Work?" *Trusteeship*, May/June 2012.

4. For additional resources from AGB, see:
- Alexander E. Dreier and Martin Michaelson, *A Guide to Updating the Board's Conflict of Interest Policy*, 2006.
- Martin Michaelson, "How is Your Institution Doing on Conflicts of Interest?" *Trusteeship*, November/December 2007.

5. For additional resources from AGB, see:
- Robert O'Neil, *Updating Board Bylaws: A Guide for Colleges and Universities*, 2012
- Lawrence White, "The Principle of Indemnification and Why Trustees Should Care About It," *Trusteeship*, March/April 2012.

- Robert O'Neil, "Updated Board Bylaws—and Beyond," *Trusteeship*, March/April 2013.

6. For additional resources from AGB, see:
- Richard D. Legon (ed.), *Margin of Excellence: The New Work of Higher Education Foundations*, 2005.
- *Institutionally Related Foundation Boards: An Introductory Guide for Board Members*, 2019.
- Christopher Connell, "Stronger Together: Building Better Relationships Between Foundations and Universities," *Trusteeship*, January/February 2020.
- Sandy Baum, "Taxing the Endowment," *Trusteeship*, May/June 2019.
- Michael J. Worth, *Foundations for the Future: The Fundraising Role of Foundation Boards at Public Colleges and Universities*, 2012.
- David Bass and Jim Lanier, "What Lies Ahead for University- Foundation Relations?" *Trusteeship*, November/December 2008.
- David Bass, "What's a Prudent Payout from an 'Underwater' Endowment?" *Trusteeship*, May/June 2009.

Chapter 6: Risks to Strategic Direction (and Shared Risks)

1. For additional resources from AGB, see:
- Kent John Chabotar, *Strategic Finance: Planning and Budgeting for Boards, Chief Executives, and Finance Officers*, 2006.
- Larry D. Shinn, *Strategic Thinking and Planning in Higher Education: A Focus on the Future*, 2017.
- Terrence MacTaggart, *Leading Change: How Boards and Presidents Build Exceptional Academic Institutions*, 2011.
- Jeff A Weiss, "Growth and Transformation: A New Era of Mergers," *Trusteeship*, January/February 2018.
- Rick Beyer, "Mergers and Affiliations," *Trusteeship*, May/June 2019.

2. Scott Jaschik and Doug Lederman, "2019 Survey of College and University Business Officers," *Inside Higher Ed* and Gallup, 2019.

3. For a primer on college and university mergers, see Sandra Sabo, *Winning Combinations: A Guide to Mergers and Acquisitions in Higher Education*, National Association of College and University Business Officers, 2019.

4. From https://www.academicimpressions.com/blog/higher-education-mergers-acquisitions/

5. For additional information, visit these websites:
- From Higher Education Compliance Alliance, https://www.higheredcompliance.org/
- From The Catholic University of America, http://counsel.cua.edu/
- From North Carolina State University, https://generalcounsel.ncsu.edu/legal-topics/compliance-ethics/compliance-reporting-calendar/

Notes

- From Washington and Lee University, https://my.wlu.edu/general-counsel/answer-center/compliance-initiatives/business-office-calendar

6. "Risk Management– Moving Beyond Compliance," Risk & Compliance, July to September 2018, https://riskandcompliancemagazine.com/risk-management-moving-beyond-compliance.

7. For additional resources from AGB, see:
   - Julie Bourbon, "University of Iowa Flooding: The Expected and the Unexpected," *Trusteeship*, September/October 2008.
   - Lyn Trodahl Chynoweth, "Creating Solutions in Times of Crisis," *Trusteeship*, November/December 2011.
   - Lawrence White, "Governing During an Institutional Crisis: 10 Fundamental Principles," *Trusteeship*, January/February 2012.
   - Terrence Mactaggart, "Leadership in a Time of Crisis," *Trusteeship*, July/August 2019.
   - Joseph A. Brennan, "Object Lesson: The Crucial Role of Trustees in Facing Crisis," *Trusteeship*, July/August 2017.
   - Steve Dunham, "Crisis Management and the Law," *Trusteeship*, November/December 2019.

8. For additional resources from AGB, see "When Governance Goes Awry: What are the Takeaways?" *Trusteeship*, September/October 2012.

Chapter 7: Risks to Institutional Resources

1. For additional resources from AGB, see Ingrid S. Stafford, *The Finance Committee* (Effective Committee Series), 2013.

2. For additional resources from AGB, see:
   - Kent John Chabotar, *Strategic Finance: Planning and Budgeting for Boards, Chief Executives, and Finance Officers*, 2006.
   - Merrill Schwartz, "Making Sense of Tuition Prices and College Costs," *Trusteeship*, July/August 2011.
   - Verne Sedlacek, "The Importance of Stress Testing in Higher Education," *Trusteeship*, September/October 2019.
   - Verne Sedlacek, "How Can Institutions Use Financial Stress Testing to Ensure Their Fiscal Health?" *Trusteeship*, January/February 2019.

3. For additional analysis on national and regional demographic and enrollment trends, see Nathan Grawe, *Demographics and the Demand for Higher Education* (Baltimore: Johns Hopkins University Press, 2018).

4. "Commonfund Higher Education Price Index: 2018 Update," Commonfund Institute.

5. For additional resources from AGB, see:
   - Lawrence Bacow and Laura Skandera Trombley, "Making Metrics Matter: How to Use Indicators to Govern Effectively," *Trusteeship*, January/February 2011.

- Gerald W. McLaughlin and Josetta McLaughlin, *The Information Mosaic: Strategic Decision Making for Universities and Colleges*, 2008.
- Sandy Baum, *Financial Aid and Enrollment: Questions for Boards to Consider*, 2015.
- Sandy Baum, "The Link between Financial Aid and Enrollment," *Trusteeship*, May/June 2015.

6. For more information on metrics and the Composite Financial Index, see *Strategic Financial Analysis for Higher Education*, published by KPMG, Prager, Sealy & Co., and Attain.

7. Some institutions set up an independent website to share information with bondholders. See Stanford University's website at https://bondholder-information.stanford.edu/home.html

8. For additional resources from AGB, see Richard L. Staisloff, *The Audit Committee* (Effective Committee Series), 2011.

9. For additional resources from AGB, see:
- Thomas K. Hyatt, "Show Me What I'm Looking For: A Trustee's Guide to Reviewing the New IRS Form 990," *Trusteeship*, January/February 2008.
- Andrea J. Loughry, "Stay Alert to Financial Oversight and Risk Assessment on the Audit Trail," *Trusteeship*, November/December 2007.
- Frank Bossle, Betty McPhilimy, and Michael Somich, "Who Audits the Auditor? Assessing the Quality of the Internal Audit Function," *Trusteeship*, May/June 2015.

10. "Report to the Nations: 2018 Global Study on Occupational Fraud and Abuse," Association of Certified Fraud Examiners, 2018, https://www.acfe.com/report-to-the-nationa/2018/default.aspx.

11. For additional resources from AGB, see Lawrence White, "The Whys and Wherefores of Whistleblowing," *Trusteeship*, January/February 2012.

12. For additional resources from AGB, see:
- Lawrence White, "Why Do So Many Lawsuits End in Settlement? Check Your E-Mail," *Trusteeship*, September/October 2011.
- Pamela J. Bernard, "Does Your Institution Need a Social-Media Policy?" *Trusteeship*, September/October 2010.
- Pamela J. Bernard, "New Federal Rules Elevate E-mail as a Risk for Boards and Presidents," *Trusteeship*, March/April 2008.

13. For additional resources from AGB, see:
- David Bahlman, John Walda, and Verne Sedlacek, "Higher Education Endowments Return," *Trusteeship*, March/April 2012.
- David Bass, "Spending and Management of Endowments Under UPMIFA," 2010.
- John R. Curry and Lyn Hutton, "Why Cash Flow Is No Longer for Wimps," *Trusteeship*, September/October 2012.

- John Griswold, "What Should We Know About Investments and Endowments?" *Trusteeship*, January/February 2013.
- Jay A. Yoder, *The Investment Committee* (Effective Committee Series), 2011.
- Nicole Wellmann Kraus, Hilda Ochoa-Brillembourg, Jay A. Yoder, *Endowment Management for Higher Education*, 2017.

14. "2018 NACUBO-TIAA Study of Endowments," National Association of College and University Business Officers and TIAA-CREF.

15. For additional resources from AGB, see:
- David Bass, "College Fundraising: Is There a 'New Normal'?" *Trusteeship*, November/December 2009.
- Peyton R. Helm, *The Development Committee* (Effective Committee Series), 2012.
- Patricia P. Jackson, *The Board's Role in Fundraising*, 2013.
- Michael J. Worth, *Securing the Future: A Fund-Raising Guide for Boards of Independent Colleges and Universities*, 2005.

16. For additional resources from AGB, see Jake B. Schrum (ed.), *A Board's Guide to Comprehensive Campaigns*, 2000.

17. "Is College President 'the Toughest Job in the Nation'?" *Chronicle of Higher Education*, May 1, 2018, https://www.chronicle.com/article/Is-College-President-the/243289.

18. "2019 Retention Report: Trends, Reasons, & A Call to Action," Work Institute, 2019, https://info.workinstitute.com/retentionreport2019.

19. "Beating Turnover in Higher Ed: New Findings from Academic Impressions," Academic Impressions, 2019, https://www.academicimpressions.com/beating-turnover-in-higher-ed/.

20. "Representation and Pay of Women of Color in the Higher Education Workforce," May 2018, CUPA-HR, https://www.cupahr.org/wp-content/uploads/CUPA-HR-Brief-Women-Of-Color-1.pdf.

21. Institutions can use segment-specific salary benchmarks to guide compensation standards, including higher education salary data from CUPA-HR, *Chronicle of Higher Education*, and HigherEdJobs, which allow institutions to compare salaries by segment and position type. Resources related to compensation data in higher education include:
- "Administrators in Higher Education," CUPA-HR, https://www.cupahr.org/surveys/results/administrators-in-higher-education/;
- "Chronicle Data," *Chronicle of Higher Education*, https://data.chronicle.com/;
- "Salary Data," *HigherEdJobs*, https://www.higheredjobs.com/salary/;
- "Representation and Pay of Women of Color in the Higher Education Workforce," May 2018, CUPA-HR, https://www.cupahr.org/wp-content/uploads/CUPA-HR-Brief-Women-Of-Color-1.pdf.

- Jeffrey Humber, Jonathan Alger, Loretta Martinez, Jeffrey B. Trammell, Marc A. Nivet, and Anne C. Berlin, "Why Boards Must Become Diversity Stewards," *Trusteeship*, May/June 2014.
- Bethami A. Dobkin, "Creating Inclusive Board Culture," *Trusteeship*, March/April 2019.
- Freeman A. Hrabowski III, "Diversity, Access, and the American Dream," *Trusteeship*, May/June 2014.
- Thomas K. Hyatt, *The Compensation Committee*, 2013.

22. "Diversity and Inclusion Defined," George Washington University, Office of Diversity, Equity and Community Engagement, 2019, https://diversity.gwu.edu/diversity-and-inclusion-defined; Marjorie Derven, Ernest Gundling, and Pamela Leri, "Diversity & Inclusion: A Few Basics You Need to Know," *CTDO Magazine*, Winter 2020.

23. For additional resources from AGB, see:
- Harvey H., Kaiser, "Protecting and Enhancing Campus Facilities: 6 Principles for Boards," *Trusteeship*, March/April 2012.
- Harvey H., Kaiser, *The Facilities Committee* (Effective Committee Series), 2012.
- Lawrence White, "What the New and Invigorated Americans with Disabilities Act Means for Boards," *Trusteeship*, May/June 2011.

24. "Taking Inventory of Your Off-Campus Real Estate," United Educators, June 2017, https://www.edurisksolutions.org/Templates/template-blogs.aspx?pageid=47&id=3337&blogid=100.

25. For an additional report from AGB, see:
- Stephen G. Pelletier and Richard A. Skinner, "Technology in Context: 10 Considerations for Governing Boards of Colleges and Universities," 2010.
- Michael Hites, George Finney, and Joseph D. Barnes, *What Board Members Need to Know About Cybersecurity*, 2018.
- John O'Brien, "IT: The New Strategic Imperative," *Trusteeship*, March/April 2018.
- Eric Denna, "Higher Education's Return on Information Technology," *Trusteeship*, special issue 2015.
- Angel L. Mendez, "Need IT With That? How one Board Effectively Oversees Technology," *Trusteeship*, special issue 2015.
- Stephen G. Pelletier, "Taming 'Big Data:' Using Data Analytics for Student Success and Institutional Intelligence," *Trusteeship*, special issue 2015.

Chapter 8: Risks to the Student Experience

1. "Don't Stop Believin' (in the value of a college degree): Committee on Education and Labor Report," U.S. House of Representatives, March 2019, https://edlabor.house.gov/imo/media/doc/FINAL%20VALUE%20OF%20COLLEGE%20REPORT.pdf.

Notes

2. For additional resources from AGB, see:
- "Faculty Governance in Higher Education," National Education Association, 2019, http://www.nea.org/home/34743.htm.
- Governance for a New Era: A Blueprint for Higher Education Trustees, American Council of Trustees and Alumni, 2014, https://www.goacta.org/images/download/governance_for_a_new_era.pdf.
- Peter Ewell, *Making the Grade: How Boards Can Ensure Academic Quality*, 2nd Edition, 2012.
- Kenneth C. Green, "Mission, MOOCs, and Money," *Trusteeship*, January/February 2013.
- "How Boards Oversee Educational Quality: A Report on a Survey of the Assessment of Student Learning," 2010.
- *Statement on Board Responsibility for the Oversight of Educational Quality*, 2010.
- Carol A. Twigg, "Transforming Learning Through Technology: Educating More, Costing Less," *Trusteeship*, September/October 2011.
- Susan Wheallor Johnston, *The Academic Affairs Committee*, 2014.
- Peter T. Ewell, "The Growing Interest in Academic Quality," *Trusteeship*, January/February 2014.
- Mary Dana Hinton, "The Importance of Academic Oversight," *Trusteeship*, September/October 2019.
- Stanley Ikenberry, Peter Ewell, and George Kuh, "Governing Boards and Student Learning Outcomes Assessment," *Trusteeship*, January/February 2016.
- Jullian Kinzie, Alexander C. McCormick, and Robert M. Gonyea, "Using Student Engagement Results to Oversee Educational Quality," Trusteeship, January/February 2016.

3. Laura Pappano, "The Year of the MOOC," *New York Times*, November 2, 2012, https://www.nytimes.com/2012/11/04/education/edlife/massive-open-online-courses-are-multiplying-at-a-rapid-pace.html; "The Future of MOOCs Must Be Decolonized," *EdSurge*, January 3, 2019, https://www.edsurge.com/news/2019-01-03-the-future-of-moocs-must-be-decolonized.

4. MOOCs Are Dead—Long Live the MOOC, *Wired*, August 2014, https://www.wired.com/insights/2014/08/moocs-are-dead-long-live-the-mooc/; "The MOOC Is Not Dead, But Maybe It Should Be," *Wonkhe*, March 4, 2018, https://wonkhe.com/blogs/the-mooc-is-not-dead-but-maybe-it-should-be/.

5. "MOOC Platforms' New Model Draws Big Bet From Investors," *Inside Higher Ed*, May 22, 2019, https://www.insidehighered.com/digital-learning/article/2019/05/22/investors-bet-big-companies-formerly-known-mooc-providers.

6. "Tenure," American Association of University Professors, 2019, https://www.aaup.org/issues/tenure.

7. "Problems Arising From Tenure Denials: A Review of Recent Claims," United Educators, June 2017, https://www.edurisksolutions.org/Templates/template-article.aspx?id=3328&pageid=134.

8. "NIH has referred 16 allegations of foreign influence on U.S. research to investigators," *Stat News*, June 2019, https://www.statnews.com/2019/06/05/nih-has-referred-16-allegations-of-foreign-influence-on-u-s-research-to-investigators/.

9. "Science vs. Security," *Inside Higher Ed*, April 2019, https://www.insidehighered.com/news/2019/04/16/federal-granting-agencies-and-lawmakers-step-scrutiny-foreign-research.

10. For additional resources from AGB, see:
- Darrell G. Kirch, "Higher Education and Health Care at a Crossroads," *Trusteeship*, March/April 2011.
- Darrell G. Kirch, "Higher Education in the Age of Obamacare," *Trusteeship*, July/August 2013.

11. For additional resources from AGB, see Shannon Ellis, *The Student Affairs Committee* (Effective Committee Series), 2012.

12. "Mental illness: Is There Really a Global Epidemic?" *The Guardian*, June 3, 2019, https://www.theguardian.com/society/2019/jun/03/mental-illness-is-there-really-a-global-epidemic.

13. "National College Health Assessment," American College Health Association, Fall 2018, https://www.acha.org/documents/ncha/NCHA-II_Fall_2018_Reference_Group_Executive_Summary.pdf; "One Small Step to Address the Student Mental Health Crisis," *Inside Higher Ed*, February 24, 2019, https://www.insidehighered.com/blogs/just-visiting/one-small-step-address-student-mental-health-crisis.

14. "Mental Health Diagnoses Rising among U.S. College Students," Reuters, November 1, 2018, https://www.reuters.com/article/us-health-mental-college/mental-health-diagnoses-rising-among-u-s-college-students-idUSKCN1N65U8; "Trends in College Students' Mental Health Diagnoses and Utilization of Services, 2009–2015," *Journal of American College Health*, online October 25, 2018, bit.ly/2CWWNN0.

15. "Mental Health and School Dropout across Educational Levels and Genders: a 4.8-Year Follow-up Study," U.S. National Library of Medicine, National Institutes of Health, September 2016, https://www.ncbi.nlm.nih.gov/pmc/articles/PMC5024430/; "Number of University Dropouts Due to Mental Health Problems Trebles," *The Guardian*, May 23, 2017, https://www.theguardian.com/society/2017/may/23/number-university-dropouts-due-to-mental-health-problems-trebles.

16. "Liability and Lessons from General Mental Health Claims," United Educators, October 2018, https://www.edurisksolutions.org/Templates/template-article.aspx?id=3789&pageid=135.

Notes

17. "Liability Lessons from Claims Involving Suicidal Students," United Educators, October 2018, https://www.edurisksolutions.org/Templates/template-article.aspx?id=3788&pageid=94.

18. For additional resources, see:
    - "Get the Facts," Higher Education Center for Alcohol and Drug Misuse Prevention and Recovery, September 2019, https://hecaod.osu.edu/about/get-the-facts/.
    - Gregory T. Eells, "Rx for Students' Mental Health: What Boards Can Do," *Trusteeship*, September/October 2011.
    - Lee Burdette Williams, "Under Pressure: The Growing Demand for Student Mental Health Services," *Trusteeship*, May/June 2017.

19. National College Health Assessment, ACHA, Fall 2018, https://www.acha.org/documents/ncha/NCHA-II_Fall_2018_Reference_Group_Executive_Summary.pdf; "Binge drinking down among young adults in college, up among those who are not," Science Daily, July 27, 2017, https://www.sciencedaily.com/releases/2017/07/170727115604.htm.

20. "Addressing College Drinking and Drug Use, A Primer for Trustees, Administrators, and Alumni," ACTA, June 2019, https://www.goacta.org/publications/addressing-college-drinking-and-drug-use.

21. "College Drug Abuse," Addiction Center, https://www.addictioncenter.com/college/.

22. "Assessing Marijuana Use, Anxiety, and Academic Performance Among College Students," Higher Education Center for Alcohol and Drug Misuse Prevention and Recovery, July 22, 2019, https://hecaod.osu.edu/assessing-marijuana-use-anxiety-and-academic-performance-among-college-students/.

23. "Get the Facts," Higher Education Center for Alcohol and Drug Misuse Prevention and Recovery, September 2019, https://hecaod.osu.edu/about/get-the-facts/.

24. "A Framework for Integrating Young Peers in Recovery into Adolescent Substance Use Prevention and Early Intervention," Higher Education Center for Alcohol and Drug Misuse Prevention and Recovery, August 29, 2019, https://hecaod.osu.edu/a-framework-for-integrating-young-peers-in-recovery-into-adolescent-substance-use-prevention-and-early-intervention/.

25. Campuses looking for additional resources may seek to connect with the JED Foundation's initiative called JED Campus, which guides nearly 200 campuses in campus-wide prevention efforts involving student mental health, suicide, and substance abuse. Additionally, campuses may partner with and review student mental health data collected by ACHA's National College Health Assessment and Healthy Minds Network, or review the nine steps for trustees in 2019 ACTA report on *Addressing College Drinking and Drug Use: A Primer for Trustees, Administrators, and Alumni*.

- JED Foundation, https://www.jedfoundation.org/; JED Campus, https://www.jedcampus.org/.
- National College Health Assessment, ACHA, Fall 2018, https://www.acha.org/documents/ncha/NCHA-II_Fall_2018_Reference_Group_Executive_Summary.pdf; "One Small Step to Address the Student Mental Health Crisis," *Inside Higher Ed*, February 24, 2019, https://www.insidehighered.com/blogs/just-visiting/one-small-step-address-student-mental-health-crisis.
- Healthy Minds Network, https://healthymindsnetwork.org/.
- "Addressing College Drinking and Drug Use, A Primer for Trustees, Administrators, and Alumni," ACTA, June 2019, https://www.goacta.org/publications/addressing-college-drinking-and-drug-use.

26. For additional resources from AGB, see Pamela J. Bernard, "Do Emergency Planners Know When and How to Share Confidential Student Records?" *Trusteeship*, May/June 2008.

27. "Safeguarding Our Communities From Sexual Predators: What College Presidents and Trustees Should Ask," United Educators, January 2019, https://www.edurisksolutions.org/Templates/template-article.aspx?id=3859&pageid=134.

28. "Safeguarding Our Communities From Sexual Predators: What College Presidents and Trustees Should Ask," United Educators, https://www.edurisksolutions.org/Templates/template-article.aspx?id=3859&pageid=134.

29. For additional resources from AGB, see Janice M. Abraham, "Heat Map: Is Your Institution at Risk? Protecting Minors on Your Campus," *Trusteeship*, March/April 2012.

30. "Excessive Force by Campus Security," United Educators, February 2017, https://www.edurisksolutions.org/Templates/template-article.aspx?id=3244&pageid=135.

31. "Firearms and Weapons Policies," United Educators, July 2019, https://www.edurisksolutions.org/Templates/template-blogs.aspx?pageid=47&id=2147483748&blogid=100.

32. "Firearms and Weapons Policies," United Educators, July 2019, https://www.edurisksolutions.org/Templates/template-blogs.aspx?pageid=47&id=2147483748&blogid=100.

33. "10 years. 180 school shootings. 356 victims," CNN, August 2019, https://www.cnn.com/interactive/2019/07/us/ten-years-of-school-shootings-trnd/.

34. "U.S. Secret Service Releases Operational Guide for Preventing Targeted School Violence," U.S. Department of Homeland Security, July 13, 2018, https://www.dhs.gov/news/2018/07/13/us-secret-service-releases-operational-guide-preventing-targeted-school-violence; https://www.dhs.gov/publication/enhancing-school-safety-using-threat-assessment-model.

35. "U.S. Secret Service Releases Operational Guide for Preventing Targeted School Violence," U.S. Department of Homeland Security, July 13, 2018, https://

Notes

www.dhs.gov/news/2018/07/13/us-secret-service-releases-operational-guide-preventing-targeted-school-violence; https://www.dhs.gov/publication/enhancing-school-safety-using-threat-assessment-model.

36. "Preventing and Preparing for School Shootings," United Educators, October 2016, https://www.edurisksolutions.org/Templates/template-blogs.aspx?pageid=47&id=3152&blogid=100.

37. For additional resources from AGB, see:
- Stephen Pelletier, "Campus Security Under the Microscope," *Trusteeship*, January/February 2008.
- Kim Krisberg, "Campus Carry Laws and the Challenges for Leadership," *Trusteeship*, September/October 2017.
- Kim Krisberg, "Can Institutions Learn to Live with Campus Carry?" *Trusteeship*, September/October 2018.

38. https://www.iie.org/Research-and-Insights/Open-Doors/Data/US-Study-Abroad/Duration-of-Study-Abroad.

39. For more information online, see:
- Center for Disease Control at https://www.cdc.gov/.
- National Collegiate Athletic Association at NCAA.org.
- Sport Concussion Library at www.sportconcussionlibrary.com or Brain Injury Alliance of New Jersey at sportconcussion.com.

Chapter 9: Advancing Reputation

1. For additional resources, see:
- Janice M. Abraham and Paul L. Walker, "ERM and Reputational Risk: More Talk Than Action?" 2017, https://www.ue.org/uploadedFiles/ERM%20and%20Reputational%20Risk%20White%20Paper.pdf.
- Janice Abraham, "Are You Sacrificing Your Reputation to Protect Sacred Cows?" *Trusteeship*, September/October 2014.
- Susan Whealler Johnston, "Risking Your Reputation," *Trusteeship*, November/December 2017.

About the Author

Janice Menke Abraham joined United Educators Insurance, a reciprocal risk retention group, as the president and chief executive officer in 1998. During Abraham's tenure, United Educators has become known as the premier risk management and liability insurance expert serving educational institutions, offering in-depth expertise on the unique risks and claims facing education. Prior to joining United Educators, Abraham served the higher education community through her work as the chief financial officer/treasurer at Whitman College and in positions at Cornell University and the National Association of College and University Business Officers (NACUBO). Abraham has also served as an international banker for J. P. Morgan.

She serves as a trustee of American University and Whitman College; a director of the Campagna Center, the Griffith Foundation, the Institutes Board, and the American Property and Casualty Insurance Association; a member of American University's School of International Service Dean's Advisory Council; and the Association of Governing Boards of Universities and Colleges' Editorial Board of *Trusteeship* magazine. She is a former president of the Western Association of College and University Business Officers (WACUBO) and a past member of the board of directors of NACUBO and the National Risk Retention Association. Abraham earned an M.B.A. from the Wharton School at the University of Pennsylvania and a bachelor's degree in international service from American University.

About the Contributors

Sarah Braughler is the associate vice president for risk management at United Educators, where she oversees consulting services, risk research, and online program development, deployment, and support. Previously, she was the associate vice president and associate general counsel for resolutions management at United Educators, supervising lawyers and claims professionals who resolve liability insurance claims for United Educators' members.

Prior to beginning her work at United Educators, Sarah was a staff attorney at the Kentucky Community and Technical College System (KCTCS). She received her J.D. from the University of Kentucky, and her B.A., in English, *cum laude*, from Wake Forest University. She is a member of the National Association of College and University Attorneys and the Kentucky Bar Association.

Liza Kabanova is a risk management consultant at United Educators who partners with schools, colleges, and universities to implement and refresh campuswide enterprise risk management initiatives and proactive risk management practices. Prior to working at United Educators, Liza worked in Pepperdine University's risk management office, where she founded the Office of Environmental Health and Safety, established holistic safety and learning initiatives, and served as the university's Threat Assessment Team archivist. She has a J.D. from Pepperdine University and graduated magna *cum laude* with a B.A. from Bucknell University.

Justin Kollinger is a risk management consultant at United Educators, where he works with universities, colleges, and schools to launch and refresh enterprise risk management initiatives, advise on risk management tactics, and restructure risk management functions. Prior to joining United Educators, Justin served at an education consulting firm, where he consulted with community colleges on enrollment, workforce development, and academic reform. He has also worked at two private colleges in the Mid-Atlantic. He has a B.A. from Gettysburg College and an M.A. from Georgetown University.

Author Acknowledgments

2020 Edition

We would like to extend special recognition and deep appreciation to the following individuals, who were interviewed for this book and so generously shared their expertise and experience:

Fran Bouchoux
Stevens Institute of Technology

Barbara Brittingham
New England Commission of Higher Education

Jeff Chasen
University of Kansas

Nim Chinniah
Prager & Co.

Tim Edwards
University of Alaska

Luke Figora
Northwestern University

Carrie Frandsen
University of California

Barbara Gellman-Danley
Higher Learning Commission

Julie Groves
Wake Forest University

Ed Hanna
RCM&D

Eric Hartman
University of the South (Sewanee)

Erin Hennessy
TVP Communications

Dawn Hess
Finger Lakes Community College

Steve Holland
University of Arizona

Anita Ingram
University of Cincinnati

Susan Jackson
Embry-Riddle Aeronautical University

Sarah Latham
University of California, Santa Cruz

André Le Duc
University of Oregon

Michael Legg
Alamo Community College District

Michael Liebowitz
New York University

Chris Messina-Boyer
Finn Partners

Morgan Olsen
Arizona State University

Mike Reca
Rider University

Susan Shaffer
Moody's Investor Services

Paula Vene Smith
Grinnell College

Cynthia Vitters
Deloitte

Heidi L. Wachs,
Aon's Cyber Solutions (formerly Stroz Friedberg)

Jessica Wood
S&P Global Ratings

Cindi Zimmerman
University of California, Merced

Our sincere thanks to United Educators colleagues who were helpful in so many ways. The book would not have been updated without the expert advice, research, and guidance of:

- Jenny Cunningham and Nikole Alcala, who assisted with gathering updated data.
- Joshua Street, who scheduled interviews and obtained interview transcripts.
- Christine McHugh, who reviewed and drafted subsections for two chapters.
- Alex Miller, Laura Wright, and Melanie Bennett, who shared insights and encouragement.